DEMOCRACY AND ITS ELECTED ENEMIES

Democracy and Its Elected Enemies reveals that American politicians have usurped their constitutional authority, substituting their economic and political sovereignty for the people's. This has been accomplished by creating an enormous public service sector operating in the material interest of politicians themselves and of their big business and big social advocacy confederates to the detriment of workers, the middle class, and the nonpolitical rich, jeopardizing the nation's security in the process. Steven Rosefielde and Daniel Quinn Mills contend that this usurpation is the source of America's economic decline and fading international power, and they provide an action plan for restoring "true" democracy in which politicians only provide the services people vote for within the civil and property rights protections set forth in the constitution.

Steven Rosefielde is a professor of economics at the University of North Carolina, Chapel Hill. His most recent books include *Russia in the 21st Century: The Prodigal Superpower* (Cambridge University Press, 2005), *Masters of Illusion: American Leadership in the Media Age* (with Daniel Quinn Mills, Cambridge University Press, 2007), *Russia Since 1980* (with Stefan Hedlund, Cambridge University Press, 2009), *Red Holocaust* (2010), *Two Asias* (edited with Masaaki Kuboniwa and Satoshi Mizobata, 2012), *Prevention and Crisis Management* (edited with Masaaki Kuboniwa and Satoshi Mizobata, 2012), and *Asian Economic Systems* (2013). He holds a PhD in economics from Harvard University.

Daniel Quinn Mills is an emeritus professor of business administration at Harvard University. His most recent books are *Masters of Illusion: American Leadership in the Media Age* (with Steven Rosefielde, Cambridge University Press, 2007), *Rising Nations* (with Steven Rosefielde, 2009), *The Financial Crises of 2008–10* (2010), and *The Leader's Guide to Past and Future: The History of the World* (2013). He holds a PhD in economics from Harvard University.

Democracy and Its Elected Enemies

American Political Capture and Economic Decline

STEVEN ROSEFIELDE

University of North Carolina, Chapel Hill

DANIEL QUINN MILLS

Harvard University

CAMBRIDGE
UNIVERSITY PRESS

Shaftesbury Road, Cambridge CB2 8EA, United Kingdom

One Liberty Plaza, 20th Floor, New York, NY 10006, USA

477 Williamstown Road, Port Melbourne, VIC 3207, Australia

314–321, 3rd Floor, Plot 3, Splendor Forum, Jasola District Centre, New Delhi – 110025, India

103 Penang Road, #05–06/07, Visioncrest Commercial, Singapore 238467

Cambridge University Press is part of Cambridge University Press & Assessment, a department of the University of Cambridge.

We share the University's mission to contribute to society through the pursuit of education, learning and research at the highest international levels of excellence.

www.cambridge.org
Information on this title: www.cambridge.org/9781107012653

© Steven Rosefielde and Daniel Quinn Mills 2013

First published 2013

A catalogue record for this publication is available from the British Library

Library of Congress Cataloging-in-Publication data
Rosefielde, Steven.
Democracy and its elected enemies : American political capture and economic decline /
Steven Rosefielde, Daniel Quinn Mills.
pages cm
Includes bibliographical references and index.
ISBN 978-1-107-01265-3 (hardback)
1. United States – Politics and government – 21st century.   2. United States – Economic
conditions – 21st century.   3. Democracy – United States.   I. Mills, Daniel Quinn.   II. Title.
JK275.R67   2013
320.97309′051–dc23   2013013920

ISBN   978-1-107-01265-3   Hardback
ISBN   978-1-107-47593-9   Paperback

In memoriam for David Rosefielde

Contents

Preface

This book elaborates a concept of "true democracy" (rule of elected representatives obedient to the people's agenda rather than politicians governing for themselves in the name of the people) derived from economic utility optimization theory and the principle of majority rule under minority property and civil-rights constraints (consistent with the U.S. Constitution). It compares the size and scope of the United States' federal government with the true democratic ideal and finds them excessive – waste, fraud, and abuse cost taxpayers approximately $2 trillion annually (see Chapter 6). *Democracy and Its Elected Enemies* then describes how the United States' elected officials across the political spectrum behave in domestic and foreign affairs, showing that their actions are motivated to a considerable degree by selling public services in collaboration with big business and big social advocacy. The economic motives that shape domestic political behavior fully apply to foreign policy and form a bridge connecting what might otherwise seem to be separate domains.

Politicians, big business, and big social advocacy collectively set the national agenda in ways that allow them not only to overtax, but also to indirectly serve themselves through fiscal and monetary leveraging, inflation, interest-rate rigging, special-interest mandates, subsidies, preferences, insurance guarantees, "tax-expenditures," grants-in-aid, bureaucratic layering, and outsourcing at home and abroad. This behavior, it is argued, is the primary source of the United States' contemporary economic woes. Proof of the thesis is provided by the bloated scale of government in all these dimensions compared with a true democratic benchmark; the system's inefficiency, waste, fraud, and abuse; bipartisan refusal to roll back and retrench in the face of declining microeconomic vitality; and a looming financial mega crisis driven by national debt. The problem isn't technical. It is systemic.

U.S. presidents, federal legislators, and judges, it is argued, have transformed their positions as the people's agents into a new form of electoral sovereignty – the rule of politicians primarily committed to the leveraged sale of public services. These nest-feathering elected officials are dubbed "politarchs" to distinguish them from their predecessors who operated on a smaller venal scale, and their rule is called "politocracy."

Scale matters because bigness strangles competition and separates the electorate from officials who are supposed to serve as the people's representatives. Moderate misconduct gave us bad democracy; gross misconduct has killed democracy and substituted politocracy.

We chronicle the domestic and foreign economic consequences of this "noiseless revolution" and offer suggestions for remedying the damage to the United States and the tarnished global cause of true democracy. A similar phenomenon can be observed in other nations with elected government, but the nuances cannot be prejudged and the topic must be left for further investigation.

The volume was originally conceived as a sequel to our *Masters of Illusion* (Cambridge University Press, 2007), but gradually became more ambitious. We view the thesis as it has finally emerged as a Kuhnian political paradigm shift in the perception and analysis of contemporary U.S. elected government and its adverse global impact.[1]

Most contemporary treatments of democracy are mired in nineteenth-century partisan, class, and social frameworks that encourage scholars and the public to choose sides between big business and big social advocacy. Others attribute contemporary government economic mismanagement to sin or institutional inertia. Our approach does not dispute these influences but places primary blame on the trans-partisan power and material self-seeking of politicians, big businessmen, and big social advocates. It constitutes a clean break with critiques attributing responsibility for bad electoral government to the class struggle, partisan wrangling, institutional determinism, and human nature, offering instead a real science of elected national, transnational, and world government based on collusive utility seeking in the presence of state, business, and social coercive power.

The book isn't idealist or utopian. It isn't Democratic, Republican, Independent; conservative, liberal, or libertarian; right, left, or middle. It is

---

[1] Thomas Kuhn, *The Structure of Scientific Revolutions*, Chicago: University of Chicago Press, 1962. A Kuhnian revolution requires both a new and a researchable paradigm. The concept of politocracy provides a new lens for reinterpreting the United States' past, present, and future and for applying the same logic to rethinking modern state governance more broadly.

neo-institutional economic science that reveals an urgent need for a new, true democratic politics aimed at curbing the trans-partisan exploitation of workers and the middle class and re-empowering everyone's personal liberty in the United States and beyond.

The claim to science isn't perfunctory. Our thesis is formulated as a testable hypothesis. We assert that: (i) The U.S. economy is microinefficient and macrodestabilized by bad governance; (ii) bad governance is primarily caused by insider self-seeking; (iii) excessive bigness is an aspect of insider self-seeking; (iv) insider goals (codetermined by politicians, big business, and big social advocacy) conflict with the people's will; (v) the people's will requires drastic governmental downsizing; and (vi) if the rollback is accomplished, the principal sources of the United States' micro- and microeconomic disorders will be significantly ameliorated. Each of these propositions can be rigorously analyzed and objectively tested. Readers are invited to confirm or refute. The approach isn't speculative. It is scientific.

Acknowledgments

The scope of *Democracy and Its Elected Enemies* is too large to permit us to thank all those who have contributed to its development, but special acknowledgment for their insightful observations is due to Jonathan Leightner, Bruno Dallago, Chiara Guglielmetti, J. Peter Pham, Torbjorn Becker, Assaf Razin, Jong Rong Chen, Szabina Czako, Stephen Blank, Stefan Hedlund, Jan Rylander, Vitaly Shlykov, Shirley E. Mills, and Steve Papa. April Lee, Chunxiao Li, and Huan Zhou provided invaluable research assistance. Susan Rosefielde gave her unstinting support.

Our project was largely self-funded, but elements have benefited from funding provided for related research. We therefore gratefully acknowledge the assistance of Harvard Business School's Division of Research and the Taiwan Visiting Scholar Program from the Ministry of Education, Taiwan (Republic of China), the UNC Institute for the Arts and Humanities, and the UNC Parr Center for Ethics.

To all, we offer our sincere gratitude.

Executive Summary

Modern U.S. democracy is not a true democracy at all, despite its outward forms – universal suffrage; opposing political parties; elections; separate powers of legislature, executive, and judiciary; and a Constitution and Bill of Rights. It is not a true democracy because these forms of democracy have been usurped by several generations of elected officials for their own benefit. The essence of true democracy is that the government acts in accordance with the people's will (for the people's benefit); it is not that there are elections or any other of the forms of democracy. It is the perversion of this essence that has made the United States a postdemocratic society – a politarchy (often mischaracterized as social democracy) – a government of politicians, by politicians, and for politicians and their associates in big business and big social advocacy. The contest between political parties, between Republicans and Democrats, is superficial. Both parties are captured by politocrats, and their policies vary little; only rhetoric and personalities differ. The result is that the nation's economy is stagnant; unemployment is high; incomes are falling; finances are in crisis; and the opportunity for peace that followed the collapse of the Soviet Union is being squandered in continual warfare. Each of these tragic results benefits the politocracy while injuring the public. Worse still, the problems are not self-healing. The costs of politocracy will continue to mount, propelling the nation toward economic ruin and a sea of needless bloodshed unless the people take back sovereign powers from their elected enemies. It may still be possible to reverse politarchy – and the place to start is with a radical rollback of big government.

PART I

THE CHALLENGE OF U.S. POLITOCRACY

ONE

Hard Times

The United States has entered an epoch of protracted paralysis, crisis and decline, mostly of its own doing.[1] The wars of the 2000s, GDP growth retardation, stubborn high unemployment, widening inequality, poverty, stealthy and open inflation, Ponzi finance, speculative bubbles, government overspending and misregulation, the 2008 financial crisis, bailouts, and a gargantuan sovereign debt are all telltale signs of the times. Public officials, Wall Street, and business economists do their best to make this degeneration seem self-healing and never tire of assuring everyone that perpetual prosperity is just around the corner, but the glad tidings are superficial.[2]

Democracy and its Elected Enemies is an inquiry into the deep causes of America's plight and its prospects. It offers an explanation based on competitive economic theory and the concept of "true democracy" (majority popular rule, subject to minority property and civil-rights guarantees) that primarily attributes the United States' contemporary economic disorders to the violation of Enlightenment principles of democracy (characterized as "true democracy") by federal elected officials collectively pursuing their own interests including private enrichment, power, parochial missions, the creation of supranational political organizations and privilege-seeking world government at the expense of the American people's wellbeing. The U.S. federal government, it will be argued, has degenerated into a system of managed popular consent where avaricious power-seeking elected federal officials arrogate control over public services for themselves and constrict individual and community choice,[3] creating a federal balloting regime devoid

---

[1] Kenneth Rogoff, *The Second Great Contraction*, Project Syndicate (http://www.project-syndicate.org/commentary/rogoff83/English), 2011.

[2] Joseph Stiglitz, *Freefall: America, Free Markets, and the Sinking of the World Economy*, W. Norton & Company, 2010. The same reassurances were given during the 1930s.

[3] There is a longstanding debate about the contending claims of communities (connected with the concept of republic) and individuals. We believe that there is ample space for

3

of democratic substance. We dub these elected politicians "politarchs"[4] and the system they control in collaboration with "big business" and "big social advocacy" "politocracy." Politarchs are politicians of a special sort. They feather their nests as politicians always have, but on a grander scale. The distinction at first glance may appear innocuous, but scale matters because bigness strangles competition and separates the electorate from officials who are supposed to serve as the people's representatives.

The politarchic model postulates that contemporary politicians, big business, and big social advocacy collectively set the national agenda and indoctrinate the public in ways that allow them not only to overtax, but to indirectly serve themselves through fiscal and monetary leveraging, infla- tion, interest-rate rigging, special-interest mandates, subsidies, preferences, insurance guarantees, "tax-expenditures," grants-in-aid, bureaucratic layer- ing, and outsourcing at home and abroad.

This insider system applies equally to domestic and foreign affairs and in its entirety diminishes economic competitiveness, efficiency, productiv- ity, and growth potential. Likewise, it places the macro economy in a state of fundamental disequilibrium through policies of perpetual deficit spend- ing, increasing national indebtedness, monetary debasement, excess credit creation, and lax financial regulation. Proof of the thesis is provided by the bloated scale of government in all these dimensions, the system's inef- ficiency, waste, fraud and abuse, trans-partisan public-service trafficking, and bipartisan refusal to roll back and retrench in the face of declining eco- nomic vitality (including falling real wages, intractable high unemployment, and excessive middle-class taxation), and a looming national-debt-driven mega-financial crisis. Hard times in the United States are not the unfortu- nate result of bad policies. They are the poisoned fruit of politocracy. [5]

---

negotiating conflicts of these sorts at the local and state levels within the framework of the U.S. Constitution.

[4] Politicians by definition are influential individuals who exert power over public policy- making and programming. They exist in all governance systems serving their masters and themselves. The concept of democracy however precludes politicians using their public authority primarily for their self-interest. They are supposed to be the people's agents and public servants. Contemporary U.S. politicians violate this principle in especially egre- gious ways and are distinguished in this book by the label politocrats. They can be thought of as criminally entrepreneurial state officials, but we avoid the adjective because entrepre- neurship nowadays has a positive connotation.

[5] For a popular version of this theme see David Roche and Bob McKee, *Democrisis*, London: Lulu, 2012.

TWO

Democracy

True Democracy

Because they conflate popular rule with balloting, Americans do not realize that elected politarchs have usurped American democracy. This lapse is understandable. Democracy is an attractive but elusive concept. It is both an icon and a mirage. Democracy literally means people's rule (*demos kratos*): a governance system where the political sovereignty of every citizen reigns without privilege or special entitlement.[1] The people cast in the role

---

[1] The Greek word *demos* and the English-language equivalent, "people," are collective singulars (pluralities of human beings) that retain the double sense of heterogeneous individual persons and their oneness. The duality is easily grasped but also can be a source of ambiguity because the sense determines the meaning of *kratos*. If the term is used as a synonym for nation without regard for individuality, then democracy is a shallow concept meaning little more than any kind of governance in the national "interest." Alternatively, if the *demos* is a collection of heterogeneous persons (of the people) who elect representatives and participate in governing (by the people), with the purpose of bettering themselves individually and collectively (for the people), then the term acquires all the modern meanings of freely competitive multiparty, elected, civic participatory state governance serving the heterogeneous needs of minority-rights-protected citizens. *Democracy and Its Elected Enemies* employs the word "democracy" strictly in the latter sense (which also is compatible with neoclassical economic theory), except when the collective meaning is intended or clearly indicated. Democracy, particularly in the American setting, is a type of republic, where the people do not carry out the tasks of government directly by themselves, but delegate this job to elected representatives, controlled by the people through periodic elections and the constitution. See James Madison, *Federalist Paper* No. 10. The American republic is a representative democracy. The term *republic* does not appear in the Declaration of Independence, but does appear in Article IV of the Constitution, which "guarantee[s] to every State in this Union a Republican form of Government." What exactly the writers of the constitution felt this should mean is uncertain. The Supreme Court, in *Luther v. Borden* (1849), declared that the definition of republic was a "political question" in which it would not intervene. In two later cases, it did establish a basic definition. In *United States v. Cruikshank* (1875), the court ruled that the "equal rights of citizens" were inherent to the idea of republic.

of sovereign ruler (*demos*) distinguishes demo-cracy from types of political rule (*kratos*) where power is variously vested in the hands of kings (autocracy/monarchy), tyrants, aristocrats (aristocracy), patricians, religious authorities (theocracy), sects, cults, clans, communities, communes, cooperatives, professions, unions, gangs (mafiocracy), or families (patriarchy or matriarchy). The sovereign *demos* is the ultimate authority, superior to any entity claiming to speak for it as is often done by powerful interest groups (describing themselves as the public),[2] the community, or societal spokesmen (associations of some of the *demos*). The *demos* is not obligated by any group's notion of what the people ought to want.[3]

The concept of democracy can be traced back more than 2,000 years, but inclusive, fully articulated, jurisdictionally segmented, balanced governance constructs that protect minority rights did not emerge until the age of absolutism. Seventeenth- and eighteenth-century Western intellectuals conversant with autocratic oppression and inspired by rationalism and empirical science devised a self-regulating, popular, representative federal governance system with participatory aspects that maximized every individual's well-being subject to a constitutionally founded social contract.[4] This ideal can be conveniently dubbed American Enlightenment democracy (democracy of the Enlightenment type), or true democracy for short, to distinguish it from prior and subsequent elected governance regimes with restricted electorates, or leaders (demagogues) that disregard the people's will. The distinction escapes many who are preoccupied with majority balloting or drumming up popular consent for causes that pit minorities against the majority, or the majority of women against the minority of men.

True democracy as conceived by Enlightenment philosophers assumes that humans are sufficiently rational, can master their instincts, forge culturally informed identities,[5] and abide by an acceptable moral order.

However, the term "republic" is not synonymous with the republican form. The republican form is defined as one in which the powers of sovereignty are vested in the people and are exercised by the people, either directly or through representatives chosen by the people, to whom those powers are specially delegated. In *re Duncan*,139 U.S. 449, 11 S.Ct. 573, 35 L.Ed. 219; *Minor v. Happersett*, 88 U.S. (21 Wall.162, 22 L.Ed 627. Republicanism is broader than democracy and not a central concern of this book.

[2] Montesquieu, *Spirit of the Laws*, Bk. II, chs. 2–3.

[3] There is an extensive literature debating the contending rights of communities and individuals in democracies. The conflict can be resolved in principle by allowing individuals the right to form communities and subordinating themselves to the group, but communities do not have the right to impose their policies on the majority of other individuals outside the group. The debate essentially is over the interpretation of minority rights.

[4] John Locke, *Two Treatises on Government*, 1728.

[5] See Sigmund Freud, *Civilization and Its Discontents*, 1930, on the issue of instincts and mind. See Rene Descartes, *Meditationes de prima philosophia*, 1641, and Georg Wilhelm

Rational faculties allow individuals to form preferences with a clear (albeit fallible) perception of right and wrong, choose consistently to enhance their well-being, and learn from experience. Their moral compass assures that they will mostly forego wrong and do right, allowing true democrats to infer that outcomes will be both individually and socially superior according to the norms of their epoch.[6]

Rational, morally principled men and women should have the right to as much freedom as possible within constraints imposed by the social contract. They, and they alone, know what is best for them.[7] They are as trustworthy as those claiming to be their "betters," and they are disciplined by market competition. Their freedom must include secure core private property and business rights because without those people cannot efficiently and exhaustively maximize their well-being. Economic freedom and markets in this way are integral aspects of true democracy.[8]

True democrats understand that private property rights and competition are not panaceas; that conflicts of interest are embedded in human relations and must be resolved by collective bodies and institutions. Government inevitably is a battleground for determining the scale, scope, and particularities of public activities, including the interpretative details of property rights and market rules.[9]

Enlightenment democrats in the eighteenth century failed to find universally best principles for resolving interpersonal conflicts in the

---

Friedrich Hegel, *Phenomenology of Spirit*, tr. A. V. Miller, 1977, on contending theories of humans as fully self-sufficient individuals and social beings.

[6] The values of one age are not necessarily the values of the next, and perhaps none are transcendental. Slavery today is a crime against humanity in international law, but was widely accepted three hundred years ago.

[7] Cf. Sigmund Freud, *Civilization and Its Discontents*, 1930. This supposition holds as well for the relaxed case where elected officials and the people are imperfectly rational in the same degree.

[8] Competitive economic theory teaches that true democracy, free from misgovernment of any type, will inter-temporally maximize individual and public utility, taking full advantage of the opportunities afforded by science and technological progress. Second- best versions of the same theory that acknowledge the unlikelihood of perfectly competitive outcomes similarly imply that true democracy will provide superior results because politicians do not really know best or care sufficiently about the people's welfare. An America free of bad or antidemocratic elected governance can dramatically outperform all its rivals as they are currently configured. For a thorough analysis of the rational and behavioral bases of this optimal result, together with mathematical proofs and qualifications, see Steven Rosefielde and R. W. Pfouts, *Inclusive Economic Theory*, unpublished draft, 2013.

[9] Government is not the only means for adjudicating interpersonal conflicts in the public domain. The Japanese rely on a tapestry of contextual shame culture rules for this purpose. See Steven Rosefielde, *Asian Economic Systems*, Singapore: World Scientific, 2013.

public domain,[10] but sought to create the second-best by establishing a Bill of Rights to protect minorities from majority usurpation and by separating branches of government to restrain abuses of power. Legislators were granted authority to write laws for the public good that could favor some citizens or groups over others. The executive, including bureaucracies under presidential authority, was charged with implementing the law, but also had the implicit power to make law through selective implementation and explicitly by emergency decree. The potential for abuse accordingly came with the territory making judicial review of legislative and executive malfeasance the people's last court of recourse.

Enlightenment democracy as it was devised in the eighteenth century consequently was not utopian. It was and remains a vision of a pragmatic ideal guided by practical reason, offering the prospect of outcomes superior to autocracy, and *the bellum omnium contra omnes* (Thomas Hobbes's war of all against all).[11] Enlightenment democracy is feasible,[12] only requiring (1) the supremacy of the people's constitutional right to govern over elected officials' penchant for ruling as they see fit;[13] (2) the supremacy of constitutional writ over legislative desires to trample property rights, misspend, overspend, overtax, and over-borrow;[14] and (3) the supremacy of constitutional writ over free judicial reinterpretation.[15] The infringement of these

---

[10] "It has always been held, in the most enlightened nations, that a tribunal will decide a judicial question most fairly when it has heard two able men argue, as unfairly as possible, on the two opposite sides of it" (Thomas Babington Macaulay, "History," *Edinburgh Review*, May, 1828).

[11] De Cive, 1642, Leviathan, 1651.

[12] For a discussion of the historical nuances see Daniel Quinn Mills, "The Reinvention of the American Constitution," draft, March 19, 2012, where it is argued that Lincoln's rationale for the Civil War and post-conflict constitutional amendments made today's big federal government possible. The Civil War in effect constituted a reinterpretation of the Enlightenment compact in America's 1787 constitution away from states' and citizens' rights toward federal authority.

[13] Adverse selection refers to a process in which "bad" results occur when buyers and sellers have asymmetric information. Elected officials who are supposed to function as the people's agents are apt to adversely select when the public lacks sufficient information to deter their representatives' misbehavior.

[14] James Buchanan emphasizes this point in his writings on public-choice theory and constitutional economics. See James Buchanan and Robert Tollison, *The Limits of Liberty Between Anarchy and Leviathan*, Chicago: University of Chicago Press, 1975. The public here means both individuals and communities, reconciling conflicts at the local level as best they can.

[15] Judicial defense of constitutional principle can be degraded in two ways. Courts can bend the meaning of constitutional provisions for diverse purposes, and legislatures can overwhelm the system with contradictory laws that give judges license for corruption. The first abuse is connected with the concept of the "living constitution." It asserts that constitutional meanings are dynamic and should be interpreted according to contemporary norms,

principles makes the federal government illegitimate in the eyes of true democrats,[16] although, of course, not in the eyes of politicians who claim to serve as the conscience and voice of the people.[17]

True democracy of the sort enshrined in America's constitution has rivals. Some overtly challenge the democratic ideal. Others pretend to support it. Challengers contend that Enlightenment pragmatism is not good

allowing courts to override constitutional protections. The principle is often applied to the equal protection and due process clauses of the Fifth and Fourteenth Amendments to the American Constitution. David Weigel, in "Ruth Bader Ginsburg Makes Banal Point, Destroys the Republic," writes, "I would not look to the US constitution, if I were drafting a constitution in the year 2012" (http://www.slate.com/blogs/weigel/2012/02/03/ruth_bader_ginsburg_makes_banal_point_destroys_the_republic.htm_February_3,2012). A recent poll reveals that most Americans believe that the Supreme Court decided the merit of the Obama administration's healthcare bill on partisan rather than valid judicial grounds. See Greg Holyk, "New Low in Support for Health Law: Half Expect Justices to Go Political," Yahoo! News, April 11, 2012: "Half the public, moreover, thinks the U.S. Supreme Court will rule on the legislation on the basis of the justices' partisan political views rather than the law. Fewer, 40 percent, think impartial legal analysis will carry the day, with the rest unsure."

[16] If these principles are violated, true democracy should be restored by applying Buchanan's and Tullock's concept of "unanimous workable" public consent. James Buchanan and Gordan Tullock argue that taxation and state expenditures should be restricted to activities where there is "unanimous workable" public consent, relaxing Knut Wicksell's concept of strict unanimity. The essence of their position is the judgment that government services are inefficient, cannot be made efficient with social-benefit/cost indicators, and too often are corrupt, which makes them chary of most government programs. Principal-agent theory demonstrates that most government programs are infeasible because objectives are too fuzzy to permit the design of effective disciplinary mechanisms. The concept of unanimous support can be softened, but only to the extent that levels of spending do not violate property right or other constitutional protections. Also, the erosion of individual economic rights must be rolled back, and courts must refrain from improperly bending constitutional safeguards and unscrupulously exploiting legislative loopholes, especially those affecting property rights, competitiveness, and abusive entitlements (for rich, poor, and the middle class). See James Buchanan, *Democracy in Deficit: The Political Legacy of Lord Keynes*. Indianapolis, IN: Liberty Fund, 1999. The rollback in Europe entails pruning "social democracy," reducing mandates (forced substitution), over-regulation, burdensome compliance, over-taxation, and restrictions on entrepreneurship. Opportunities for legislative and executive misconduct, including excessive, bubble-inducing financial and monetary leveraging must be curtailed. "Over the 50-year period from 1954 to 2003, Congress enacted 16,015 laws; state laws, one million laws passed" (Clark Neily, "The Myth of Judicial Activism," *Wall Street Journal*, Sept. 28, 2011). Government straitjackets individual economic freedom by imposing unwarranted regulations, mandates, reporting, and tax obligations.

[17] Douglass North and Robert Thomas, *The Rise of the Western World: A New Economic History*, Cambridge: Cambridge University Press, 1973; Milton Friedman, *Capitalism and Freedom*, Chicago: University of Chicago Press, 1962; Jean-Pierre Chauffour, On the Relevance of Freedom and Entitlement in Development: New Empirical Evidence (1975–2007); Policy Research Working Paper 5660, World Bank, 2011; Chauffour, *The Power of Freedom: Uniting Human Rights and Development*, Washington, DC: Cato Institute, 2009.

enough. They claim the right to rule for the people with people's consent, or subordinate the *demos*'s interests to their own, even though this often is said to be for the people's own good (prosperity, social justice, fairness, equitable entitlements, etc.).[18] This means different things to different advocates, but amounts broadly to affirmative action for those claiming privileged status and repression of allegedly socially harmful elements. Socialists champion the cause of the working poor (vulnerable people), and communists the welfare of the proletariat (industrial working class). Fascists promote collectivism, and modern politicians the mediated demands of assorted entitlement seekers.[19]

These goals may be compatible with true democracy, but only when approved by the majority on issues that do not infringe constitutional and minority property and civil rights. Otherwise, entities and associations other than the *demos* (understood as the will of heterogeneous persons) rule in their own interest, purporting to represent the will of "society" (sociocrats) as distinct from the will of the people (community of all persons).[20] If the American electorate desires affirmative action and chooses to restrict personal liberties for the greater good without violating the Bill of Rights, then "socio-cracy" and demo-cracy come to the same thing. If not, programs imposed by social advocates (socio-crats) are antidemocratic,[21] even though champions of particular social causes and shame cultures like Japan's do their utmost to disregard the distinction.

---

[18] This issue is argued from multiple perspectives. David Hume disputed the existence of a social contract. Rawls and Sandel devised Kantian categorical imperatives for social activism. This has been accompanied by efforts to continuously widen the circle of deserving (privileged) minorities coupled with affirmative action. "Hume, Essays, Moral, Political, and Literary, Part II, Essay XII, Of the Original Contract," Library of Economics and Liberty; John Rawls, *A Theory of Justice*, Cambridge, MA: The Belknap Press of Harvard University Press, 1971; Michael Sandel, *Justice: What is the Right Thing to Do?*, New York: Macmillan, 2010.

[19] Democracy was the darling of Enlightenment political theory until shortly after 1800 when it started to be challenged by socialists like Saint Simon, Robert Owen, and Karl Marx, who began claiming that virtuous causes trumped popular sovereignty.

[20] These distinctions are fundamental in economic theory because they affect the scope of unencumbered individual utility maximizing. See Steven Rosefielde, *Inclusive Economic Theory*, unpublished manuscript, 2013.

[21] The people are free to voluntarily associate. Their associations create societies with distinct characteristics. The merit of these characteristics however is not innate, but derives from the people who in democracies are the true sovereigns. One can admire or reject democratically formed societies as a matter of personal taste, but a single individual's taste does not justify his or her sovereignty over the *demos*. The issue, and the related question of moral imperative, are fixtures of neoclassical welfare economics. See Abram

AMERICAN TRUE DEMOCRACY

America's founding fathers, grasping these essentials and motivated by "the love of humanity,"[22] sought to transform theory into practice by constructing a constitutionally based, majority-elected government (the form) acting strictly in accordance with the people's will (the content), upholding an inviolable bill of rights, resting on the Enlightenment premise that mankind is rational, morally disciplined, and willing to abide by a voluntary social contract under the rule of law in the unencumbered pursuit of happiness.[23] They strove to design a government that was the people's instrument,[24] not one for the benefit of the elected.

Abraham Lincoln in the Gettysburg Address, on November 19, 1863, described the essence of this democracy as "government of the people, by the people and for the people," meaning that authority derives directly from the people whose will created the constitution; that elected officials are the people's agents, and that agents operate solely for the people's benefit, not their own or that of those seeking supra-constitutional entitlements.

SOCIOCRACY

Early-nineteenth-century European intellectuals starting with Claude Henri de Rouvroy, comte de Saint Simon, admired aspects of Enlightenment democracy but sought to improve upon the vision by transforming the Bill of Rights into a Bill of Entitlements that compel the people to accept a common set of priorities, which too often infringe basic constitutional protections. They demanded that democracy dedicate itself to improving

Bergson, "A Reformulation of Certain Aspects of Welfare Economics," *Quarterly Journal of Economics*, Vol. 52, No. 1, February 1938, pp. 310–34; Bergson, "Social Choice and Welfare Economics under Representative Government," *Journal of Public Economics*, Vol. 6, No. 3, October, 1976, pp. 171–90. Steven Rosefielde, *Inclusive Economic Theory*, unpublished manuscript, 2013.

[22] "The love of humanity has become the true concern of government." See Condorcet, *Life of Voltaire, in Works*, Vol. IV, pp. 176–77. Condorcet attributes the phrase to Voltaire.

[23] Cf. Michael Lewis, *Boomerang: Travels in the New Third World*, New York: W. W. Norton Company, 2011. Cf. Frank Knight , *The Ethics of Competition and Other Essays*, New York: Harpers and Brothers, 1935.

[24] Toward this end, John Adams insisted that the composition of the legislature mirror each representative's constituency. Representatives should be from all walks of life, not predominantly lawyers as they are today. "The representative assembly ... should be in miniature an exact portrait of the people at large" (John Adams, "The Foundation of Government," 1776). Democracies are "good" when balloting is fair, administration is constitutional, and agents are faithful to the people's will. They are "bad" when they violate one or more of these tenets, even if they are well meaning.

the welfare of the class that is most numerous and most poor, to providing a comfortable living standard to everyone regardless of effort, and to
eradicating inequalities of income and wealth, even when these conditions compromise fundamental minority property rights, stifle the market,
impair productivity, stultify economic growth, and create myriad hidden
injustices.[25]

---

[25] The form and substance of U.S. and European elected government are broadly similar at
the national level. All have popular constitutions with bills of rights. Powers are divided
among executive, legislative, and judicial branches tasked to carry out the people's will. The
size and scope of government activities everywhere are huge, and insider government is
rampant. Nonetheless, they differ profoundly in one critical regard: the United States is a
federation of semiautonomous states under central legislative, judicial, and executive control with an unitary monetary regime and formidable fiscal powers, whereas the European
Union is a supranational organization with weak transnational authority. The distinction
is crucial because eurozone supranationality handcuffs EU macroeconomic-management
capabilities. The story of how Europe's elected governments ensnared themselves illustrates
the destructive consequences of politocratic social-democratic zealotry and self-seeking.
    It begins more than two centuries ago when socialism emerged as a rival to Enlightenment
democracy. The United States was founded on the Enlightenment premise that all men
are rational, have reliable moral compasses, inalienable economic and human rights, are
best positioned to ascertain the determinants of their well-being, and can do so most
effectively in well functioning democracies. European democratic republicanism (where
the people as a whole constitute the public), however, came to doubt the efficacy of the
common person's rationality, the virtue of Adam Smith's invisible hand, and the potency
of Lockean democracy to assure satisfactory social outcomes. Many social thinkers didn't
reject private property, markets, entrepreneurship, and democracy but took a jaundiced
attitude toward them. They demanded virtuous results, not promises, and when outcomes
were unacceptable devised utopias of their own based on principles like state planning and
mutual aid. Thus, while Americans and Europeans share many Enlightenment premises,
Europeans leaders gradually came to reject the idea that free individuals limited solely by
the rule of virtuous law (John Locke's social contract) and balloting are the nation's rightful sovereigns, substituting the rule of "society's" acknowledged spokesmen.
    Society as Europeans came to conceptualize it is an association of individuals operat-
ing under a common set of rules that has value in its own right and therefore serves as
a basis for asserting the primacy of social over individual welfare. While Enlightenment
thinkers accept the claim that men should be the arbiter of their actions, relying on reason
and science, many concluded that rational and seemingly virtuous private self-seeking too
often harms society. Adam Smith's invisible hand has its merits but is not good enough.
Rational democratic balloting, where every individual votes his or her conscience, likewise is deemed inadequate because people are said to vote selfishly in their own interest.
Therefore, contrary to Locke, many European Enlightenment thinkers in the nineteenth
century fretted that liberty and democracy might impair social welfare, even if minorities
were protected and states were governed by majority rule. They demanded social justice
over democratic sovereignty.
    Philosophers understand that social justice is an elusive concept. Nonetheless in the
European context from the start of the nineteenth-century thinkers who described themselves as socialists like Claude Henri de Rouvroy, comte de Saint Simon (1760–1825),
Francois Marie Charles Fourier (1772–1837), Robert Owen (1771–1858), and Karl Marx

This counterapproach to elected government today is interchangeably called social democracy, or democratic socialism, in Europe. The term is an oxymoron in the Enlightenment sense because the *demos* and society can

(1818–1883) insisted that "reason" required just societies to eradicate the exploitation of man by man, encourage the full actualization of individual human potential (renaissance men and women), assure personal freedom, equal opportunity, egalitarianism (equality of outcomes), protection of fundamental human rights, women's liberation, and the provision of basic needs.

Economic and social justice including egalitarianism of outcomes trump prosperity whenever choices must be made between them. For example, egalitarianism of outcomes (everyone receives similar income and wealth) necessitates taxing the highly productive and transferring receipts to those who contribute less. This could easily discourage effort, investment, and entrepreneurship, reducing per-capita income. Socialists understand the problem, but insist that "less, but equal" is better than "more, but unfair." Likewise, Marxists ardently defend basic human rights, but not the right to private property and business because in their view both entail labor exploitation.

Socialism thus is not just a matter of condemning the side effects of Adam Smith's invisible hand and the libertarian preference for small government (without Marx's harmonist presumption); it is a philosophy that absolutizes basic principles like exploitation-free societies and egalitarianism. Where democrats tolerate conflicting claims about the *summum bonum* (highest good), socialists contend that sovereigns have a superior duty to protect that which transcends personal freedom and choice. Both share common humanist and Enlightenment views about the primacy of the individual and the virtue of autonomy in building worthy existences, but for socialists individual fulfillment takes a backseat to the higher good of egalitarianism and societal well-being.

The fine print of these socialist duties, however, is subject to debate. Robert Owen thought human ills could be cured by banning market prices and requiring goods to be exchanged according to the labor time expended in their production. Karl Marx first preached the gospel of communal harmony, but then stressed the need for scientific public economic administrators to choose technologies, allocate factors, determine production and distribute outputs after private property, business, and entrepreneurship were criminalized.

Democratic socialists by contrast are less categorical. They believe that ideal consensus priorities can be determined through competitive multiparty socialist governments, where rival people's spokesmen press their interpretation of society's will. At first glance, this seems tantamount to pluralist democratic republicanism, but is not because while nonsocialist parties may participate in elections, "true society" must be socialist, an implication that has crept into the U.S. polity and caused cognitive dissonance.

Enlightenment thinkers like Emmanuel Kant (*Answering the Question: What is Enlightenment?*, 1784) argued for the free unimpeded use of one's own intelligence as a superior guide to righteous behavior, justice, and the optimal design of human institutions compatible with the "rights of man" (*French Declaration of the Rights of Man and the Citizen*, 1789). Just at the moment when European monarchs were claiming to rule by "divine right of kings," Enlightenment philosophers insisted democracy was better (John Locke, Jean-Jacques Rousseau, Montesquieu), and when the French Revolution erupted, many interpreted the event as the harbinger of impending global democracy. See Perry Anderson, *Lineages of the Absolutist State*, London: Verso, 1974; Michael Kimmenl, *Absolutism and Its Discontents: State and Society in Seventeenth-Century France and England*, New Brunswick, NJ: Transaction Books, 1988; Hillary Zmora, *Monarchy, Aristocracy, and the State in Europe – 1300–1800*, New York: Routledge, 2001; Milan Zafirovski, *The Enlightenment and Its Effect on Modern Society*, 2001.

simultaneously rule only by coincidence, but can be understood nonetheless as societal rule with popular consent. Extreme variants like those of Robert Owens and Karl Marx were tried and failed, but the notion that good democracy requires the *demos* to sacrifice some basic liberties to achieve superior social priorities, also commended by Alexis de Tocqueville,[26] continues to flourish in Europe, Canada, Australia, and New Zealand, and has become a major force in the United States. Elected governments that fail to achieve the social priorities of the moment from a socio-cratic perspective are bad (uncaring) democracies,[27] even when they accurately reflect the people's will. "Social democrats" (who are not democrats at all; they are sociocrats) in this way often succeed in fooling the public into believing that they are the true democrats and that those pressing insider minority agendas are the voice of the people.

DEMOCRATIC PERPLEXITIES

American democratic practice departed from true democratic theory, even before the advent of politocracy, blurring its merit. Many have tried to separate the wheat from the chaff by identifying true democracy's essence. James Russell Lowell, for example, stressed equal opportunity – "that form of society in which every man had a chance and knew that he had it"[28] – and John Stuart Mill championed individual rights over majority tyranny.[29] However, neither these nor other suggestions[30] have proven adequate because the concept of true democracy itself is riddled with perplexities.

Steven Rosefielde and R. W. Pfouts, "Egalitarianism and Production Potential in Postcrisis Russia," in Steven Rosefielde, ed., *Efficiency and the Economic Recovery Potential of Russia*, Aldershot: Ashgate, 1998; Amartya Sen, *The Idea of Justice*, Cambridge, MA: Harvard University Press, 2009; Karl Marx, *The Communist Manifesto*, New York: Penguin, 1998 (1848). Karl Marx, *Das Kapital*, Verlag von Otto Meisner, 1867; Alec Nove, *The Economics of Feasible Socialism*, London: Routledge, 1983.

[26] Hugh Brogan, *Alexis De Tocqueville: A Life*, New Haven: Yale University Press, 2008.

[27] Advocates of social democracy in its various guises disparagingly label Enlightenment democrats as "conservative," even though they champion liberty over political privilege. This political labeling is obscurantist, but the intention is plain. Those promoting the empowerment of the underprivileged against constitutional rights of everyone else call themselves liberals and social democrats. Enlightenment democrats are stigmatized as conservative libertarians.

[28] Address, Birmingham, England, October 6, 1884. James Russell Lowell, *Democracy*, New York: Riverside Press, 1902.

[29] John Stuart Mill, *On Liberty*, 1859.

[30] Andrei Okara, *Sovereign Democracy: A New Russian Idea or PR Project, Russia in Global Affairs*, Vol. 5, No. 3, July–September 2007, pp. 8–20.

Who are the people (republicans, the proletariat, the oppressed, the nation, every living person)? How informed and competent are they? How do they forge their intentions (individually, collectively, communally, imitatively, deferentially, rationally, emotionally, intuitively, impressionistically, neurotically, psychotically, reflexively, eclectically, or haphazardly)? What is democracy's proper scope (politics, economics, society, religion, culture, identity, values, or private behavior)? Ought democratic governments create, promote, administer, control, and defend unpopular (and therefore minority) values like reparations for social injustices of prior generations? Should they take stands on controversial issues like abortion and homosexual marriage? How extensive are the freedoms and protections of the Bill of Rights, including first-amendment freedoms of religion, speech, press, assembly, petition, and ninth-amendment nonenumerated rights (sexual orientation, abortion, right to life, prostitution, incest, suicide, right to mock the "prophet," and the right to teach creationism)?

What is true democracy in practice, and what are its ideal forms? Does it require the rule of contract law? Does it require bureaucracy? Does the rule of law take precedence over democratic authority? Does bureaucracy take precedence over democratic authority? Does divine law trump human law? On balance, do the media facilitate or impede informed democratic choice? Can political elections provide agents with enough information for them to ascertain the people's wants with market-like precision (Arrow's Paradox)?[31] Is electoral balloting reliable? If it is, are representatives the people's voices, and do they act as agents with broad discretionary powers, nannies, custodians, or guardians of incompetent wards obliged to rule in their interest? Are elected officials pawns of the powerful, or co-conspirators with them? If elected officials and their privileged partners rule in their own behalf, does civic participation (participatory democracy) offset the damage?

Must the people and electoral agents be morally upright? Should prisoners be permitted to vote? Is democracy a means rather than an end? If it is a means, do higher ends (isms) justify repressing democracy in favor of one-party rule (contemporary China)? Is popular consent sufficient to make government democratic?[32] Can the *demos* restrain usurpers in the United States and other popularly elected governments across the globe? Do the

---

[31] Kenneth Arrow famously proved mathematically that democratic voting almost always allows the preferences of losers to determine some policy decisions. See Kenneth Arrow, *Social Choice and Individual Values*, New York: Wiley, 2nd ed., 1963.

[32] Russian slavophils contended that tsarism was autocracy with popular consent. Also, see Edward Herman and Noam Chomsky, *Manufacturing Consent: The Political Economy of the Mass Media*, Boston: Pantheon, 1988.

people have the right to vote democracy out of existence as the Germans unwittingly did in 1932 when Hitler finished second in the presidential race, or by approving complex institutions too opaque to be effectively monitored? Is agonism (irreconcilability of social conflict) an inextricable aspect of democracy?[33]

These questions, which reflect the paradoxes of the human condition, contradictory individual aspirations, and irreconcilable differences within the body politic (agonism), should give pause to those who conflate "ocracies," including anarchy, sociocracy, and true democracy, with harmonious utopias. No human institution, including Karl Marx's property-free and stateless communism, guarantees social bliss. Nonetheless, despite considerable skepticism, most contemporary Westerners feel in their bones that the problems associated with true democratic state governance can be surmounted for most intents and purposes. Those with a pragmatic bent are persuaded that the benefits of fair electoral systems greatly outweigh deficiencies even when officials violate their trust, while idealists incline toward faith in the icon's miraculous self-healing powers. They consider pragmatists allies, scoff at doubting Thomases, and scorn anyone who believes that nonelectoral forms of governance are superior.

True democracy for them is an either-or proposition pitting balloting on one hand against authoritarianism on the other. They may prefer the majority rule of true democracy over social democracy, or vice versa, but these nuances are considered secondary. They believe that fair elections are sufficient for assuring satisfactory popular outcomes.

However, suppose that the people vote, but are not informed that their elected representatives act self-interestedly as their masters. The resulting regime would have a popular form, but would be devoid of true democratic substance regardless of whether it billed itself as Enlightenment democracy, social democracy, sovereign democracy, or people's democracy.[34] The

---

[33] Agonism is a political theory based on the insight that many elements of social conflict are irreconcilable. This implies to the European left that fora must be created that give progressive voices a fair hearing, otherwise the electorate will become inert. Chantal Mouffe, *The Democratic Paradox*, London: Verso, 2000. Mouffe argues that democratic theories stressing the possibility of harmonious politics conceal core conflicts and distort democratic purpose (finding acceptable solutions to hard problems without sweeping the details under the rug). The Enlightenment view is that the task of creating fora should be left to the people and not assigned to the government against the majority's expressed will.

[34] People's democracies like China, North Korea, Vietnam, and Cuba claim that they legitimately reflect the will and consent of the proletariat of the future, regardless of what today's capitalist-tainted citizens might think. Sovereign democracy is a term coined by Vladislav Surkov that conflates the assertion of popular consent with the people's sovereignty. It was offered in 2006 to rationalize Russian President Vladimir Putin's claim that authoritarian Russia is a superior form of democracy.

appearance of true democracy fostered by formal balloting would be a mirage, the antithesis of what it seemed to be.

DEMOCRATIC CAPTURE

It is the central thesis of this book that true democracy (majority rule subject to minority property and civil-rights guarantees) in the United States largely has been captured by elected officials and collaborators including sociocrats (social democrats) for their own benefit (politocracy);[35] that although balloting remains, the reality has been debased,[36] causing today's economic, social, and international woes. The new system controlled by democracy's elected enemies is not bad democracy attributable to partisanship, institutional imperatives, or error. It is politocracy, the sovereignty of elected politicians who place their self-interest ahead of their democratic duty. This judgment will be substantiated in subsequent chapters, especially 3, 5, 6, 8, and 9.

Our thesis has a double sense. First, it implies that operational control over the purpose and conduct of federal governance has shifted from the people to self-seeking politicians. Second, Americans are losing their autonomy by allowing political rhetoric to uncritically shape their perceptions, identities, and judgments. It is fallacious to call the U.S. governance system democratic in part because the *demos* is becoming whatever its masters want it to be. Such systems are not democracies of autonomous, free-thinking persons.[37] Insider self-seeking that masquerades as sage policy making has displaced the public interest, denials to the contrary

---

[35] Darrell Issa, Republican Representative from California's 49th Congressional district, and reputedly Congress's richest member, provides a case in point.

Even as he has built a reputation as a forceful Congressional advocate for business, Mr. Issa has bought up office buildings, split a holding company into separate multibillion-dollar businesses, started an insurance company, traded hundreds of millions of dollars in securities, invested in overseas funds, retained an interest in his auto-alarm company and built up a family foundation. As his wealth and public power have grown, so too has the overlap between his private and business lives, with at least some of the congressman's government actions helping to make a rich man even richer and raising the potential for conflicts. He has secured millions of Congressional earmarks for road work and public works project that promise improved traffic and other benefits to the many commercial properties he owns here north of San Diego. ("Helping His District and Himself," *New York Times*, August 15, 2011).

[36] Balloting in Russia and sundry people's democracies likewise masks antidemocratic rule, but it is widely understood that Russia's government is authoritarian, and that communist parties control "people's republics."

[37] Erick Hoffer, *The True Believer: Thoughts on the Nature of Mass Movements*, Hew York: Harper and Row, 1951.

notwithstanding.[38] "Your leaders are ... the companions of thieves; all of them take bribes" (Isaiah 1:23).

Abuse of the public interest of course is nothing new. Partisans and opportunists always have sought political help for their causes, or so-called worthy projects, seeking to impose their will on the majority and enrich themselves with unmerited benefices, grants, sinecures, usufructs, rents, incomes, and wealth transfers. Ideologues have foisted their programs on the public, while unscrupulous constituents solicited, and politicians obligingly sold, favors. These peccadilloes degraded true democracy's substance, but the corruption was kept in check by higher standards of public virtue (Puritanism and Enlightenment idealism) and the relatively small size and limited reach of pre-New Deal U.S. government.

NOISELESS USURPATION

President Franklin Delano Roosevelt (FDR) changed the dimensions and character of the United States' true democracy in the course of fighting the Great Depression by constructing an antieconomic royalist (antiplutocratic) regime. Pursuing this mission, however, FDR's administrations and Democratic congresses overreached (ruling roughshod over minority protections), and in the process increased the potential for social zealotry and corruption by re-engineering social attitudes and enlarging government's scale and scope. FDR condoned expedient and often unconstitutional behavior ("packing" the Supreme Court) on dubious lofty grounds (those of social emergency),[39] encouraged judicial usurpation (under the banner of a living constitution), and most importantly embraced social protection and national prosperity management over individual liberty as government's central missions.[40]

---

[38] The traditional ideal in Tacitus's characterization of the Germans in the period before they overthrew the Roman Empire is "They live in a state of chastity well secured; corrupted by no seducing shows and public diversions.... Nobody turns vices into mirth... nor is the practice of corrupting and of yielding to corruption called the custom of the Age" (J.B. Rives, *Tacitus: Germania*, Oxford: Oxford University Press, 1999).

[39] Franklin Roosevelt proposed asking Congress for the power to appoint one additional judge to the federal judiciary (including the Supreme Court) for every justice who had reached the age of seventy but declined to retire on March 9, 1937, under the guise of easing the backlog of cases that faced the "aged, overworked justices." While his ostensible purpose was to increase the efficiency of the judiciary, it was clear that Roosevelt was targeting six of the nine Supreme Court justices who had challenged his domestic programs.

[40] Steven Rosefielde and Assaf Razin, "Currency and Financial Crises of the 1990s and 2000s," *CESifo Economic Studies*, Vol. 57, No. 3, 2011, pp. 499–530.

At first these developments benefited and enriched few, but subsequently, with numerous twists and turns (including the unifying effects of World War II),[41] evolved into a shadow elite politocracy.[42] During the New Deal, fledgling politocrats limited themselves to peddling parochial influence (especially via the Congressional pork barrel) but gradually learned how to transform the mundane sale of public services into a mega private business by managing the macroeconomy and expanding abroad. Just as bigness altered the American business landscape, it radically changed the nature of government influence-brokering.

Local political bosses, who were once content to be big fish in little ponds, gradually became an aspiring political class,[43] as Gaetano Mosca labeled it long ago, detached from control of those who elected them. They no longer were satisfied with using chattel slavery, or wage slavery (Lowell Mill girls, 1836) to steer fortunes their way.[44] Politicians today employ more sophisticated means, providing low-interest subsidies to banks and Wall Street, promoting financial speculation, deficit spending, inflation, stealthy taxation (excessive health care and education costs), grants-in-aid, mandates, and manipulating public programs under the banner of consumer sovereignty.[45] They have learned how to exploit high-minded

---

[41] Nathan J. Brown, ed. *The Dynamics of Democratization: Dictatorship, Development and Diffusion*, Baltimore: Johns Hopkins University Press, 2011.

[42] The term "shadow elites" was coined by Janine Wedel. See Janine Wedel, *Shadow Elite: How the World's New Power Brokers Undermine Democracy, Government and the Free Market*, New York: Basic Books, 2009.

[43] The term "political class" was coined by Gaetano Mosca (1858–1941) and refers to a small group of career political participants who not only dominate policymaking (both as politicians and public-administration experts) but enrich themselves from it (Max Weber). See Gaetano Mosca, *The Ruling Class*, 1896; Max Weber, "Politics as a Vocation," in H. Gerth and C. Wright Mills, eds., *From Max Weber*, London: Routledge and Kegan Paul, 1970; Robert Putnam, *The Comparative Study of Political Elites*, New York: Prentice Hall, 1976; Peter Osborne, *The Triumph of the Political Class*, New York: Simon and Schuster, 2007; C. Wright Mills, *The Power Elite and the State: How Policy is Made in America*, New York: Oxford University Press, 1956; David Horowitz, *America's Political Class Under Fire: The Twentieth Century's Great Culture Wars*, New York: Routledge, 2003; Jens Borchert and Jurgen Zeiss, eds., *The Political Class in Advanced Democracies*, New York: Oxford University Press, 2003. Private-interest governments were identified in the 1980s as a special form of public regulation in selected economic sectors, rivaling conventional market, state, or community-based forms of public order. For a survey of the phenomenon's evolution see Claudius Wagemann, *Breakdown and Change of Private Interest Governments*, New York: Routledge, 2011.

[44] Lowell mills girls were mostly female textile employees in nineteenth-century Lowell, Massachusetts, famous for descrying low wages and other abusive working conditions through their newspaper, *Voice of Industry*.

[45] Consumer sovereignty is an economic term referring to a state where consumers' preferences (demand) govern supply without external manipulation.

altruism,[46] game income transfers, rig regulations, and dole out tax breaks in the name of prosperity, accelerated economic growth, full employment, empowerment, and social justice. The siren song of this new order has been disingenuously called the Great Society,[47] the Welfare State, the Just Society,[48] or as John Kenneth Galbraith preferred, the New Industrial State partnership of labor, business, and academia (technocrats),[49] but these "doublespeak" labels, however idealistically intended, are mostly eyewash.[50]

The phenomenon in its entirety continues to elude many because it is the result of a "noiseless revolution,"[51] an evolutionary political reeducation process, rather than a palace coup d'etat. Neither the executive committee of the capitalist class, as Marxists would have it,[52] nor a partisan faction seized the reins from the electorate and usurped power as Bolsheviks did when the Soviets criminalized markets and substituted central planning. There

---

[46] The end of democracy is the collective advancement of individual welfare. President John Kennedy turned this idea on its head by exhorting citizens to sacrifice themselves for the state. "Ask not what your country can do for you. Ask what you can do for your country." Inaugural Address, January 20, 1961. Shadow elites include academic advisors, businesspersons, organized labor, NGOs, and sundry activists at home and abroad bent on harnessing the possibilities of partisan social engineering, trading favors, and hijacking aggregate demand management and regulation to achieve their causes and enrich themselves.

[47] The Great Society was President Lyndon Baines Johnson's policy of using the instruments of state governance to build a prosperous society for all, including those left behind, that is, the poor and those victimized by racial discrimination.

[48] James Meade, *Principles of Political Economy: The Just Society*, Chicago: Aldine Press, 1965.

[49] John Kenneth Galbraith, *The New Industrial State*, New York: Houghton-Mifflin, 1967; *Economics and The Public Purpose*, New York: Houghton-Mifflin, 1973; *The Good Society*, New York: Mariner Books, 1997. Notice that government is omitted from this formula and that workers have been displaced by a heterogeneous entity often described as the disadvantaged.

[50] Doublespeak is an euphemism that not only softens the meaning of a concept, but reverses it, calling black white, or dystopia utopia. Although the term is similar to George Orwell's concept of doublethink, he does not use it explicitly in *1984*. See George Orwell, *1984*, New York: Signet Book, 1949; and William Lutz, *Doublespeak: From "Revenue Enhancement" to "Terminal Living": How Government, Business, Advertisers, and Others Use Language to Deceive You*, New York: Harper & Row, 1987.

[51] "The circumstances which have most influence on the happiness of mankind – the changes of manners and morals, the transition of communities from poverty to wealth, from ignorance to knowledge, from ferocity to humanity – are for the most part noiseless revolutions" (Thomas Babington Macaulay, "History," *Edinburgh Review*, May 1828). The contemporary noiseless revolution has unfolded differently than Macaulay anticipated, proceeding from knowledge to ignorance and humanity to ferocity.

[52] There are innumerable books blaming democracy's failures on capitalism. For a recent work of this type see Bruce Scott, *Capitalism: Its Origins and Evolution as a System of Governance*, Berlin: Springer, 2011.

was nothing this noticeable. Instead, elected officials today act stealthily behind a facade of virtuous intentions. How precisely did this coup d'etat by indoctrinated consent happen? How has true democracy been stolen unnoticed right from under our noses?

The answer is gradually and almost imperceptibly through insider guile and public inattentiveness that cannot be easily reversed. Self-seeking elected officials, shadow elites, and accomplices do not want to relinquish their grip on power. Their bread and butter is promising favors to the electorate in return for votes and selling the spoils of government to backers and collaborators under the table. Drastically rolling back government therefore might seem to provide a partial solution, but it is difficult to achieve because large segments of society have become addicted to big government. Leaders do not want independent small government because it would radically diminish their clout. Shadow elites, favor-seekers, and plutocratic partners are fighting hard to preserve their privileges, and many ordinary people are hooked by government largesse.

Moreover, most Americans are conflicted. For more than eighty years they have been misled into believing that although big government is wasteful and corrupt, on balance individuals each get more (public services and charity) than they grudgingly contribute. Voters can be counted upon to demand the curtailment of programs they do not like, but also to insist on preserving or expanding those that they deem indispensable, including tax breaks. Many do not want their pipedreams debunked, preferring to believe that the Ponzi scheme of stealing now and shifting the debt burden to future generations somehow increases the collective pie by accelerating aggregate economic growth.[53] They do not want to know that sustainable prosperity is diminished by self-serving government middlemen of sundry descriptions, who charge exorbitant agent fees, or that pervasive government inefficiency degrades national welfare.

Alvy Singer expressed the bittersweet absurdity of the American predicament with a quip about his relationship with Annie Hall:

I thought of that old joke, y'know, this guy goes to a psychiatrist and says, "Doc, uh, my brother's crazy, he thinks he's a chicken." And, uh, the doctor says, "Well, why don't you turn him in?" The guy says, "I would, but I need the eggs." Well, I guess that's pretty much how I feel about relationships, y'know, they're totally irrational, and crazy, and absurd, and ... but, uh, I guess we keep goin' through it because, uh, most of us ... need the eggs.[54]

---

[53] This is a Ponzi scheme because transfers do not cause value-adding growth. Future generations, like Madoff's shareholders, are going to get stuck with the bill.

[54] *Annie Hall.* http://www.imdb.com/title/tt0075686/quotes

That's the way Americans feel about their crisis-prone, economically stultifying big governments and government capture. They know that Washington is "irrational, and crazy, and absurd," and that the extra eggs exist only in their imagination, but they persist because they "need the eggs."

This is the specific sense in which contemporary American true democracy is a mirage. The government that the people perceive is not the individually empowering, libertarian, virtuous free enterprise (or optimally managed) system they have been misled to believe.[55] Americans know this.[56] Nonetheless, they do not want to accept it, will not easily forsake their denial, and fail to vote in their true long-term self-interest.[57]

---

[55] Also, it should not be forgotten that the people themselves are not always virtuous. It was the British commons, not the king, who pressed to overtax the colonials (Americans).

[56] People in Eastern democracies have lower expectations about their participation in and influence on state government than their Western counterparts.

[57] This is classic doublethink, a corollary of doublespeak.

To know and not to know, to be conscious of complete truthfulness while telling carefully constructed lies, to hold simultaneously two opinions which cancelled out, knowing them to be contradictory and believing in both of them, to use logic against logic, to repudiate morality while laying claim to it, to believe that democracy was impossible and that the Party was the guardian of democracy, to forget, whatever it was necessary to forget, then to draw it back into memory again at the moment when it was needed, and then promptly to forget it again, and above all, to apply the same process to the process itself – that was the ultimate subtlety; consciously to induce unconsciousness, and then, once again, to become unconscious of the act of hypnosis you had just performed. Even to understand the word "doublethink" involved the use of doublethink. (George Orwell, *1984*, London: Martin Secker & Warburg Ltd, London, 1949, part 1, chapter 3, p. 32).

Cf. Voltaire's seventeenth-century satire of the same mentality, as Dr. Pangloss explains why syphilis is really good for you: " it was a thing unavoidable, a necessary ingredient in the best of worlds; for if Columbus had not caught in an island in America this disease, which contaminates the source of generation, and frequently impedes propagation itself, and is evidently opposed to the great end of nature, we should have had neither chocolate nor cochineal" (Voltaire, *Candide, or the Optimist*, 1759).

THREE

Politocracy

POLITARCHS

Contemporary U.S. government is "politocratic;" a regime where elected officials usurp the people's sovereignty, primarily running the state as a private business and foisting their policy agendas on the majority.[1] The system is customarily called democracy because multiparty representatives are popularly elected, implying that the services rendered by the federal government are "of," "by," and "for" the people, even though the *demos* has been disempowered by its elected enemies. Politarchs often deceive themselves into believing that they are true democrats, but in actuality have become masters by transforming the democratic facade into a government of elected officials, by elected officials, for elected officials.[2] Fareed Zakaria dubs the regime "illiberal democracy," a term that conveys one important aspect of the phenomenon.[3]

Politocracy is furtive. Politarchs rule in their own interest, but portray themselves as people's agents, humble representatives, leaders, statesmen,

---

[1] It is an organization of legislators, executives, judges, administrators, regulators, and public-service providers; overseen, performed and controlled by elected politicians in collaboration with professional jurists, administrators, regulators, officials, technocrats, civic actors (including NGOs), external experts, and lobbyists serving the people generally, constituents, and other motivated parties (including foreigners, business, organized labor, social action, and religious groups), all in the name of the *demos*.

[2] Cruder versions of politocracy occur in less developed nations, including India. See Emmanuel Oneyemaghani Owah, "Government of the Crooks, by the Crooks, for the Crooks, Kleptocracy Nigeria Expose," Xlibris, 2011, and Alan Heston and Vijay Kuman, "Institutional Flaws and Corruption Incentives in India," *Journal of Development Studies*, Vol. 44, No. 9, 2008, pp. 1243–61.

[3] Fareed Zakaria, *The Future of Freedom: Illiberal Democracy at Home and Abroad*, New York: W.W. Norton, 2007. Zakaria, "The Rise of Illiberal Democracy," *Foreign Affairs*, November/December, 1997, pp. 22–43.

and popular coalition builders guiding the ship of state for the *demos's* good.[4] They often are intelligent, competent, congenial and persuasive, making it difficult to pierce the facade. The Bush and Obama administrations' mismanagement of the 2008 financial crisis provides a window into their hidden agendas. The crisis was not a figment of anyone's imagination. The entire financial system was on the cusp of imploding. Emergency methods were required to staunch the hemorrhaging without putting long-term well-being at risk.

This called for surgical intervention in the financial sector, coupled with a reduction of the ruinous national debt.[5] The government's response was just the reverse. Instead of intervening only where essential, Washington chose to bail out the financial sector and vastly expand deficit spending beyond what was required, and then continued spending at the new levels as the Troubled Asset Relief Program (TARP) wound down because the excesses served politicians best.[6] This disregard for the national interest in favor of political symbolism, parochial causes, and insider enrichment epitomizes politocracy[7] and distinguishes it from both legitimate public agency and

[4] Politarchs often do not see any contradiction in serving themselves for the benefit of special interests, taking the position democracy requires them to service their constituencies even when this is at the expenses of the people and the Constitutional guarantees that protect them.

[5] Politarchs counter unpersuasively that the greater the national debt, the faster GDP grows, creating the wherewithal to finance perpetually expanding debt. Empirical evidence disconfirms the claim.

[6] The "fiscal cliff" agreement changed nothing. See Martin Hutchinson, "Global Investing Strategist," *Money Morning*, January 3, 2013: "In the end, the agreement reached on Tuesday night will only reduce the deficit by about $60 billion annually over the next 10 years. That's less than 10% of the total projected deficits, which means well before 2020 we will likely have a real crisis on our hands."

[7] Peter Yost and Thomas Beaumont, "Gingrich Says He Received Freddie Mac Compensation," Associated Press: "Gingrich said he didn't remember exactly how much he was paid, but a former Freddie Mac official said it was at least $1.5 million for consulting contracts stretching from 1999 to 2007." Margaret Chadbourn, "Fannie, Freddie Executives Defend Pay Packages," Reuters, November 16, 2011: "Top executives at Fannie Mae and Freddie Mac on Wednesday defended their companies' pay practices which have drawn opposition after it was disclosed the government-controlled firms were paying out nearly $13 million in executive bonuses." Michael Tarm, "Any Defiance Could Hurt Blagojevich at Sentencing," Yahoo! News, December 4, 2011: "As Rod Blagojevich steps before a sentencing judge, the impeached Illinois governor might do well to suppress the cocksure, perpetual campaigner in him and conjure up a lesser-known figure: The humble, contrite family man. Whether he can pull that off at the hearing beginning Tuesday may play a role in determining the sentence imposed for his 18 convictions, including that Blagojevich sought to auction off the Senate seat Barack Obama was vacating to become president."

"Blagojevich Sentenced to 14 years," ABC News, December 7, 2011: A federal judge today sentenced impeached Illinois Gov. Rod Blagojevich to 14 years in prison, giving

mundane favor peddling.[8] Politocracy is a governance culture that trans-
forms occasional individual bad behavior into the full-time business of selling public services heedless of collateral damage,[9] effectively decoupling the
supply of government services from the *demos's* demand.[10] Politacracy dis-
enfranchises the people even though there are elections because the usurpation is trans-partisan. Democrats and Republicans distribute the spoils
differently but collaborate in indoctrinating the public and placing their
joint agenda in collaboration with big business and big social advocacy

little weight to Blagojevich's first-ever apology this morning since his arrest three years
ago. "The jury didn't believe you and neither did I," U.S. District Court Judge James Zagel
said. Blagojevich was convicted on 18 corruption charges, including the scheme to peddle
the vacated Senate seat of Barack Obama. Prosecutors argued that he has failed the people
of Illinois and instead "further eroded the public's confidence in government and government officials." "He knew from a very early date exactly what he could do to help the people of Illinois and he didn't do it," federal prosecutor Reid Schar said. "Instead, what he
did was first to seek personal benefits, jobs, millions of dollars, and things for him in rela-
tion to the Senate seat. He lied repeatedly, concretely, and on issues that went to the heart
of the case and he lied on every episode that he was questioned," Schar said. "He is incredibly manipulative, and he knows how to be." Judge Zagel earlier sided with prosecutors
in key rulings that could help determine the prison sentence. Zagel agreed that evidence
showed supporters of U.S. Rep. Jesse Jackson Jr., D-Ill., were offering $1.5 million in cam-
paign contributions in exchange for the Senate appointment, a dollar figure that factors
into sentencing even though Blagojevich never got the money. If Blagojevich is sent to
jail today, he will join George Ryan, a Republican who was governor from 1999 to 2003,
who is serving a prison sentence. After a scandal involving the illegal sale of government
licenses, contracts and leases by state employees, Ryan was convicted of corruption in
2006. But Ryan was merely following in the footsteps of those who came before him. Otto
Kerner Jr., a Democrat who was governor from 1961 to 1968, was convicted in 1973 on 17
counts of bribery, conspiracy, perjury and related charges. Dan Walker, a Democrat who
was governor from 1973 to 1977, pleaded guilty to bank fraud, misapplication of funds
and perjury in 1987. Walker was sentenced to seven years in prison.

8 The counterargument is that the United States' financial system would have imploded
without TARP. The claim is implausible and cannot be proven. The Federal Reserve had
alternative means for creating money to replace the losses caused by the bankruptcy of
firms like AIG.

9 The failure of the Joint Select Committee on Deficit Reduction (super committee) to reach
a deficit reduction agreement in November 2011, despite the clear and present danger of a
financial meltdown, is emblematic of politocracy's disregard for the people's welfare.

10 James Copland, *Trial Lawyers Inc.: Attorneys General – A Report on the Alliance between
State AGs and the Plaintiffs' Bar 2011*, Manhattan Institute's Center for Legal Policy, 2011.
James R. Copland shows how State attorney generals (AG) enter into contingency-fee
contracts with private plaintiffs' firms, who often rake in windfall fees – and just as often
fill the officials' campaign coffers. In general, it is not the state AGs but the plaintiffs' bar
that designs the legal theories used to litigate on behalf of the states. The contingency-fee
arrangements entered into by many state AGs allow the economic interests of private-sector
lawyers to influence state law-enforcement priorities. Statewide campaigns demand rich
war chests, making it difficult for state AGs to resist the prospect of hefty campaign donations from the plaintiffs' lawyers. www.triallawyersinc.com.

ahead of the people's well-being,[11] devitalizing and destabilizing the nation's economy.[12]

Jon Corzine, Newt Gingrich, and Al Gore are politar-chic archetypes.[13] Like an army of Tweedledum and Tweedledee

---

[11] Their collaboration is compatible with "gridlock." Often the failure of Democrats and Republicans to compromise to the people's detriment is not about partisan principle. It is motivated by the conviction that both parties are better off judged in terms of narrow personal interests.

[12] Laura Litvan, "Congress Getting Failing Marks on Economy in Year of Gridlock," *Bloomberg*, December 16, 2011:

Congress is ending what may be its least productive year on record after government shut-down threats, the collapse of debt-reduction talks and little action to fix the worst U.S. economy since the Great Depression. Just 62 bills were signed into law through November this year, meaning that 2011 may fall short of the 88 laws enacted in 1995, the lowest num-ber since the Congressional Record began keeping an annual tally in 1947. In 1995, as in this year, a new House Republican majority fought a Democratic president's agenda.

[13] Peter Lattman and Nelson Schwartz, "In Corzine Comeback, Big Risks and Steep Fall," *Wall Street Journal*, November 1, 2011: "Mr. Corzine, with a fortune estimated at half a bil-lion dollars at its peak, did not confine his future ambitions to Wall Street. Even as he was seeking to revive his financial career, Mr. Corzine, a Democrat, had long styled himself as a financial executive moving seamlessly between Washington and Wall Street." Corzine was a top executive of Goldman Sachs, then a Democratic senator for the state of New Jersey, then governor of New Jersey, and then CEO of MF Global, a financial firm that bet big with its own and customers' money on the European debt crisis, lost, and is now bank-rupt. Corzine may face criminal charges. MSNBC reported that Jon Corzine had been the biggest single contributor to President Obama's reelection campaign until the collapse of Corzine's firm on November 3, 2011. Azad Ahmed and Ben Protess, "As Regulators Pressed Charges, Corzine Pushed Back and Won," *New York Times*, November 4, 2011:

As a former United States senator and a former governor of New Jersey, as well as the leader of Goldman Sachs in the 1990s, Mr. Corzine carried significant weight in the worlds of Washington and Wall Street. While other financial firms employed teams of lobbyists to fight the new regulation, MF Global's chief executive in meetings over the last year per-sonally pressed regulators to halt their plans.

As a former sovereign debt trader at Goldman Sachs, Mr. Corzine wagered that the European regulators would backstop any default. So even as dark clouds circled over Europe, he sensed an opportunity. Starting in late 2010, MF Global began to accumulate short-term sovereign debt of countries like Italy, Spain and Portugal. MF Global financed these pur-chases through complex transactions known as repurchase agreements. In these, the bonds themselves were used as collateral for a loan to purchase them. The interest paid on that loan was less than the interest the bonds paid out, earning the firm a profit from the spread.

$630 million is missing.

Aron Task, "Jon Corzine: Taken to Task for Excessive Chutzpah," Yahoo! Finance, August 22, 2012:

Russell Wasendorf of Peregrine Financial was indicted last week on 31 counts of lying to regulators and robbing his firm's clients of about $200 million. Wasendorf, who plead "not guilty" to the charges, faces up to 155 years in jail. Meanwhile, the *New York Times* reports, NO charges are likely against Jon Corzine or other senior execs of MF Global – where $1.6 billion of customer funds remain missing nearly a year after the futures brokers

look-alikes,[14] they are personable, polished, glib, and unscrupulous,[15] putting on airs and aspiring to become members of a parvenu aristocracy (Roosevelts, Kennedys, Gores, Rockefellers, Bushes).[16] They pursue causes that allow them to transform public service into private businesses.[17] Their

filed for bankruptcy. Which brings us back to a segment we call Taken to Task. Look, I get that proving a crime is tough, but when the guy accused of stealing $200 million goes to jail and the guy who can't account for $1.6 billion is likely to get off scott [sic] free, something is very wrong.

Newt Gingrich is another dramatic example. He takes much money for himself (directly and indirectly via a not-for-profit) from private interests (especially Fannie Mae and Freddie Mac) while attacking them publicly and supporting them privately and defending himself on the grounds that he is operating within the letter of the law. He enriches himself and postures for the electorate without regard to any consistency in his public positions.

[14] Eric Lichtblau, "Economic Downturn Took a Detour at Today's Capitol Hill," *New York Times,* December 27, 2011: "Rarely has the financial divide appeared so wide between lawmakers and those they represent. Lichtblau reports that nearly half of all members of Congress (250) are now millionaires; and that the wealth gap between Congress and constituents has never been larger." *Palm Beach Post,* January 23, 2012: "In the Senate 67 of 100 members have a net worth of more than $1 million, not counting home equity. In the House, 42% have a net worth of more than $1 million and the average is $756,765, not counting home equity."

[15] "Some say compar'd to Bononcini That Mynherr Handel is but a Ninny Others aver, that he to Handel Is scarcely fit to hold a Candle Strange all the Difference should be 'Twixt Tweedle-dum and Tweedle-dee," John Byron (1692–1763). See *John Byron Epigrams on the Feud between Handel and Bononcini, Poems,* The Cheltham Society 1984–895, Literature Online.

[16] Our congress is not composed of distinguished people who have contributed to our country in science, technology, art, commentary, business, or numerous other ways. Our congress is composed of inferior, poorly educated, little experienced, third-rate members of various professions – usually law but sometimes medicine or real estate. Such people seek election to public office as a way to make their fortunes. Such persons, who are habitually meddling and of unquiet minds and litigious disposition, join in any project of legislation that lays open to them lucrative opportunities. It does not matter to which political party each Congressperson declares himself or herself to belong. The momentum of Congress is driven by its members' ignorance and lust for plunder, not by any concern, other than pretended, for the public interest. Most disturbing is the liberal elite who professes such great concern for the U.S. public but who, when they are not on their guard, treat the poor with the greatest contempt. At the same time they pretend to make the poor the depositories of all power and the beneficiaries of all their activities. Their liberalism is not egalitarian. Their supposed knowledge is ignorance; their poverty of imagination is revealed in political correctness; their pretended caring is savage, brutal, and always self-serving. They have sponsored in America a revolution in attitudes, manners, and moral opinions that has enfeebled our nation.

[17] Curt Anderson, "Fla. Ponzi Schemer Implicates Many Others in Crime," Associated Press, January 5, 2012: "Over two grueling weeks, convicted Florida Ponzi schemer Scott Rothstein laid out in incriminating detail how far the tentacles stretched in his $1.2 billion fraud, pointing the finger at numerous lawyers, bankers, business people, relatives, friends and unnamed law enforcement officials and politicians." "Rothstein implicated his former partners, staff and others at his now-defunct Fort Lauderdale law firm. He pointed the

strategy is to construct a transnational insider, state-private governance outsourcing partnership in which select members compete for electoral office, crafting personas and platforms that match malleable constituent identities within boundaries fixed by a pliable public consensus. This allows officials and non-elected privilege seekers to codirect an agenda guided by their pocketbooks,[18] relying on media imagery and attitude management to conceal their self-interest.[19] Victorious politicians governing by consent are free to continuously remake their public images, change stripes, switch parties, accept support from all quarters (foreign as well as domestic) as if they actually heeded the people's will, [20] sell favors and blackmail any way

finger at unnamed local politicians, judges, police officers and sheriff's deputies, claiming he paid at least $1 million in cash bribes and allowed them to live his 'rock-star lifestyle' of private jets, prostitutes, sporting events and strip clubs."

[18] Larry Margasak, "Investigators Say that 4 Reps Got Discounted Loans," Yahoo! News, December 19, 2011: "Congressional investigators said Monday that four House members received VIP discounted loans from the former Countrywide Financial Corp., the lender whose subprime mortgages was largely responsible for the nation's foreclosure crisis. Countrywide also processed VIP loans to public officials and others in position to help the company." Also see Mike McIntire, "Conservative Nonprofit Acts as Stealth Business Lobbyist," *New York Times*, April 22, 2012.

A whistleblower at Common Cause provided documents to the New York Times revealing that 200 private sector businesses gave the non-profit American Legislative Exchange Council $7,500 each to lobby for business friendly legislation. "Some companies give much more, all of it tax deductible: AT&T, Pfizer and Reynolds American each contributed $130,000 to $398,000, according to a copy of ALEC's 2010 tax returns, obtained by *The Times*, that included donors' names, which are normally withheld from public inspection. The returns show that corporate members pay stipends – it calls them "scholarships" – for lawmakers to travel to annual conferences, including a four-day retreat where ALEC spends as much as $250,000 on child care for members' families.

[19] The Supreme Court voted 5–4 in Citizens United that corporations and unions had First Amendment rights to spend as they wished to favor or oppose candidates, regardless of the government's view that such expenditures could corrupt elections for Congress and the presidency. In that opinion, Justice Anthony Kennedy wrote that the government failed to show that independent political expenditures by corporations actually had corrupted federal elections. "Indeed, 26 States do not restrict independent expenditures by for-profit corporations. The Government does not claim that these expenditures have corrupted the political process in those States," Justice Kennedy wrote. It may not be churlish to suggest that the justice department, courts, politocrats, and lobbyists colluded in a smokescreen (that is, that the government suit against Citizens United was not truly a hostile suit, but rather that it was conducted for the purpose of losing the issue and enhancing the corruption of elections) that disempowers voters for the benefit of big corporations and unions.

[20] David Goldstein, "Super PACS channel flood of money into 2012 elections? *Miami Herald*, September 30, 2011. http://www.miamiherald.com/2011/09/30/2432786/super-pacs-channel-flood-of-money.html#ixzz1ZSxLarYV:

Relaxed campaign spending rules unleashed a torrent of cash in the 2010 elections. In 2012, it could be a deluge. Court rulings and revised regulations have made it easier for

they can.[21] They are adept at blaming failures like the sovereign debt crisis on others or on forces beyond their control and promising to make things right, regardless of who is stuck paying the piper. [22]

BIG GOVERNMENT

Politicians can fleece the people in organizations of any size, but rewards are strongly correlated with government's size and scope. From their perspective, the bigger the government, the greater the reward. Collaborators never tire of asking and paying for more favors. American political leaders press the public to support programs expanding domestic entitlements, mandates and regulations, international trade partnerships, customs unions, economic communities, supranational organizations, and world government. Larger government itself is not necessarily bad. The governments of some true democracies may be bigger than others in accordance with the *demos's* will, but oversized politarchic big government is always toxic.

The U.S. federal government today is immense and politarchic. It employs 4.7 million people, including 2.8 civilian workers, 1.2 million active duty military personnel, and 740,000 Defense Department civilians.[23] In 2010,

donors to give as much money to campaigns as they want – and keep it secret. That could shape next year's race for the White House, and very likely the battle to control Congress.

21 Carol Lee and Damian Paletta, "White House Steps Up Push to Toughen Rules on Banks," *Wall Street Journal*, May 17, 2012. Peter Henning, "JP Morgan's Loss: Illegal or Just Bad Judgment?" *New York Times*, May 14, 2012:

A JP Morgan hedge trader made a $2 billion bad bet that prompted the Obama administration to threaten tighter regulations. Of course, you cannot regulate hedge fund risk taking without destroying the business and hence the motive was mundane politicking, which also created an opportunity to blackmail campaign contributions from Wall Street to forestall regulation no sensible party really wants.

22 In a genuine democracy, government programs and living constitutions perpetually adjust to changing public demand, just as supply does to consumer demand in the market place, but in politocracy the politarchs call the tune on the public supply-and-demand side while they pretend to satisfy the people. Also, it should be noted that politocrats aren't always solicitous of the rich. They are quite prepared to have ordinary investors lose substantial sums, as long as interests closer to home are appeased. In the aftermath of the dot-com bubble's collapse, suits were filed on behalf of shareholders in Delaware courts against some eighty-five dot-com companies (each of which was incorporated in Delaware). The litigation consumed a decade and ended only recently. The final settlement provided virtually no money to shareholders but many millions to their attorneys. The Delaware courts approved the settlement. The politarchy (here attorneys and courts) is now at the point of devouring all of the substance of investors. Cf. Aaron Task, "26B Mortgage Settlements: Good for Banks, Not so Goods for Homeowners," Yahoo! Finance, February 9, 2012.

23 U.S. Office of Personnel Management, Federal Employment Statistics, Historical Federal Workforce Tables, Federal Government Employment Since 1962 online. Department of Defense Personnel and Procurement Reports, http://siapapp.dmdc.osd.mil. Total federal

federal tax receipts (including social security) were $4 trillion and outlays $5.3 trillion,[24] $3.4 trillion of which went to labor compensation and direct purchases. Total expenditure as a share of GDP ($14.7 trillion) was 36 percent, equaling nearly 9 percent of the entire world's national income. State and local government spending (excluding federal transfers) substantially augment these aggregates.

U.S. big government is not a myth, regardless of its rationale.[25] Moreover, its reach goes far beyond the employment and expenditure numbers. Government agencies wield power over state-private collusion (including job rotation between the state and private sectors), outsourcing, regulation, mandating (product characteristics, compulsory health insurance, social security insurance), and cost sharing. They regulate the money supply, interest rate, foreign exchange rate, credit, banking, finance, insurance guarantees, taxation, tariffs, quotas, subsidies, transfers, pardons, rules, and preferences (affirmative action, veterans, and the handicapped). The federal government oversees immigration, education, health, social services, food safety, energy, social security, the environment, international trade, foreign aid, foreign policy, international institutions (IMF, World Bank, WTO, NATO, United Nations), and private behavior.[26]

STRATEGY OF PUBLIC MANAGEMENT

U.S. big government has two distinct economic aspects, one transparent, the other opaque. The first component, often called on-budget, includes federal employment, tax revenues, and expenditures. Statistics on these activities are readily available and politically sensitive because the public can be aroused by steadily rising federal employment rolls and spending. Attuned to this

civilian employment in 2006 was 2.7 million, including 29,000 legislative branch and 34,000 judicial-branch employees. Executive-branch workers totaled 2.6 million, including 757,000 postal workers. Men constituted 56 percent of the civilian federal labor force. The average age was 47, and 43 percent had bachelor degrees. The Defense Department employed 740,000 non-civilian employees. The civil, non-defense occupational breakdown in 2004 was: professional, 26 percent; administrative, 41 percent; technical, 23 percent; clerical, 7 percent; other, 3 percent.

[24] U.S. Department of Commerce, Bureau of Economic Analysis, National Income Accounts Government Receipts and Expenditures (seasonally adjusted rates), January 24, 2011, www.bea.gov. The expenditure statistics include all government programs plus negative income taxes ("earned income credits," that is, minimum income support payments, which, for a family with more than three children, could reach $5,761 in 2011. Six million parents and 15 million children receive assistance. A million families with a single mother receive a supplement. Total expenditures should be in the vicinity of $10 billion).

[25] Richard Rosecrance, "Bigger is Better: the Case for a Transatlantic Economic Union," *Foreign Affairs*, Vol. 89, Issue 3, May 2010.

[26] Private behaviors include gay marriage, abortion, drugs, prostitution, and legally protected sex workers.

electoral risk, politicians have chosen to hold the line on federal employment and civil service compensation, concentrating instead on expanding grants-in-aid that shift blame for overstaffing to the states. Politicians
are chafing at the bit to spend more, and periodically do whenever a real
or imaginary national emergency allows them to cover their tracks. The
global financial crisis of 2008 and the subsequent Great Recession (GDP
fell 5.1 percent top to trough) provided just such an excuse.[27] Federal outlays surged $1.5 trillion annually from 2009–2011 and won't be significantly
curtailed any time soon despite promises to the contrary,[28] as the looming
sovereign debt crisis menacingly attests.[29]

This splurge spending, compounded by off-budget federal activities,[30]
including unfunded obligations totaling more than $104 trillion for social
security and Medicare, is expanding rapidly.[31] Big government has been
anything but quiescent. The spiraling intrusion by the federal government
into every nook and cranny of what is supposed to be constitutionally protected private life is happening, even though ordinary citizens do not have
the tools at their disposal to quantify its invasiveness.[32]

PROFESSIONAL FAÇADE

Elected officials have been able to deflect public misgivings in large part by
constructing a professional image that lends plausibility to their actions.

[27] Greg Robb, "Great Recession Even Deeper than Thought," *MarketWatch*, July 29, 2011.
"As part of an annual revision of data on U.S. gross domestic product, the Commerce
Department said that the economy contracted by 5.1% between the fourth quarter of 2007
and the second quarter of 2009, more than the 4.1% previously estimated. It ranks as the
most severe recession in the post-World War II era."

[28] See note 6 to this chapter.

[29] Among other things, the Obama administration is itching to make higher education an
entitlement and in the process absorb a trillion dollars of student-loan debt. See Morgan
Korn, "Student Loans Could be the Next Housing Bubble: Robert Reich," Yahoo! Finance,
March 30, 2012.

[30] Off-budget federal expenditures are officially defined as social security, Medicare, and
post-office obligations (excluding the Social Security Administration's costs). The term
is used more broadly here to include other unfunded federal expenditure promises. See
"Dallas Federal Reserve President: US Unfunded Liabilities over 100 Trillion," http://feed-
proxy.google.com, February 12, 2010. The exact figure reported by Richard Fisher is $104
trillion calculated in present discounted value terms (i.e., adjusted downward to account
for foregone interest). It refers only to social security and Medicare obligations. Medicare
constitutes 85 percent of the total.

[31] These obligations include mandates (subprime loans), insurance guarantees, regulations,
and social policy initiatives (affirmative action, gay marriage, abortion "services").

[32] Thomas Miller, "The Individual Mandate: Ineffective, Overreaching, Unsustainable,
Unconstitutional and Unnecessary," *American Enterprise Institute*, March 23, 2012.

Politicians, executives, policymakers, advisors, agencies, regulators, administrators, bureaucrats, and technicians insist that they make innumerable tough decisions and do their job right. Every bureaucracy has a legislatively assigned mission, divided into specific programs and tasks. The governing statute is written by legislators and their staffs, most of whom are lawyers. Responsible bureaucracies are required to establish formal procedures for organizing, implementing, monitoring, auditing, supervising, and evaluating program fulfillment, including affirmative-action aspects of personnel employment. Just as in the former Soviet Union, success is measured with diverse quantitative indicators such as the number of subprime loans issued, without regard to their consequences. There are no market tests, only take-it-or-leave-it outcomes, and because bureaucracies in the big picture simply obey political commands, they may well do their jobs right on this narrow ground.

However, as the ghost of the Kremlin past tells us, working to rule with internally contradictory directives (federal statute and inscrutable tax codes) seldom translates into anything rational beings can recognize as success.[33] The Drug Enforcement Agency publishes copious statistics on narcotics seizures, yet admits that in the past few decades it has made virtually no progress in the war on drugs. Fannie Mae and Freddie Mac have fulfilled and over-fulfilled their toxic mortgage plans year after year to the people's detriment (See Chapter 8). The Security and Exchange Commission and bank regulators regulate but accomplish little and less than that on a social-cost-benefit basis. The State Department and Department of Commerce press the United States to open its markets while doing little to deter China from closing its ports to U.S. exports to the cumulative tune of more than $3 trillion.[34] The United States has spent hundreds of billions of dollars to build a modern democratic Iraqi nation on quicksand. Responsible elected officials would have learned from these failures and downsized, but impervious government is an integral aspect of politarchic self-seeking.[35]

---

[33] "Tax System Too Complex to be Constitutional," *Wall Street Journal*, January 26, 2011. The American tax code has 3.8 million words. This is only a small part of IRS regulations and court rulings. The language often is so obscure as to be literally unconstitutional because the Supreme Court ruled in 1926 that no one can be held accountable for inscrutable regulations.

[34] Steven Rosefielde, "China's Perplexing Foreign Trade Policy: Cause, Consequences, and a Tit for Tat Solution," *American Foreign Policy Interests*," Winter 2011.

[35] See "The Ruling Ad-Hocracy," *Wall Street Journal, Review and Outlook*, January 21, 2011: "Federal regulators have made it official: The 2010 Dodd-Frank law to reform Wall Street has already failed on its most fundamental promise." The new overseers confirmed that "there could be more 'exceptional' market interventions and that regulators will continue

The essential point to grasp is that while Americans may want the efficient services that they are told big government alone can deliver, they do not want the toxic outcomes that they get.[36] The prevailing system merely provides the semblance of authentic value added (judged from the standpoint of people's preferences), not the genuine coin of the realm. This is not bad luck. Principal-agent theory demonstrates that electoral government of any size that flouts the boundaries imposed by true democracy cannot optimally allocate funds to best public use or otherwise efficiently regulate.[37] Legislative directives (mandates) and bureaucratic processing are intrinsically unscientific. Elected officials do not know in detail which services individual Americans need. They do not know how to find out and wouldn't care if they could. Nor, if they had the requisite information, do they possess the technical planning skills to compute optimal solutions. And even where contemporary government has some capabilities, they are ignored. A

---

to exercise their discretion to identify 'systemic risks'. Regulators will also be able to discriminate among creditors and bail out short-term lenders too-big-to-fail firms, which will be protected from bankruptcy."

[36] Simon Johnson, *White House Burning: The Founding Fathers, Our National Debt, and Why It Matters*, New York: Pantheon, 2012. Daron Acemoglu and James Robinson, *Why Nations Fail: The Origins of Power, Prosperity, and Poverty*, New York: Crown Business 2012. Johnson, Acemoglu, and Robinson stress the big business side of the problem. Their views are compatible with those expressed here.

[37] Indeed, it is easily proven with principal-agent theory that it is impossible for the United States' bloated federal government to be efficient because its objectives are too vague, and the incentives it uses are too blunt. Steven Rosefielde, "The Impossibility of Russian Economic Reform: Waiting for Godot," in Stephen Blank, ed., *Russian Reform*, Carlisle Barracks: US Army War College, 2012. Oliver Williamson, *Markets and Hierarchies*, The Free Press, New-York, 1975. Martin Weitzman, "The New Soviet Incentive Model," *The Bell Journal of Economics*, 7, 1976, pp. 251–57. S. Ross, "The Economic Theory of Agency: The Principal's Problem," *American Economic Review*, 63, 1973, pp. 134–39. Eric Maskin, and Jean Tirole, "The Principal-Agent Relationship with an Informed Principal, I: Private Values," *Econometrica*, 58, 1990, pp. 379–410. Eric Maskin, and Jean Tirole, "The Principal-Agent Relationship with an Informed Principal, II: Common Values," *Econometrica*, 60, 1992, pp. 1–42. Tracy Lewis and David Sappington," Ignorance in Agency Problems," *Journal of Economic Theory*, 61, 1993, pp. 169–83. Jean-Jacques Laffont, and Jean Tirole, *A Theory of Incentives in Procurement and Regulation*, MIT Press, Cambridge, 1993. Joseph Berliner, *Innovation in Soviet Industry*, MIT Press, Cambridge, 1975, Douglass North, *Understanding the Process of Economic Change*, Princeton: Princeton University Press, 2005; Elizabeth Ostrom, *Understanding Institutional Diversity*, Princeton NJ: Princeton University Press, 2005, Oliver Williamson, *The Economic Institutions of Capitalism: Firms, Markets and Relational Contracting*, New York: Free Press, 1985, and *Williamson, Mechanisms of Governance*, Oxford: Oxford University Press, 1996; Williamson, "The New Institutional Economics: Taking Stock, Looking Ahead," *Journal of Economic Literature*, Vol. 38, No. 3, September 2000, pp. 595–613. Also see Ronald Coase, The New Institutional Economics," *American Economic Review*, Vol. 88, No. 2, May 1998, pp. 72–74 and Donald McCloskey, *The Bourgeois Era*, Chicago, IL: University of Chicago Press, 2010.

single example illuminates the larger truth. The United States government has developed a comprehensive set of input-output tables for the national economy,[38] regions, states, and locales capable of providing legislators with detailed, interactive, online, rule-of-thumb information on the employment impact of every deficit dollar spent to stimulate the economy. Was this tool used to guide the TARP in October 2008, so that each dollar spent had maximum employment benefit? Of course, it was completely ignored.[39] Elected officials had other priorities. The last thing they wanted was to be constrained by hard data on job-creation possibilities.

POLITARCHIC BIG GOVERNMENT

Politarchic big government is doubly injurious to national welfare. It is 1) intrinsically underproductive, necessarily reducing per-capita GDP below potential, and 2) it is unjust. Its *raison d'être* is imagining public needs and pretending to fulfill them, paying attention to its own desires without concern for impacts on others.

The charade comes with the territory. Lawyers bill regally by the hour whether or not clients are served. Bureaucrats process paper. Statesmen burnish images of self-assurance while understanding little. Shadow elites provide intellectual cover. Political theater sells media copy. Hollywood and Madison Avenue volunteer their entertainment skills, and majorities are gulled. It is a confidence game. There are no definitive failures or tests of success. When the White House assured us that Kim Jong-il had no nuclear weapons, it didn't matter that he detonated one the next day. We were simply told that he only had one or two nuclear bombs.[40] If after safeguards are installed, program trading caused the Dow Jones Industrial Average to plummet a thousand points in thirty minutes; not to worry. We do not know why the system malfunctioned, but it won't happen again. Americans are inept at connecting the dots, coming to terms objectively with politocracy because they are too easily fooled by the façade of

---

[38] www.bea.gov/industry

[39] "The Ruling Ad-Hocracy," *Wall Street Journal*, January 21, 2011: "A new report from Neil Barofsky, special Inspector General for the Troubled Asset Relief Program (TARP), underlines the fact-free analysis behind the bailout judgments of 2008."

[40] Choe Sang-Hun, "South Korean Official Warns of 'Existential Treat' from the North," *New York Times*, October 12, 2012. "In a paper published by the RAND Corporation earlier this month, an analyst, Markus Schiller, said that there were strong indications that North Korea's missiles served largely as 'a bluff' to 'create the impression of a serious missile threat and thereby gain strategic leverage, fortify the North Korean regime's domestic power, and deter other countries.'"

professionalism, partisan symbolism, doublespeak, and their own wishful thinking.

ECONOMIC SCLEROSIS AND CRISES

Politocracy blots out a million points of light,[41] each constituting a missed opportunity to democratically enhance national welfare. The consequences of these failures can be classified into three broad categories: 1) diminished microeconomic efficiency (well-being), including inferior GDP growth; 2) macroeconomic disorder including mass unemployment, financial, and sovereign debt crises, and 3) waning U.S. great power.

With respect to individual well-being and aggregate national utility (welfare), optimal results depend on allocating factors to best use, taking account of democratically approved transfers. Elected officials claim to promote this objective by encouraging free enterprise and assisting it with the best public services, but fail to follow up on these claims. U.S. living standards and quality of life consequently are pale semblances of what they ought to be. Burgeoning income and wealth inequalities exacerbate the failure. Most humanitarian supporters of big government assume that U.S. national policies diminish inequality in myriad ways and enhance living standards of the working class, but neither has happened because macroeconomic regulation has been targeted to benefit politicians and their collaborators. It might seem that exempting 47 percent of American households from federal taxation should do the trick, but politocratic fiscal stimuli and subsidies favoring the rich negate the positive effects of these exemptions (see Chapter 6).

Politarchs have gradually discovered through a process of learning by doing that monetary and fiscal policy can be used to line their pockets when they collude with various segments of the private sector on a winner-take-all basis. They reduced tax rates, increased business subsidies, abolished wealth and inheritance taxes, artificially bolstered demand with structural fiscal deficits and loose monetary policy, and promoted risky financial deregulation (including legalized insider trading in Congress),[42] accompanied by

---

[41] Cf. George Bush, Jr., 1988 Republican National Convention Acceptance Speech, August 18, 1988, Superdome, New Orleans waxed ecstatic about a million points of light.

[42] Henry Blodget, "Outrage of the Day: Insider Trading in Congress," *Scottsdale Trade*, November 16, 2011: "You cannot read the description of the personal stock trading allegedly conducted by Rep. Spencer Bachus and other members of Congress during the financial crisis and conclude anything other than that our government is corrupt. Yes, this behavior may be technically legal, because of an absurd loophole that some argue makes insider-trading rules not apply to Congress."

too-big-to-fail bailouts. The net result has been an anything-goes, excess-aggregate-demand strategy that sometimes stimulates overfull production and employment, but periodically causes bubbles, catastrophic financial crises, sovereign debt crises, intractable unemployment, gargantuan income and wealth disparities, social disgruntlement, and global economic contagion. These disorders aren't unprecedented, but have worsened steadily as politarchic capture increased.[43]

The deterioration of the United States' macroeconomy in the financial crisis of 2008, and the aftermath of the crisis, have diminished the country's global clout. In 1945 the United States was an undisputed superpower, a position that it shared with the Soviet Union after 1949, and regained as sole possessor in 1991 when the USSR went belly-up. Today, after a series of seemingly endless new-millennium foreign-policy debacles, waning military might (compared with China),[44] and ebbing economic influence, one can question whether the United States' power status can be salvaged. Part of the problem lies with the American left, which has always been inclined toward utopian pacifism, unilateral disarmament, and democratic socialist world government guided by its moral light. Stalin, Mao, and Pol Pot were shrugged off as aberrations, and socialists are always ready to put everyone at risk for their vision. Another part of the problem lies at the other end of the partisan spectrum with Wall Street and globalizing business, which can conceive the national interest only in terms of its bottom line. However, the decisive factor is the synergy created by the closet marriage between

Many members of Congress are said to have made suspiciously timed trades, including John Kerry, Dick Durbin, and Jim Moran. But Rep. Spencer Bachus takes the cake. According to a new book called *Throw Them All Out* by Peter Schweizer, as relayed by Dave Weigel at Slate, Rep. Bachus made more than 40 trades in his personal account in the summer and fall of 2008, in the early months of the financial crisis. The fact that Bachus personally traded while getting private government briefings is bad enough. The fact that he was the ranking member of the House Financial Services Committee at the time is simply outrageous. In one case, the day after getting a private briefing on the collapsing economy and financial system from Ben Bernanke and Hank Paulson, Rep. Bachus effectively shorted the market (by buying options that would rise if the market tanked.)

[43] Democratic capture of the contemporary type is analogous to the corporate capture identified by Adolf Berle and Gardner Means in the late 1920s and widely discussed in the early 1930s, where corporate boards of directors hired as agents by company owners became their masters, employing shareholders' assets for the directors' primary benefit. Shareholders' powers continue eroding, and the phenomenon is an important aspect of diminishing Western economic vitality and stability. It was inevitable that politicians tutored by Wall Street would grasp the concept of capture and seize the opportunity, just as is now being done.

[44] Office of the Secretary of Defense, Annual Report to Congress, *Military and Security Developments Involving the People's Republic of China 2011.* www.defense.gov/pubs/pdfs/2011_cmpr_final.pdf

big social advocacy and big business.[45] Increasingly throughout the postwar years, this ill-sorted couple have learned how to spruce up each other's lives by borrowing aspects of the other's persona.

Today's left thinks of itself as an integral part of the rich and famous, while business magnates bask in the prestige of their social concerns (corporate responsibility). Moreover, big social advocacy's and big business's identities tilt them toward trading favors with counterparts in other countries, and they distain any suggestion that national interest goes deeper than promoting their own agendas and self-enrichment (on patriotic grounds). These attitudes permeate the State Department, Department of Defense, National Security Council, Central Intelligence Agency, United States Agency for International Development (USAID), World Bank, International Monetary Fund (IMF), and World Trade Organization (WTO), making it impossible to devise responsible, national security strategies.

Politocracy can give all its policies public-interest glosses, making it easy to claim that true democracy is universally sovereign; that despite shredding the Constitution big government is doing everything the people desire within the limits of bounded rationality,[46] and that grievances are the result of misunderstanding or partisan pettiness. The danger is that the people may continue to be outfoxed and suffer the consequences.[47]

The reality behind the mask is a domestic system of insider self-enrichment and empire buildings expanded to encompass a so-called rules- and institutions-based foreign policy that promotes politicians', big business's, and big social advocacy's ends at the majority's expense by overtaxing workers and the middle class and abetting destructive financial speculation, bubbles, unsustainable debt burdens, other macroeconomic risks, and stealthy foreign protectionism[48] while issuing golden parachutes to themselves.[49] Many endorse the big government's idealist

---

[45] For those who remember the 1960s, this can be likened to a marriage between Woodstock and Wall Street. As the Woodstock generation aged and eventually prospered, it became a strong supporter of progressive government social-welfare programs.

[46] The term means that rational people are as informed as best they can be, given the opportunity costs of additional searching.

[47] The phenomenon was foreseen by Jean Jacques Rousseau. See Maurice Halbwachs, *The Social Contract, Book III*, chapter XV, pp. 339–40. Rousseau insisted that democracy and representative government were incompatible: "The instant a people gives itself representation it is no longer free."

[48] Steven Rosefielde, "China's Perplexing Foreign Trade Policy: Causes, Consequences and a Tit for Tat Solution," *American Foreign Policy Interests*, 2011.

[49] Cf. Nassim Taleb's assessment of the potential cause of a "Black Swan" economic catastrophe. Nassim Taleb, *The Black Swan: The Impact of the Highly Improbable*, New York: Random House, 2007. Taleb has compiled a list of the macro risks for Western economies:

objectives,[50] but idealism alone does not assure virtuous outcomes, even though insiders want us to believe it.[51]

Instead, idealism provides a cover for politocracy easily discerned in what otherwise should be major paradoxes. The reality of politocracy explains:

1. Why there is so much big business support for the party of social democracy in the United States (the Democrats): Sophisticated business executives understand that there is no real difference between the parties. Both are politarchic.
2. Why the George W. Bush administration overspent so much: The Republicans are as politarchic as the Democrats.
3. Why there was no fiscal dividend from the end of the Cold War: The politarchy continued spending.
4. Why the end of the Cold War was not followed by a reduction of military conflict: The politarchy sponsored other wars. (The terrorist attack on the World Trade Center in New York could have been dealt with as a terrorist attack, not as a cause for two wars in Iraq and Afghanistan.
5. Why the subprime mortgage effort that was supposed to help the poor ended up driving them deeper into poverty: Both the program and the rescue effort (mounted after the financial collapse of the program) were designed to benefit the banks, and did so. The poor were merely the vehicle for the politarchy's enrichment of itself.
6. Why U.S. democracy now imposes no effective limits at all on political contributions: The politarchy is increasingly greedy and brash in its activities.
7. Why elections do not seem to change anything important: Both parties are politarchic.
8. Why so many people are discouraged about politics and have become apathetic: Elections do not change anything important.

(1) "too big to fail" notions; (2) the socialization of losses and privatization of gains; (3) "nothing succeeds like failure" attitudes; (4) incentivizing regulatory incompetents to manage risk; (5) excessive complexity; (6) empowering government to play with matches; (7) allowing government to play the confidence-building con game; (8) giving governmental excess-spending addicts further doses to assuage their pain; (9) canonizing charlatan experts; and (10) patchwork reform used as a substitute for fundamental systems redesign.

50 Richard Rosecrance, "Bigger is Better: the Case for a Transatlantic Economic Union," *Foreign Affairs*, Vol. 89, Issue 3, May 2010, pp. 45–50.
51 This echoes the Soviet experience. See Ludwig von Mises, "The Economic Calculation in the Socialist Commonwealth," in Fredrich von Hayek, ed., *Collectivist Economic Planning*, London: Routledge, 1935; Von Mises, *Socialism: An Economic and Sociological Analysis*, London: J. Cape, 1936, Von Mises, *Omnipotent Government: The Rise of the Total State and Total War*, New York: Libertarian Press, 1985.

9. Why there seems a vibrant contest between the two political parties, but nothing changes: The contest is largely staged for the electorate, as the recent "fiscal cliff" farce amply testifies – the rhetorical issues are postures, not real commitments of either party.
10. Why the U.S. government continues to support the United Nations and other multinational organizations despite their evident corruption, inefficiency, and ineffectiveness in both general and U.S. interest: They provide the politarchy with opportunities for self-enrichment.
11. Why politicians who profess to care for the poor and the middle class accomplish so little on their behalf: The caring is all posturing – it's feigned and dishonest.

FOUR

Silver Lining?

By preferring the support of domestic to foreign industry, he intends only his own security, and by directing that industry in such a manner as its produce may be of the greatest value, he intends only his gain, and in this, as in many other cases, is led by an invisible hand to promote an end that was no part of his intention. Nor is it always the worse for the society that it was not part of it. By pursuing his own interests he frequently promotes that of society more effectually than when he really intends to promote it. I have never known much good done by those who affected to trade for the public good [politarchs]. It is an affectation, indeed, not very common among merchants, and very few words need be employed in dissuading them from it. (Adam Smith, *The Wealth of Nations*, Book IV, Chapter II, paragraph IX, 1776).

We have defined American politarchs as popularly elected officials who forsake their public trust, transforming themselves from elected professional agents serving local constituencies into closet businessmen.[1] They stop acting as civil servants, behaving instead like entrepreneurs hawking state services to customers of all descriptions. This makes them businessmen like any other, privileged with extraordinary political powers.

Adam Smith tells us in the *Wealth of Nations* (1776) that vendors, dealers, brokers, merchants, entrepreneurs, and speculators in the private sector are fortune-hunters driven by the lure of profits, avidly pursuing the good life that affluence can provide. While they are bound formally by the

---

[1] Politarchs strive to transform public services into private businesses, subject to weakly binding voter and constitutional constraints. This government capture is analogous to the usurpation of shareholders by corporate boards of directors widely discussed in the early 1930s. See Adolf Berle and Gardner Means, *The Modern Corporation and Private Property*, New York: Macmillan, 1932. Berle and Means contended that U.S. capitalism was being corrupted by the separation of ownership from control. We are hypothesizing analogously that the people (owners of the government) have surrendered control to their hired agents.

Constitution and rule of law and informally by custom, wheelers and dealers of all types including peddlers of public services higgle, plot in restraint of trade, and bend the rules. They are unsavory characters whose misdeeds warrant social condemnation, and it would seem to follow that the actions of the United States' politicrats should harm the people.

However, Smith insists that businessmen's ignoble intentions are seldom realized. He famously asserts, perhaps inspired by Leibniz,[2] that moral turpitude may be irrelevant in the larger scheme of things. As he phrases it, there is an invisible hand that "promotes an end that was no part of their [businessmen's] intention." Smith adds, "By pursuing his own interests he frequently promotes that of society more effectually than when he intends to promote it."

Smith contended, and many of his supporters today concur, that while businessmen's proclivity to misbehave naturally leads us to infer that they harm society, just the reverse outcome is the better part of the truth. Many businessmen in all likelihood do selfishly and unscrupulously pursue their own interests, letting society be damned, but nonetheless, Smith claims that the market not only presses avaricious higglers into society's service, but yields superior results, better than if the same tasks had been assigned to professional public agents, officials, and administrators.[3]

Do the mysterious workings of the invisible hand similarly let politicians off the hook? Although they seek to enrich themselves by informally privatizing the public-service business through all means fair and foul, should we counterintuitively surmise that the providential invisible hand assures that politicians will outshine professional public agents, officials, and administrators? Must we conclude that honest elected agents and public servants are intrinsically inferior to entrepreneurial politicians, and therefore that politocracy is a blessing in disguise?

These conundrums may baffle but are easily resolved if we recognize that they are founded on the erroneous premise that politarchic public service is governed by free and open competition like Smith's private business sector. If the premise were valid, then politocracy might be preferable to

---

[2] Gottfried Wilhelm Leibniz (1646–1716) was a German mathematician and rationalist philosopher widely noted for his claim that our civilization is the best possible because God would not have made it otherwise.

[3] Georg Wilhelm Friedrich Hegel (1770–1831) developed a similar phenomenological approach showing how seemingly bad events ultimately led to divine results through dialectical historical process. He often called this "the cunning of reason." See Hegel, *Lectures on the Philosophy of World History: Introduction, Reason in History*, New York: Cambridge University Press, 1975.

noncompetitive professional administration on efficiency grounds, but the assumption is false.[4]

Politarchs are not ordinary business service providers. They control demand, supply (production), and distribution. They spend taxpayer money (and borrow more on their own behalf [politarchic demand]), acquiring goods and services as intermediaries (supply) from privileged vendors in the politarchic network, and then distribute the goods to final recipients (distribution). The United States' politocrats have the legal power to pick pockets that private businessmen and honest professional administrators in true democracies are not allowed to touch. They have the right to select intermediate goods and service providers who pay them the highest commissions (directly and circuitously) and to distribute these goods

---

[4] As a matter of historical fact, U.S. politocracy didn't begin in 1776, and was not established in a coup d'état later. There always may have been elected officials who were the people's enemies, but they were not sufficiently powerful to exert strong politocratic influence until the twentieth century. The exact date politocracy became a potent force is debatable, but precision is not critical for our purposes. The transformation could have begun with Franklin Delano Roosevelt's New Deal, which marked the beginning of the United States' big government, but bigness does not preclude democracy. The increased social consciousness of the New Deal also was not decisive because democracies can be socially conscious, nor were politocracy's characteristics cast in stone by changes in technology, knowledge, cultural, population size, composition and location (rural, urban, suburban, exurban), and social mood. Americans during the depression, World War II, Cold War, and post-Soviet eras held very different attitudes than their contemporaries today about personal responsibility, integrity, morality, social priorities, religion, ideological duties, national security, and foreign engagement. The emergence of politocracy thus is best understood as a gradual evolutionary process that began modestly in the 1930s and then relentlessly expanded as information and control technologies advanced. During the 1950s, 1960s, and 1970s, when operations research and mathematical planning were in vogue, it was fashionable to stress centralization and downplay entrepreneurship (including government-outsourcing possibilities). Thereafter, as faith in centralized computopia waned, the pendulum swung the other way toward dispersed processing and initiative. Attitudes toward human needs and rights followed a similar pattern. In the early years of emergent politocracy, basic human needs like shelter, food, clothing, and vocational training were emphasized, but this goal gradually morphed into the more ambitious one of providing everyone with a decent middle-class standard of living including higher education, medical services, congenial environments, and an array of social services. The good life as an affordable, democratic human entitlement became an article of faith. The concept of appropriate macroeconomic management has expanded in the same way. New Deal macroeconomic policymakers restricted their attention for the most part to creating jobs (Works Projects Administration), keeping the interest rate low (monetary policy), and modest deficit spending, all aimed at stimulating recovery to the 1929 benchmark. However, after World War II, the agenda shifted to supporting full employment, containing inflation, managing the foreign-exchange rate, nurturing globalization, fostering liberalization, deregulation, and accelerating the sustainable long-run rate of aggregate economic growth.

and services for a fee (directly and indirectly) to collaborators and gratis to themselves. The politarchic control process, including negotiated exchange among insiders, operates like a Soviet-type command system (or mafia), where communist officials (including state-appointed enterprise managers) tax, commandeer enterprise profits directly into the government budget, choose suppliers (including foreign market vendors), and distribute production to themselves and other final claimants, falsely claiming to act on people's behalf.[5]

The invisible hand in Adam Smith's universe, despite participants' selfish intentions, provides purchasers with the best characteristics, assortments, and volumes of goods and services they can afford. The politarchic visible hand, by contrast, mostly enriches insiders and their circles, leaving everyone else with mal-distributed, poorly assorted, inferior goods (forced substitution) at exorbitant cost. Democratic free enterprise and politocracy may seem interchangeable to optimists, but beneath what appears to be a common facade, they are polar opposites.

The difference is night and day, utopia and dystopia. Malfunctioning true democracies could yield the same perverse outcomes,[6] if the people were

---

[5] Steven Rosefielde, *Russian Economy From Lenin to Putin*, New York: Wiley, 2007.

[6] One good way to distinguish inept from true democracies from politocracies is with the principle of rational adaption (learning). In economics and most social sciences, it is assumed that people, including politarchs, know that failure is possible, are capable of searching for evidence of poor performance, designing and implementing appropriate tests, and reforming institutions and behavior to achieve better results. It is rational to prefer better outcomes to inferior ones (Pareto utility seeking), and when individuals, organizations, and governments persistently refuse to learn by choosing less rather than more or intensifying destructive programs on the pretext of eradicating inefficiencies, then this should be treated as proof for the hypothesis that the people are being deceived or coerced by powerful self-seeking actors (politarchs), a point made long ago by Vilfredo Pareto. The old saying "Nothing succeeds more than failure in Washington" says it all. U.S. government has been captured to an important degree because our politicians persistently disregard lessons that could improve national well-being in order to advance their private welfare, while the "rational" *demos* has been unable to do anything about it for more than half a century. Public-choice theorists have long attributed the misbehavior of government officials to moral weakness in a morally hazardous bureaucratic universe. Their outlook is compatible with our concept of politocracy, but tends to be more general and deemphasizes the potential significance of corrupt official networks and empire building. One can argue that the defects of U.S. democracy are sufficiently explained by moral hazard, without having to introduce stronger politarchic causation, but this is only so if the persistence of the phenomenon is ignored or rationalized. When the colossal magnitude of the consequences of moral hazard are transparent, and rational "democrats" fail to do anything about them, there is more to the story than human frailty. Cf. Vilfredo Vilfredo Pareto, *Cours d'économie politique professé a l'université de Lausanne.* Vol. I, 1896; Vol. II, 1897. Cf. James Strachey, ed., *The Standard Edition of the Complete Psychological Works of Sigmund Freud*, New York: Vintage, 1999; Sigmund Freud, *Introduction to Psychoanalysis*,

misinformed and irrational, and loyal officials told them what they wanted to hear. But politarchic behavior is not just a possibility; it is politocracy's raison d'être. Politarchs usurp authority precisely because they put their own interests ahead of the people's (and society's), and if they are true to themselves (*telos*), they will rob the people to the hilt and foist their causes on the *demos* in a multitude of cunning ways.[7]

They can finance education and promote cultural values that create artificial excess demand for government services. They can allay public concerns about excess debt or the financial products Warren Buffet calls "weapons of mass destruction." They can manufacture speculative bubbles for their private profit at the community's expense in the name of high-minded goals. They can create overseas fortune-seeking networks under the guise of engagement and globalization. They can conspire with the media so that most of the government's egregious failures are excused or portrayed as triumphs (propaganda). In short, politarchic power prevents competitive processes from transforming bad intentions into virtuous outcomes. There is no invisible hand to make things right, and therefore there can be no silver lining.

New York: W.W. Norton & Co., 1917, Freud, *Beyond the Pleasure Principle*, New York: Bartleby, 1920, Freud, *The Ego and the Id*, 1923, Freud, Civilization and its Discontents, W.W. Norton & Co. 1930. Freud claims that with notable exceptions, people are capable of effectively organizing their behavior around the pleasure principle. After 1920 he developed a more complex view deemphasizing sexuality. Cf. Vilfredo Pareto, *Trattato Di Sociologia Generale* (4 vols.). G. Barbéra, 1916; Vincent J. Tarascio, *Pareto's Methodological Approach to Economics: A Study in the History of Some Scientific Aspects of Economic Thought*, 1968 online edition. Pareto argued that governments are ruled by foxes and speculators, who with the passage of time become effete and "humanitarian."

[7] Self-enrichment and zealotry both increase politarch's utility. They are complementary, not mutually exclusive causes.

FIVE

Road to Ruin

THE UNITED STATES' GOVERNMENTAL STRATEGY

U.S. federal governance today is primarily a grants-in-aid, tax-transfer, insurance-type administrative and regulatory process providing few direct civilian services. The legislative branch writes laws; the executive branch monitors compliance and enforces statutes, issues edicts, establishes and administers programs jointly authorized by the House of Representatives and Senate, transfers incomes, and regulates business, with the judiciary umpiring the laws and enforcement.[1] The government does not manufacture goods and plays a limited role as primary service provider other than for defense and intelligence.

The two big-ticket items, social security and Medicare, are federal insurance operations that collect premiums and pay out claims. Medicaid and grants-in-aid are similar. These programs, accounting for more than half of federal outlays, are relatively simple check-writing operations to individuals, states, and local authorities. The remaining programs mostly involve monitoring, supervising, administering, implementing, and enforcing federal statute. The supply of public goods and services is mostly determined by the legislators and bureaucrats, with little guidance from consumer demand. Market forces can and are disregarded.[2]

---

[1] The appropriation and expenditure of federal funds are compatible with the founding fathers' constitutional intent, if and only if grants-in-aid, tax-transfer, regulation, and collective services fully accord with the *demos*'s preferences, as government spokesmen steadfastly maintain. Similar services can be provided by charities, nongovernmental organizations, and individuals themselves. Government services therefore should be limited strictly to tasks where the state has a comparative advantage.

[2] See Kenneth Arrow, *Social Choice and Individual Values*, Wiley: New York, 2nd ed., 1963.

The determination of who pays and who receives is broadly a political matter settled by legislative infighting and fraught with conflicts of interest. The same principle applies to other aspects of federal regulation, including those affecting banks, financial institutions, insurance companies, monetary policy, and deficit spending. The headlines ballyhoo worthy missions; the subtext is mostly about how insiders dispense tax preferences and distribute tax revenues and favors to themselves, allies, and constituencies. Politicians never tire of discovering burning needs providing pathways to their private enrichment.

TRAJECTORY

The public services provided by the federal government over the past half-century have varied widely with a distinct liberalizing pattern of partial privatization (U.S. Postal Service), promotion of freer market entry (breakup of AT&T in 1982), increased competitiveness (elimination of most import tariffs), and permissive bank and financial deregulation (Gramm-Leach-Bliley Act, 1999). The federal government has championed enhanced choice within complex tax-planning and medical-service regulation as well as select civil rights (racial, religious, ethnic, abortion, sexual preference, gender), but also has simultaneously restricted choice in other areas by proliferating regulations, reporting requirements, mandates, subsidies, and entitlements. The net result has been mixed. On the negative side, the state has abnegated its duty to protect the nation against speculative endangerment, and transformed many Constitutional rights into Orwellian doublespeak directives. On the positive side, it has increased choice and selectively fostered competition.

LIBERALIZATION

The strategy strives to put people on leashes of appropriate length that benefit federal distributors of tax revenues and favors. It also promotes representatives' political and social causes. Civic and individual choice (often subsidized) has expanded immensely in matters of contraception, birth control, abortion, marriage, divorce, and personal lifestyles. Politicians found that this brand of liberalization paid double dividends in cash and voter support. The leash here has become very long, limited mostly by lingering taboos and legal prohibitions on some forms of consensual behavior harmful to minors (seduction), vulnerable women (prostitution), and

family members (incest).[3] Restrictions on entitlements have been loosened too, claims to the contrary notwithstanding. You can now buy almost
anything, from caviar to condoms, with food stamps, but budgetary constraints have prompted health-care regulators to move in the other direction
by reducing discretionary nip-tuck medical options. Controls on business
activities like gambling, alcohol, soft drugs (including marijuana), and adult
entertainment also have been relaxed (although restrictions on tobacco use
have tightened), and a tolerant attitude has been adopted toward abuses
of the separation of ownership from management (exorbitant pay, golden
parachutes,[4] leveraged buyouts), reckless financial practices (excessive bank
leverage, derivatives), [5] and the repression of worker wages, fringe benefits,
and job rights.

ILLIBERALIZATION

However, leashes elsewhere have been tightened to repress religious and
racial (but not secularist) intolerance, promote affirmative action, protect
society, spur litigation for the legal profession's benefit, and squeeze taxpayers. Cases can be made for restricting individual rights and imposing duties
in some of these regards, but excesses have been rampant on mundane
political and bureaucratic grounds, aggravated by political machinations.

The burden of these changes has fallen in equal measure on individual
consumers and businesses (politarchs feed big business with one hand, but
also take back part with the other for their own purposes and those of big

---

[3]   There is some support for decriminalizing prostitution and incest. For example, see www.
mpicc.de/ww/en/pub/forschung/...projekte/.../inzest_krim.htm. Also, some agitation for
social liberalization is unscrupulous. See Christopher Shea, "Pop Psychology," *Chronicle of
Higher Education*, November 16, 2011:

The discovery that the Dutch researcher Diederik A. Stapel made up the data for dozens
of research papers has shaken up the field of social psychology, fueling a discussion not
just about outright fraud, but also about subtler ways of misusing research data. Such
misuse can happen even unintentionally, as researchers try to make a splash with their
peers – and a splash, maybe, with the news media, too. Consider just two of his most
recent papers: "Power Increases Infidelity Among Men and Women," from *Psychological
Science*, and "Coping With Chaos: How Disordered Contexts Promote Stereotyping and
Discrimination," from *Science* – two prestigious journals. The first paper upended a gender stereotype (alpha-female politicos philander, too?!), while the second linked the physical world to the psychological one in a striking manner (a messy desk leads to racist
thoughts!?). Both received extensive news coverage.

[4]   Wailin Wong, "Motorola Mobility's Sanjay Jha leaving with $64.3 million golden para-
chute," *Chicago Tribune*, May 26, 2012.

[5]   See Assaf Razin and Steven Rosefielde, "Currency and Financial Crises of the 1990s and
2000s," *CESifo Economic Studies*, Vol. 57, No. 3, 2011, pp. 499–503.

social advocacy). Both are compelled to force substitute (a form of ration-ing), that is, they are coerced without just cause into accepting things they do not want in lieu of those they desire.[6] For example, mandatory unisex life expectancy tables arbitrarily award higher net annuity benefits to women than men. The unregulated competitive alternative is a gender neutral expected equal return for equal premiums.[7] Likewise, standard incandes-cent light bulbs are scheduled to be phased out starting 2014 in the United States under the Energy Independence Act of 2007 because they fail to meet the new energy efficiency standard. Proponents claim that this saves con-sumers money even though bulb prices for substitutes are much higher, but why not let the market decide? If it is really cost-efficient to switch, consum-ers should be rational enough to do so.

The issue in both cases of course is not that special pleadings are merit-less, but that officials have overstepped their Enlightenment constitutional mandate by curtailing personal choice.

Viewed in isolation, these and millions of other minor abuses seem triv-ial. However, their cumulative impact on economic efficiency and vitality can be lethal. Witness the American automobile industry, which was driven into bankruptcy by federal pension and health-care mandates, or the fed-eral government's ham-handed assault on tobacco companies. Business today is beset with mountains of unnecessary and democratically improper mandates (controls), regulations (guidance), and reporting obligations that drive up production costs, impair international competitiveness, aggravate unemployment, and diminish consumer welfare. To add insult to injury, taxpayers are compelled to pay for the multilayered administrative cost of this government overreaching, and matters are made worse by politocracy. Elected officials do not just badly regulate. They use regulations, mandates, subsidies, compliance cost obligations, and preferences as devices to reward

---

6   See "Bill Would Make Price Gouging a Federal Crime," Yahoo! News, December 6, 2011:

    Price gouging on prescription drugs already in short supply would become a federal crime under legislation about to be introduced. Sen. Charles E. Schumer, D-N.Y., said he's pro-posing a bill that that would give the U.S. Department of Justice authority to crack down on "unscrupulous drug distributors" who sell hospitals life-saving prescription medicines in short supply at huge markups. The problem has been growing this year, as shortages have dramatically worsened for normally cheap generic injected medicines that are the lifeblood of hospitals: drugs for cancer, pain, infections, even liquid nutrition and anesthe-sia for surgery. Schumer's bill is to be introduced next week, an aide told the AP. It would allow penalties of up to $500 million for each case of price gouging.

7   Female life expectancy in the United States is longer than male life expectancy. Consequently, if men and woman pay equal premiums, women receive higher annuity returns. Feminist groups disregard the result and insist that equality means only that they pay equal premiums. The government has sided with them.

supporters, partners, and themselves. This is the essence of trafficking in public services, and politocracy's raison d'être.

The term sclerosis is widely used by economists to convey the aggregate debilitating effect of excessive regulations, mandates, subsidies, compliance costs, and preferences on national well-being. Just as in medicine, where alien intrusions stiffen normal tissue and harden arteries, government overreaching can severely impair vital functions. Victims of physiological sclerosis are afflicted with paralytic strokes and fatal heart attacks. Their economic counterparts face analogous risks.

The phenomenon is called Euro-sclerosis on the other side of the Atlantic. It has different historical roots, but the mechanics are the same. More ails the European Union and the United States than business-cycle crises.[8]

---

[8]   Sclerosis in Europe is caused by its sociocratic mindset (socio-kratia: rule of "society"). First, leaders disregard majority preferences whenever socialist principle dictates. Second, they flout Lockean minority property rights and business protections. As a consequence, European governors feel duty-bound to not only overprogram, overregulate, misprogram, and misregulate, but also to curtail economic liberty and overtax. These democratic abuses take their cumulative toll in reserved effort, red tape, and inefficiency. The work ethic is dampened by entitlements (including barriers to dismissal that make hiring more like marriage with stiff alimony payments in case of divorce), and investors are daunted by regulatory monkey business and overtaxation. Choices of all kinds are warped, and government administrative layering adds cost but not value.

The adverse effects of the European Union's preference for equity (egalitarianism and affirmative action) over growth (long-term prosperity) can be illustrated with the example of its Lisbon educational reform strategy. EU leaders, recognizing that its higher education was lagging behind the international "knowledge economy" competition, devised a plan to make it the world's best by emphasizing research, innovation, expanded student access and lifelong learning opportunities. This should have entailed concentrating resources in the advanced sciences, entrepreneurship, and skills needed for adding value in the contemporary workplace. However, hard choices were essential because with its citizens already overtaxed, there were no new funds available to support the agenda. The EU's solution was to increase class size (typically in the hundreds) and require professors to meet a battery of contradictory chores like improving course content while paying more attention to individual student needs and increasing the quantity and quality of their research.

Needless to say, this wishful thinking was a nonstarter. The EU was not going to get more for less, but a mechanism was needed to report favorable results. This was accomplished by creating a new layer of bureaucratic testing and monitoring using standardized statistics that penalized and therefore discouraged real creativity and innovation. The winners in the shell game were rent-seeking politocrats and their partners in the educational establishment. The losers were students, professors, and EU citizens at large saddled with an educational system designed to do nothing whatsoever right. The EU's social-democratic version of politocracy is a juggernaut that cannot be successfully reformed without embracing the United States' democratic basics.

Most contemporary Europeans consider their national governments and the European Union to be social democracies in precisely this sense, without appreciating that social democracy has morphed into social politocracy. They believe that sovereignty abides with

Politarchic government has increased the chances that both economies will soon be paralyzed despite subsidies that simultaneously overstimulate some big-business sectors like Wall Street.

society, not self-seeking individuals, and the politarchic heads of Europe's socialist parties are people's deputies. Euro-socialists, both true believers and politocrats, fight tenaciously for their Enlightenment vision of virtuous state governance and have been successful but also have preserved pluralist options because elections are open to parties of all persuasions, including politarchic supporters of republican free enterprise.

Judged from the standpoint of non-Western per-capita income, European social politocracy has fared well. It has managed to combine high living standards with lavish public-spending programs including socialized medicine and education, labyrinthine regulation, high taxes, and labor rigidities without completely arresting economic growth, while convincing majorities that "socialism" is best, that republicanism without socialism is a booby prize. These tendencies are evident in the United States, but on a reduced scale.

Europe's performance relative to the United States, however, has been subpar 1776–2010 (Figure 5.1), despite conspicuous advantages. These advantages include its relative economic backwardness (especially among new EU members), the widening of the European common space (the European Common Market), the formation of the EU (1993), and the adoption of the euro in 1999 as a common currency facilitating investment among less developed member states.

Unemployment rates similarly have been loftier than in the United States. Other things equal, the EU should have converged to the United States' high per-capita income frontier, but instead fell back.

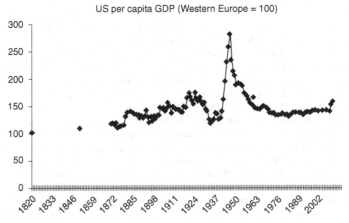

Figure 5.1 U.S. per-capita GDP: EU benchmark 1990 Geary Khamis dollars (Western Europe = 100).
Source: Angus Maddison, *World Economy: Historical Statistics*, Paris: OECD, 2003, and Web site updates.
Note: The West European series above includes only core nations: The UK, Germany, Austria, France, Italy, Belgium, Netherlands, Switzerland, Denmark, Norway, Sweden and Finland.

MACROECONOMICS

America's deteriorating economic performance however cannot be ascribed entirely to government induced sclerosis. Its macroeconomy is afflicted with another disorder: double arrhythmia. The system's heart rate alternately is too high (tachycardia) and too low (bradycardia), making it susceptible to cardiac arrest on both scores, triggered respectively by hypertension and hypotension. Deficit spending, excess sovereign debt, lax financial regulation, leveraging, loose monetary policy, and the monetization of the national debt induce the hypertension; overtaxation, stultifying regulation, and lost public confidence (liquidity trap) [9] cause the bradycardia. In economics, but not medicine, tachycardia and bradycardia may occur simultaneously as stagflation (stagnation and inflation), or "depflation" (depression in business and employment combined with inflation). The therapy appropriate for one condition necessarily aggravates the other, creating a "lose-lose" situation for bedeviled policymakers.

Economic sclerosis and bradycardia are caused by many of the same factors: debilitating regulations, mandates, effort-depressing subsidies (entitlements), compliance costs, and preferences. At the microeconomic level, they impair efficiency, productivity, entrepreneurship, innovation, and effort. In the macroeconomic sphere, they do the same, but additionally diminish aggregate effective demand through purchasing power imbalances, risk aversion, and cash hoarding. This means that while trimming bloated government should improve economic performance in all regards,

See European University Association, 2010, *Trends 2010: A Decade of Change in European Higher Education*, EUA Publications, p.15, available at http://www.eua.be/eua-work-and-policy-area/building-the-european-higher-education-area/trends-in-european-higher-education/trends-vi.aspx, retrieved on September 26, 2011. See László Csaba, "Innovation, Imitation and Adaptation: The Experience of Fifteen Years of Upscaling Hungarian Economic Higher Education," paper presented at the World Bank-CEU Conference Scaling Up the Success of Capacity Building in Economic Education and Research, June 14–15, 2005, Budapest. See Van Vught, Frans, "The EU Innovation Agenda: Challenges for European Higher Education and Research," *Higher Education Management and Policy*, Vol. 2, 2009. See OECD, "Tertiary Education for the Knowledge Society," *The OECD Thematic Review of Tertiary Education: Synthesis Report*, Overview, 2008. Available at http://www.oecd.org/dataoecd/20/4/40345176.pdf, retrieved on September 22, 2011. See "The Brains Business," *The Economist*, September 8th, 2005. Available at http://www.economist.com/node/4339960?story_id=4339960, accessed on September 30, 2011.

9 The liquidity trap in Keynesian economics is a situation where monetary policy is unable to stimulate an economy through lowering interest rates or increasing the money supply. It is caused by the expectation that adverse events such as deflation, insufficient aggregate demand, and civil or international war will induce people to increase their holdings of idle cash balances and thereby reduce aggregate effective demand.

weight-reduction programs alone are not enough to restore full-employment equilibrium. Policymakers must also grapple with issues of consumer and investor confidence, including the painful task of deleveraging; that is, reducing budgetary deficits, sovereign debt, and excess money creation, all anathemas to orthodox Keynesian theorists focused on promoting full employment.[10]

Economic tachycardia is different. Although it too is rooted in bad politocratic governance, the nation's economic heart is overstimulated by permissive regulations, mandates, and business-spurring subsidies and preferences, instead of being depressed. Banks are allowed and encouraged to engage in speculative lending and they are bullied into making subprime loans (see Chapter 8). Unworthy "go green" energy-environment projects are underwritten by the government,[11] and contracts are issued to high-rolling insiders addicted to gambling with other people's money. All these distortions momentarily may be misdiagnosed as signs of health but invariably yield unhappy endings.

As in the case of economic bradycardia, the disease has micro and macroeconomic dimensions. The micro aspect is ascribable to overreaching democratic constitutional limits, bad judgment, and project-specific politocratic self-seeking with different segments of big business. The macro element involves the micro causes, plus excessive deficit spending (fiscal policy), national debt, money emission (monetary policy), and indulgent financial regulation. U.S. leaders never are at a loss when it comes to overstimulating the economy. They can be counted on to do the wrong thing whether the nation's economic heart is racing or faltering. Only equilibrium seems unthinkable.[12]

EARTHLY PARADISE

Economic sclerosis and arrhythmia are considered pathological by most people on some grounds. Few openly praise corruption, nor urge unbounded deficit spending, excessive sovereign debt, and unbridled monetary

---

[10] Deleveraging necessarily entails reducing fiscal and monetary stimulus. Keynesians correctly insist that both adjustments will diminish consumer and investor demand. Nonetheless, the bullet must be bitten as long as the adverse effects of leveraging outweigh the positive effects of stimulus.

[11] The Solyndra loan controversy is a political scandal involving U.S. President Barack Obama's administration's authorization of a $535 million loan guarantee to Solyndra Corporation in 2009 as part of a program to spur alternative energy growth. www.gogreeninitiative.org

[12] See Robert Hetzel, *The Great Recession: Market Failure or Policy Failure?* Cambridge: Cambridge University Press, 2012.

expansion (QE-infinity).[13] Everyone bemoans high unemployment, depression, stagnation, growth retardation, excessive income disparities, and inflation. Accordingly, American leaders cannot publicly acknowledge that their micro and macroeconomic policies are paralytic and lethal. They are compelled by electoral necessity instead to insist that policies are as good as they can be and that mild tachycardia is socially best. They must also insist that regulations, mandates, subsidies, and preferences as they characterize them are not significantly flawed and claim that overstimulating the nation's economic heart is beneficial because it promotes full employment and fosters rapid growth. Price stability and balanced growth might seem superior on paper, but politicians contend that this is not the case because both inure unemployment and impede productivity gains. Without perpetual macroeconomic overstimulus and government economic (mis)management, the U.S. economy, it is averred, would be less efficient, productive, dynamic, and stable.

Federal government denials of serious economic wrongdoing on multiple grounds can be dismissed out of hand. Economic sclerosis is real and mostly Washington's fault. The macroeconomic rationale is plausible, but cannot be adequately gauged until Americo-sclerosis is eliminated. If government-generated microeconomic impediments to full employment were removed, deficit spending and expansionary monetary policies might turn out to be superfluous.

Politicians, big business, and big social advocates have no desire to concede this or to accept cogent professional evidence (Ricardian equivalence)[14] that deficit spending and inflationary monetary expansion often are counterproductive. They have worked hand and glove to craft and proselytize the idea that big government, aggressive deficit spending, mammoth sovereign deficits, and loose monetary policy are the touchstones of national health, validating their antidemocratic agendas and paving the way for permanent paralysis and mega crises. Many fully understand the costs but are unconcerned because the pain will be borne by others while they dance between the raindrops.

---

[13] QE is an acronym for quantitative easing, that is, doublespeak for printing money. QE-infinity represents a policy of unlimited monetary debasement.

[14] The Ricardian equivalence proposition (also known as the Barro–Ricardo equivalence theorem) is an economic theory holding that consumers internalize the government's budget constraint: as a result, the timing of any tax change does not affect their change in spending. See Robert Barro, "The Ricardian Approach to Budget Deficits," *The Journal of Economic Perspectives* Vol. 3, Issue 2, 1989. http://www.ukzn.ac.za/economics/viegi/teaching/uct/barro.pdf.

GRAND BARGAIN

The road map guiding U.S. government today reflects a grand bargain between big business, big social advocacy (across the political spectrum), and big politocracy. It permits business to pursue profits, fortified with lucrative government contracts, lax regulation, tax preferences, subsidies, expansionary macroeconomic policy, wage repression, and gradually weakening organized labor and bailouts (TARP), but imposes concessions. Big businesses have been compelled to grudgingly tolerate some aspects of worker protection, high multi-source taxation, excessive microregulation and oversight, overreporting, mandates, and expensive compliance costs. They also have agreed to collaborate with social advocates' broad civil rights, antipoverty, anti-abortion, public arts, and environmental agendas, and to abet government officials trafficking in public services.

The results between 1990 and 2008 appeared acceptable from various perspectives, even to many losers. Per-capita GDP growth surpassed the long-run trend,[15] inflation was mild,[16] and unemployment rates tame.[17] The rich got richer, but the poor and minorities were better protected. Only the blue-collar workers and much of the heterogeneous middle class and passive rich were excluded from the party; their living standards diminished.[18]

RUDE AWAKENING

The federal government's contribution to this growth, full employment, and low inflation was diverse. Deregulation, wage repression, enhanced competitive access, and the promotion of trade liberalization (including outsourcing) spurred entrepreneurship, investment, and innovation, all essential for a surge in economic growth and employment. This stimulus was augmented by the reawakening of China, India, and Brazil, which catapulted global productivity higher, augmenting demand for Western goods and providing lucrative investment opportunities for U.S. companies. The

---

[15] Per-capita GDP grew 4 percent per annum during this interval. Many economists put the U.S. full employment rate at 5.5 percent, taking account of transitory factors.

[16] Inflation (CPI) fluctuated widely 1990–2008, but was mostly in the 2–3 percent range.

[17] The unemployment rate in the United States 1990–2008 was mostly below 5.5 percent, often in the 4 percent range.

[18] In 2010, the top 10 percent of wage earners made as much as they did in 2002. By contrast, the 50th percentile hasn't earned this little since 1996, and the bottom 10 percent since 1994. The last decade has set everyone back, but the richest Americans have been better protected than others. But, don't blame the recession alone for the inequality gap: the trend started during the mid to late 1990s.

United States also was flooded with inexpensive imports that dampened inflationary pressures and derivatively created immense imbalances in global dollar reserves (mostly with China), allowing the U.S. Treasury to borrow funds cheaply. Real gains were not as great as they seemed because politocratic programs added less value than competitive alternatives (people were forced to purchase mandated substitutes for the goods they preferred). Nonetheless progress was made, and in an imperfect world seemed adequate until the 2008 financial crisis raised questions about the grand bargain's sustainability. Was America living in a fool's paradise that traded transient prosperity today for a blighted future?

The evidence that the grand bargain was ill-advised is compelling. Politicians have embraced a strategy that continuously decreases national microeconomic efficiency (including mountains of superfluous paperwork), waste, fraud, and abuse while creating conditions for a catastrophic macroeconomic crisis that will make the 2008 depression look like child's play. As the cataclysmic cracks in Japan's nuclear energy strategy revealed by the March 11, 2011 tsunami make plain, it is easy for nations to be lulled into complacency. Building the Daiichi nuclear reactor in the Fukushima earthquake zone provided benefits for many decades, but we now know that the stress tests were not failsafe.

MACROECONOMIC OPPORTUNISM

The United States' economic version of Fukushima's disabled reactor cooling mechanism is its macroregulatory system. Nuclear reactors are cooled to maintain thermal equilibrium. Cooling systems can be modified or diverted for other purposes but not without consequences for nuclear safety. Politicians chose to modify the nation's macroeconomic cooling system by amending the Employment Act of 1946 into the Humphrey-Hawkins Full Employment and Balanced Growth Act of 1978, prioritizing full employment and growth over competitive equilibrium.[19] They, together with many social-protectionist academics and politicians, contended that the expected employment and growth benefits of a little overheating exceeded the expected losses in consumer purchasing power and accumulating federal debt. Everyone knew that there was a remote possibility of an economic meltdown, but politicians assured the public that they understood how to prevent this from ever happening.

[19] See Murray Weidenbaum, "The Employment Act of 1946: A Half Century of Presidential Policymaking," *Presidential Studies Quarterly*, Summer 1996, Vol. 26, Issue 3, pp. 880–85.

These assurances were credible. The federal government has the discretionary authority to tighten credit, run a budgetary surplus, impose conservative financial regulations, and devalue the dollar without dire consequences under ordinary circumstances. However, this does not guarantee that they will do so if insiders have golden parachutes, are purblind, or in crisis situations politicians are paralyzed when confronted with a host of unattractive options.

The United States today finds itself in a parlous state precisely because politicians (now including Federal Reserve Chairman Ben Bernanke)[20] have abused the good intentions of the Humphrey-Hawkins 1978 Full Employment and Balance Growth Act by transforming it into a vehicle for leveraging their public service business through excess and perverse deficit spending, printing money, loose credit (subsidies to Wall Street connected banks and financial institutions), and indulgent financial regulation. As a consequence, both the deficits on and off the books are at critical levels, monetary policy has become ineffectual (for macro stimulatory purposes), the dollar's value is eroding, and the risks associated with speculative derivative trade continue unabated.

Politicians seem to be presuming that they can tough things out, that excesses will generate stable disequilibria (a few Daiichi-scale explosions and moderate radiation leakages) rather than nuclear winter,[21] either because they can always stick someone else with the bill or join Dr. Strangelove in a radiation-proof shelter.[22] They refuse to curtail deficit spending or restrict

---

[20] See John Carney, "Three Things Fed Did Today It's Never Done Before," Yahoo! Finance, September 13, 2012:

If the outlook for the labor market does not improve substantially, the Committee will continue its purchases of agency mortgage-backed securities, undertake additional asset purchases, and employ its other policy tools as appropriate until such improvement is achieved in a context of price stability,' the Fed said in its official statement. This explicit tying of the LSAP to the labor market is unprecedented. Not only has the Fed never done this in the past, but no other central bank has launched a quantitative easing program with such an explicit link to jobs.

[21] Nuclear winter is a term coined to describe the catastrophic effects on the climate of detonating large numbers of nuclear weapons. It is conjectured that the explosions could place a cloud of dust in the atmosphere that might cause cold weather and reduced sunlight for a period of months or even years, especially over flammable targets such as cities, where large amounts of smoke and soot would be ejected into the Earth's stratosphere. At its most extreme, the climate change could be severe enough to kill most living creatures, as happened for other reasons to the dinosaurs.

[22] The reference is to the central figure of Stanley Kubrick's black comedy *Dr. Strangelove or: How I Learned to Stop Worrying and Love the Bomb,* who gleefully retreats to a nuclear-resistant bomb shelter with a bevy of beauties to wait out nuclear winter. The film was released in 1964.

it to employment-promoting programs, despite the unfolding PIIGS (Portugal, Italy, Ireland, Greece, Spain) and Cyprus sovereign-debt crises and their roiling effects on international markets.[23] An assessment of President Barack Obama's budget released March 18, 2011 by the nonpartisan Congressional Budget Office (CBO) found that the White House is underestimating future budget deficits by more than $2 trillion 2011–2020. His February 2011 budget was estimated to produce deficits totaling $9.5 trillion, or $1 trillion per year, ballooning the national debt toward 160 percent of GDP.[24] Subsequent data indicate that even this bleak scenario is too hopeful, and the recent "fiscal cliff" agreement has done nothing to fundamentally change this prognosis.[25]

---

[23] See Steven Rosefielde and Assaf Razin, "PIIGS," in Steven Rosefielde, Masaaki Kuboniwa and Satoshi Mizobata, *Prevention and Crisis Management: Lessons for Asia from the 2008 Crisis*, Singapore: World Scientific, 2012. For an example of the pot calling the kettle black, see http://www.dailymail.co.uk/news/article-2062258/European-debt-crisis-Obama-reads-riot-act-eurozone-leaders-AGAIN.html#ixzz1dsjBDOip, November 16, 2011: "Obama said that whilst there had been progress in putting together unity governments in Italy and Greece, Europe still faced a 'problem of political will'. 'We're going to continue to advise European leaders on what options we think would meet the threshold where markets would settle down. It is going to require some tough decisions on their part.'" Michalis Persianis and Stelios Bouras, "Blame Game Widens in Cyprus Crisis, *Wall Street Journal*, April 12, 2013.

[24] See "CBO: Obama Understates Deficits by $2.3 Trillion," Yahoo! Finance, March 18, 2011: "Obama's budget saw deficits totaling $7.2 trillion over the same period. The difference is chiefly due to the CBO's realist view of future American GDP growth and federal tax collections. Republican Congressman Paul Ryan, Chairman of the House Budget Committee, commenting on his draft 2012 federal budget proposal, said that spending reductions would be "a lot more" than $4 trillion. President Obama's debt commission recommended a plan that reduced the deficit by $4 trillion over the coming decade. The debt commission's plan called for freezing nondefense discretionary spending, whereas Ryan would return to 2008 levels and thus cut an additional $400 billion over ten years. It should be noted that Ryan's plan would still leave the U.S. federal debt at 100 percent of the GDP." See Douglass Daniel, "GOP 2012 Budget to Make $4 Trillion-plus in Cuts," Yahoo! News, April 3, 2011. See Andrew Taylor, "Democrats, Republicans Far Apart on Deficit Deal," Associated Press, November 16, 2011. "The backbiting has intensified since the exchange of offers. The Democrats' most recent plan called for $2.3 trillion in deficit cuts, including a $1 trillion tax increase over the coming decade. Republicans countered with almost $300 billion in new tax revenues as part of a $1.5 trillion debt plan, an offer that even a top Democrat, Majority Whip Dick Durbin of Illinois, called a breakthrough."

[25] The national debt exceeded $16 trillion in September 2012 and is now 107 percent of the GDP. See Andrew Taylor, "US National Debt Hits $16 Trillion as Republicans Blast Obama's Handling of the Economy," Yahoo! Finance, September 4, 2012: The "fiscal cliff" agreement changed nothing. See Martin Hutchinson, "Global Investing Strategist," *Money Morning*, January 3, 2013: "In the end, the agreement reached on Tuesday night will only reduce the deficit by about $60 billion annually over the next 10 years. That's less than 10% of the total projected deficits, which means well before 2020 we will likely have a real crisis on our hands."

Politarchs also are insensitive to hyperinflationary risk; dollar depreci-
ation, the danger of beggar-thy-neighbor protectionism,[26] and destructive
social turmoil. They seem to suppose, and sometimes publicly declare, that
the unemployed and wage-repression victims should adjust to the new normal.[27] Bondholders, bank deposit holders and pensioners should anticipate
taking haircuts (partial repayment on corporate, sovereign bonds and bank
deposits), and everyone except politicians and Wall Street insiders should
brace themselves for financial ruin. The public is assured that politocratic
leveraging is manageable, and if it is not, most will just have to deal with the
problem themselves, including expiring without ever retiring.[28]

The preposterousness of these attitudes should be self-evident but seldom is
because the majority of economists and the public assume that politicians are just
naughty boys who in the breech will do the right thing. Economists in particular
fail to appreciate how a well-intentioned desire to promote full employment
has been gradually transmuted into a blank check for politarchic mischief. The
United States' long day's journey into night is easily documented.[29]

LONG DAY'S JOURNEY INTO NIGHT

The transformation of full employment goals into political license was gradual and at every step condoned by adaptive changes in macroeconomic
theory. Immediately after World War II, the U.S. government passed the
Employment Act of 1946 prioritizing the attainment and maintenance of full

---

[26] See Uri Dadush, "Global Rebalancing: The Dangerous Obsession," *Carnegie Endowment for
International Peace, Policy Brief 90*, February 2011. Dadush contends that international efforts
to rebalance global imbalances and fend off beggar-thy-neighbor protectionism is misguided
because the problem is better addressed by macroeconomic reforms in the United States.

[27] The "new normal" is a term coined by the brain trust at the giant bond fund PIMCO.
Anthony Crescenzi, a PIMCO vice president, strategist, and portfolio manager, is part of that
brain trust. He contends that by contrast to past norms, the U.S. economy could grow 2 percent a year without adding any new jobs because the productivity of current workers is rising
at about 2 percent a year. Among the unemployed in the United States today, 64 percent have
been out of work for 27 weeks or more, a figure double that of prior postwar recessions. See
John Ydstie, "What the 'New Normal' Means for Americans," *NPR*, March 11, 2012.

[28] See Emily Brandon, "Why You Should Plan to Work Until Age 70," *U.S. News and World
Report*, July 9, 2012:

Only about half of households are on track to maintain their current standard of living
upon retirement at age 66. However, if workers are willing to delay retirement until age
70, 86 percent can expect to enjoy a comfortable retirement, according to recent Center
for Retirement Research at Boston College calculations. "I think everybody needs to aim
to work longer," says Alicia Munnell, director of the Center for Retirement Research at
Boston College. "If everybody works about five years longer than they had planned, most
people would find themselves with adequate retirement income."

[29] See Eugene O'Neill, *Long Day's Journal into Night*, New Haven: Yale University Press, 2002.

employment (further codified and expanded in the Humphrey-Hawkins Full Employment Act, 1978). The law didn't fix quantitative targets but marked the Truman administration's expansion of federal powers to include macroeconomic administration, management and regulation, without explicit constitutional sanction, and established the Council of Economic Advisors to aid presidential policymaking, as well as the Joint Economic Committee of Congressmen and Senators to review executive policies.

These actions enabled Washington to go beyond the perimeters of Keynesian orthodoxy, whenever full employment could not be sustained with trans-cyclically balanced federal budgets. The exclusion remained moot throughout much of the 1950s until William Phillips discovered[30] and Paul Samuelson popularized the notion that full employment could only be maintained with excess monetary and/or fiscal stimulation accompanied by inflationary side effects (Phillip's Curve). Keynes, many concluded, was almost right. Deficit spending was essential, but it also should be applied no matter how much inflation is generated to realize the higher goal of full employment. Full-employment zealots insist that governments are morally obliged to deficit spend forever, a position still widely maintained despite Edmund Phelps's demonstration that Phillips and Samuelson were wrong in the long run, confirmed by today's high intractable unemployment.

The orthodox Keynesian straitjacket was loosened further by Walter Heller, Chairman of President John Kennedy's Council of Economic Advisors, 1961–1964, who introduced across-the-board tax cuts as a counter-recessionary stimulus, even though this meant creating credit not just for investment, but for consumption as well. Keynes's employment and income-multiplier theory required stimulating investment as the only legitimate method for combating deficient aggregate effective demand.[31] The Works Projects Administration 1932 (WPA) provided 8 million jobs, and later investment tax credits were utilized for the same purpose. Keynes argued that new investment creates jobs, bolsters wages, and derivatively increases consumption, whereas deficit consumption spending via diminished marginal propensities to consume transfers purchasing power from one recipient to another, without increasing employment. Heller's revisionist substitution of across-the-board tax cuts for investment tax credits brushed Keynes's concerns aside, making it possible for politicians to claim that any deficit spending that benefited them and their constituents would stimulate

---

[30] See William Phillips, "The Relationship Between Unemployment and the Rate of Change of Money Wages in the United Kingdom 1861–1957," *Economica*, Vol. 25, No. 100, 1958, pp. 283–99.

[31] See John Maynard Keynes, *The General Theory of Employment, Interest and Money*, London: Macmillan Cambridge University Press, for Royal Economic Society, 1936.

aggregate economic activity and employment, including inter-temporal income transfers from consumers' pockets tomorrow to today's big spenders.

This logic was extended by falsely contending that deficit spending and expansionary monetary policy accelerate long-term economic growth. Although there are no grounds for claiming that structural deficits, the debasement of money and lax financial regulation accelerate scientific and technological progress (the ultimate source of sustainable economic growth), policymakers couldn't resist the temptation to assert that deficit spending and inflation are indispensable for maximizing current and future prosperity. Perhaps what this doublespeak really meant was that nominal growth (inflation) lightened the debt burden and indirectly raised taxes with muted public complaint. The ploy has been successful in making deficits and inflation seem more palatable but also has opened the door to compounding past abuses by upping the ante whenever the economy sours. Bureaucrats' reflex is not to retrench, but to do more of what caused problems in the first place.

Academic macroeconomists likewise succumbed to wishful thinking, brushing aside the speculative momentum embedded in postwar institutional liberalization and fiscal indiscipline. Influenced by Robert Lucas,[32] the conventional wisdom 2000–2008 came to hold that business-cycle oscillations were primarily caused by productivity shocks that lasted until price- and wage-setters disentangled real from nominal effects. These shocks sometimes generated inflation, which it was believed was best addressed with monetary policy. Accordingly, central bankers were tasked with the mission of maintaining slow and stable, Phillips curve-compatible inflation. Although central bankers were supposed to be less concerned with real economic activity, many came to believe that full employment and 2 percent inflation could be sustained indefinitely by divine coincidence.[33] This miracle was said to be made all the better by the discovery that real economic performance could be regulated with a single monetary instrument, the short-term interest rate. Happily, arbitrage across time meant that central bankers could control all temporal interest rates, and arbitrage across asset classes implied that the U.S. Federal Reserve could similarly influence risk-adjusted rates for diverse securities. Fiscal policy, which had ruled the roost under the influence of orthodox Keynesianism from 1950–1980, accordingly was relegated to a subsidiary role aided by theorists' beliefs in the empirical validity of Ricardian

---

[32] See Robert Lucas, "Macroeconomic Priorities," *American Economic Review*, Vol. 93, No. 1, 2003, pp. 1–14.

[33] The term divine coincidence is used explicitly by economists and has fueled continuing debate. See "Divine Coincidence and the Fed's Dual Mandate," *Economist's View*, January 29, 2011:

John Taylor says the Fed should adopt a single mandate. In his view, which seems to be fairly common on the political right, the Fed should abandon targeting the output gap and restrict its attention it keeping the inflation rate stable: Former U.S. Treasury Department

equivalence arguments and skepticism about lags and political priorities. The financial sector likewise was given short shrift, but this still left room for other kinds of nonmonetary intervention. The consensus view held that automatic stabilizers like unemployment insurance should be retained to share risks, that is, to assist in case there were any unpredictable shocks. Commercial bank credit similarly continued to be regulated and federal deposit insurance preserved to deter bank runs, but otherwise finance was lightly supervised, especially shadow banks, hedge funds, and derivatives.

THE EMERGENCE OF THE KEYNESIAN AND MONETARIST COMA

It was a long time coming, but by 2008, theory had evolved to the point where almost any self-enriching politocratic policy could be construed as socially desirable:

1. regulatory safeguards could be scrapped,
2. deficits could pile sky high,
3. real wages could stagnate,
4. mandates that caused the housing crisis and drove GM and Chrysler into bankruptcy could be expanded,
5. full-employment goals could be given priority over inflation,
6. politicians could safely pretend that structural deficits promote accelerated economic growth,
7. government insurance guarantees, off-budget unfunded obligations like social security, and mandated preferences to savings and loans banks could be deemed innocuous, despite the $160 billion savings and loans debacle in the late 1980s–1990s,
8. subprime loans (the extension of public housing into privately owned homes for the poor), adjustable rate mortgages (ARM), and tolerance of finance-based credit expansion that flooded the globe with credit could be portrayed as progressive (capitalization of derivatives),[34]
9. Post-Bretton Woods restrictions on international capital flows could be relaxed (early 1970s),
10. the deceptively labeled shareholder primacy movement of the 1980s, which partnered Wall Street with CEOs to increase management's ability to enrich itself at shareholder expense, widening the gap

---

undersecretary John Taylor on Wednesday called for overhauling the Federal Reserve's dual mandate of ensuring stable prices and maximum employment, saying that the central bank should focus on prices.

[34] Subprime mortgages involved loans to people likely to encounter difficulty maintaining their repayment schedules. ARMS allowed homeowners to borrow inexpensively, but

between ownership and control first brought to light by Adolf Berle and Gardner Means in 1932, could be fostered,[35]

11. an indulgent attitude could be taken toward destructive financial innovation apparent in the 1987 program trading and 2000–2002 dot-com bubble stock-market crashes[36] as well as the 1998 Long-Term Capital Management hedge fund collapse,[37]

12. a permissive approach to financial auditing could be adopted,[38] including mark-to-face valuation for illiquid securities,

13. a consensus could be forged to rescind the Glass Steagall firewall separating commercial and investment banking (the 1999 Gramm-Leach-Bliley Act),[39]

14. a one-way-street, too-big-to-fail mentality that transformed prudent business activity into a speculative game on Wall Street, Main Street, and Washington could be applauded,

obligated them to pay more if interest rates rose. Additionally, during the new millennium it was common for banks to waive down payments, enabling "owners" to walk away from their properties when housing prices (and values) fell, leaving banks with a huge inventory of bankruptcy repossessions and distressed sales. The Clinton administration pushed subprime lending. The value of U.S. subprime mortgages in 2007 was $1.3 trillion. In an inflationary environment, driven in part by people borrowing from their home's inflationary premium, home buying was transformed into a speculative game. The ratio of global liquidity to global GDP quadrupled 1980–2007; doubling 2000–2007. Cross-border capital flows dectupled 1990–2007 from $1.1 to $11.2 trillion. Derivatives rose from virtually zero in 1990 to $684 trillion in 2007. U.S. nonfinancial debt outpaced GDP growth since 2007 by $8 trillion. See Quinn Mills, *World Financial Crisis 2008–2010: What Happened, Who is to Blame and How to Protect Your Money*, Create Space, 2009, p. 51.

[35] See Adolf Berle and Gardner Means, *The Modern Corporation and Private Property*, New York: Macmillan, 1932.

[36] The dot-com bubble began shortly after Federal Reserve Chairman Alan Greenspan's "irrational exuberance" speech on December 5, 1996. For proof that dot-com stocks were grossly overvalued, see J. Bradford Delong and Konstantin Magin, "A Short Note on the Size of the Dot-Com Bubble," *National Bureau of Economic Research Working Paper 12011*, January 2006. The Nasdaq Composite Index peaked at 5,132.52 on March 10, 2000 and bottomed at 1,108.49 on October 10, 2002. It was at 3,296 on April 14, 2013. The Enron accounting scam, tied to energy deregulation and lax accounting by Arthur Anderson, also contributed to the slaughter.

[37] Myron Scholes and Robert Merton, famous for devising a new method for valuing derivatives, were members of LTCM's board of directors.

[38] Richard Bowen III testified to the Financial Crisis Inquiry Commission that mortgage underwriting standards collapsed in the final years of the U.S. housing bubble (2006–2007). Sixty percent of mortgages purchased by Citicorp from some 1,600 mortgage companies were defective. Clayton Holdings reported in parallel testimony that only 54 percent of mortgage loans met their originators' underwriting standards.

[39] See K. Sabeel Rahman, "Democracy and Productivity: The Glass-Steagall and the Shifting Discourse of Financial Regulation," *Journal of Policy History*, Vol. 24, No. 4, October, 2012, pp. 612–643.

15. the institutionalization of hard assets (commodities, land, natural resources, precious metals, art, antiques, jewelry), which paved the way for the subordination of individual stock-market investment to institutional speculation, could be ignored,[40]

16. the side effects of post-dot-com-bust credit easing could be belittled,

17. the Iraq War, which swelled the U.S. federal budget deficit and triggered a petro bubble, could be treated as a plus,

18. Chinese stealthy beggar-thy-neighbor renminbi undervaluation and dollar-reserve hoarding could be portrayed as a minor irritant,[41]

19. the 2006 U.S. housing bust, which toxified mortgage and derivative financial instruments, could be blamed on technical errors,[42]

20. the emergence of institutional as distinct from ordinary depositor bank runs, where financial and nonfinancial companies flee repurchase (repo) agreements, could be attributed to inadequate stress tests,

21. rapidly mounting sovereign debt in Iceland and several European Union states could be ascribed to foreign blunders,[43]

---

[40] Jack Boogle, founder of Vanguard Group, privately estimated that $40 trillion of the $41 trillion traded on world stock exchanges in 2009 was speculative. The institutional share of U.S. stock-market investment has risen in the last two decades from 8 percent to 70 percent. Wall Street was complicit in manipulating the rise of commodity prices. See Tatyana Shumsky and Andrea Hotter, "Wall Street Gets Eyed in Metal Squeeze: Some Say Warehousing Inflates Prices," *Investor Shub*, June 18, 2011.

[41] See Steven Rosefielde, "China's Perplexing Foreign Trade Policy: Causes, Consequences, and a Tit for Tat Solution," *American Foreign Policy Interests*, Vol. 33, No. 1, January–February, 2011, pp. 10–16. Chinese dollar-hoarding is widely mischaracterized as financing imports. See Ken Miller, "Coping with China's Financial Power: Beijing's Financial Foreign Policy," *Foreign Affairs*, Vol. 89, No. 4, July 2010, pp. 1–8.

[42] U.S. housing prices peaked in early 2005, and the Case-Shiller home price index began falling in 2006. Prices plunged 34 percent thereafter, bottoming out in 2009, and were expected to continue declining in 2011 despite more than a trillion dollars of government support. On December 24, 2009, the Treasury Department pledged unlimited support for the next three years to Fannie Mae and Freddie Mac, despite $400 billion in losses. The bubble was predicted by Robert Shiller in 2000. See Robert Shiller, *Irrational Exuberance*, Princeton NJ: Princeton University Press, 2000 and Shiller, *The Subprime Solution: How Today's the Global Financial Crisis Happened, and What to Do About It*, Princeton, NJ: Princeton University Press, 2008. As early as 1997, Federal Reserve Chairman Alan Greenspan fought to keep derivatives unregulated, a goal codified in the Commodity Futures Modernization Act of 2000. Derivatives like credit default swaps (CDS) were used to hedge or speculate against particular credit risks. Their volume increased 100-fold 1998–2008, with estimates of the debt as high as $47 trillion. Total over-the-counter derivative notional value rose to $683 trillion by June 2008. Warren Buffet described the phenomenon as "financial weapons of mass destruction" in *The Economist*, September 18, 2008.

[43] Debt obligations issued by nation states are called sovereign debt. Superficially, it might be supposed that sovereign bonds are more secure than their corporate equivalents, but the

22. macroeconomic-policy mismanagement could be attributed to a misplaced faith in divine coincidence,

23. the disastrous imposition of mark-to-market valuation (Fair Accounting Standard: FAS 157) of illiquid assets from November 15, 2007 could be glossed as a timing error,[44]

24. the increased separation of ownership from corporate control encouraging CEOs to gamble with shareholders' money at negligible personal risk could be lauded as wise, and

reverse often is the case because countries cannot be forced to honor their obligations under the doctrine of sovereign immunity. Creditors' only recourse is to passively accept rescheduling, interest reductions, or even repudiation. See Jonathan Eaton and Raquel Fernandez, "Sovereign Debt," in G. Grossman and K. Rogoff, eds., *Handbook of International Economics*, Vol. III, Amsterdam: Elsevier Science B.V., 1995, chapter 39. Sovereign debt initially played a subsidiary role in the 2008 financial crisis. The collapse of Iceland's main banks and 77 percent stock plunge in September 2008 prompted rating agencies to drastically cut Iceland's sovereign debt rating from A+ to BBB-. The IMF arranged a rescue package on November 19, 2008, but the cat was out of the bag. Suddenly, investors became aware that the global financial crisis's scope might be much wider than earlier supposed, raising the specter of a worldwide financial collapse that was not reversed until March 2009. Nonetheless, sovereign debt fears reemerged in 2010 due to credit rating reductions for Greek, Irish, Portuguese, and Spanish sovereign debt that forced an EU to intervene in defense of these members. The rescue involved loans for conditionality, where credit-impaired sovereigns were compelled to pledge the adoption of austerity measures reducing their "structural deficits." The problem, which could easily expand to include Italy and others, does not appear to jeopardize the international financial system immediately but is a bad omen for the future. Additionally, many worry that if rating cuts contingent on budgetary debt reductions do not cease, it could force the European Union to abandon the euro as a common currency and even result in the EU's dissolution. The root cause of the EU's problem is not excessive debt per se, but the ability of less productive members to run EU-threatening deficits in a common currency regime without the option of individual country currency devaluation. See Bruno Dallago and Chiara Guglielmetti, "The EZ in the Prospects of Global Imbalances: Two Europes?" in Steven Rosefielde, Masaaki Kuboniwa and Satoshi Mizobata, eds., *Two Asias: The Emerging Postcrisis Divide*, Singapore: World Scientific, 2012. As we know from the theory of optimum currency areas, there are benefits and costs to currency integration. Benefits are the reduced costs of doing business. If they are large, forming currency areas lead to large increases in trade. This is not what happened in the eurozone after the monetary union was established. The key problem is building a consensus on how best to restore price equilibrium after asymmetric shocks, booms, and slumps that disparately affect individual member states. Labor mobility (Robert Mundell), fiscal integration (Peter Kenen), a strong central bank serving as lender of last recourse, and a fiscal unit to bail out sovereign debts lubricate equilibration, but do not automatically resolve conflicting member interests. The EU sovereign debt issue is tutoring members about the tradeoffs that must be made if the monetary union is to survive.

[44] FDIC Chairman William Issac places much of the blame for the subprime mortgage crisis on the SEC for its fair-value accounting rules, misapplied in times of crisis. The Emergency Stabilization Act of 2008, signed October 7, suspended mark-to-market asset pricing during crises. The new regulation is FAS 157-d.

25. bank deposits could be arbitrarily confiscated in Cyprus by EU edict, a harbinger of the shape of things to come.

The 2008 global financial crisis and the looming sovereign debt crisis thus are not garden-variety white swan business cyclical events.[45] They mark politocracy's coming of age within an accommodative body of new orthodox economic theory.

PROSPECTS

A great deal of blood has flowed under the bridge in the past two decades. There were two distinct types of financial crisis in Western democracies: (1) a worldwide debacle rooted in reckless aggregate demand management and financial deregulation by a partnership of politicians, big business, and big social advocacy in significant part for personal gain that started in the United States but spread almost instantaneously across the globe, mostly through international financial networks (except Asia where export shocks were primary); and (2) a sovereign debt crisis concentrated initially in Iceland and the EU PIIGS that spread to the United States and threatens the entire global system.[46]

---

[45] See Nassim Taleb, *The Black Swan: The Impact of the Highly Improbable*, New York: Random House, 2007. "Morici: Down Grade US Treasury to Junk," Yahoo! Finance, December 20, 2010. Peter Morici contends that Congress and the White House made no comprise whatsoever in extending and expanding the Bush tax cuts, including a temporary 33 percent cut in poor and middle-class social-security taxes, ballooning the federal deficit to $1.5 trillion in 2011, to say nothing of off-budget deficits ten times as large.

[46] See Uri Dadush, William Shaw, "Preparing for Eurogeddon," Carnegie Foundation, December 8, 2011: "A collapse of the euro would be a tragedy for Europe and a calamity for the United States. Given the extensive economic ties between the United States and Europe, urgent steps are required to guard against a collapse of the financial system, a severe reduction in external demand, and a seizing up of international transactions." "Massive support from the European Central Bank for economies facing prohibitively expensive borrowing terms, coupled with expansionary policies in Germany and an agreement on fiscal union, could still save the euro. Absent such huge policy reversals, however, the financial conditions of peripheral countries may continue to deteriorate, and their governments will likely refuse to undertake a decade of austerity to save the common currency, an option no politician loyal to nation or party should contemplate." "Assessments of the likely impact of a eurozone breakup on the United States range widely. The IMF found that a 2.5 percent reduction in European GDP would result in a 0.7 percent fall in U.S. GDP, while the OECD calculated that disorderly sovereign defaults in some euro countries could reduce U.S. GDP by more than 2 percent. However, these models cannot capture all of the indirect effects of a systemic crisis, particularly through the financial system, which can be more important than the direct impact. One example of the potentially extreme implications of a euro breakup is given by a UBS analysis suggesting that a weak country leaving the eurozone could lose half its GDP in the first year, while

Both are likely to recur and reinforce each other soon because high-rolling losers were compensated out of public funds,[47] self-interested aggregate demand managers are unrepentant, Western politicians remain steadfastly in denial, and publics are dazed by fast talk.[48] Public-private partnerships are using all means fair and foul to create favorable speculative financial conditions for their personal enrichment. The Dodd-Frank bank regulation act for example has the effect of underwriting derivative trading losses.[49] At the same time the government is resisting significant reductions in deficit spending (and consequently continues expanding the national debt),[50] which, when combined with open-ended money printing (QE-infinity), underregulated white hot international money flows, Chinese dollar-reserve hoarding, and stealthy protectionism, in the best scenario will seriously degrade global economic performance, and in the worst culminate a black swan catastrophe.

Germany's exit would reduce its GDP by 20 to 25 percent, implying a much larger shock for the United States and the global economy. A collapse of the euro would be a tragedy for Europe and a calamity for the United States. Given the extensive economic ties between the United States and Europe, urgent steps are required to guard against a collapse of the financial system, a severe reduction in external demand, and a seizing up of international transactions."

[47] See "Why Bank of America Must be Thrilled to Pay a 3 Billion Dollar Penalty," Yahoo! Finance, January 4, 2011. The U.S. government provided the Bank of America with a $20 billion "back-door" bailout by relieving it of all but $3 billion of its liability for Fannie Mae's and Freddie Mac's likely cumulative bad mortgage losses. See Stacy Curtin, "Why Obama Lacks Political Will to Crackdown on Wall Street," Yahoo! Finance, May 8, 2012: "Despite his populist posturing, the president has failed to pin a single top finance exec on criminal charges since the economic collapse. Are the banks too big to jail – or is Washington's revolving door to blame? ... Financial-fraud prosecutions are at 20-year lows and down 39% since the Enron and Worldcom scandals of 2003."

[48] See Matthew Kaminski "A Silver Lining in Europe," *Wall Street Journal*, December 9, 2011:

In a paper presented at a Witherspoon Institute conference this week, German finance ministry official Ludger Schuknecht, who previously headed fiscal policy surveillance at the ECB, notes that the U.S. increase in its size of government over the past decade was on par with those of Italy, Spain, Portugal, Greece, Ireland and the U.K. All the others have tried to rein it in, he writes, but the U.S. "stands out as the country that seems to be quite oblivious to the need for adjustment over the near future."

[49] Editorial, *Wall Street Journal*, May 24, 2012, 1:

As we noted in May 2010, the authority for this regulatory achievement was inserted into Congress's pending financial reform bill by then-Senator Chris Dodd. Two months later, the legislation was re-named Dodd-Frank and signed into law by Mr. Obama. One part of the law forces much of the derivatives market into clearinghouses that stand behind every trade. Mr. Dodd's pet provision creates a mechanism for bailing out these clearinghouses when they run into trouble.

[50] See Morgan Korn, "Student Loans Could be the Next Housing Bubble: Robert Reich," Yahoo! Finance, March 30, 2012.

The U.S. constitution strictly interpreted in the spirit of the founding fathers does not preclude the present danger, but would make the prospect unlikely. The *demos* is supposed to behave more rationally than politicians do today. The Bill of Rights should protect private property, empower economic liberty, and foster competition at the same time checks and balances limit the ability of the few to pursue their causes and material interests to the detriment of the many.

Politocracy, however is another matter. Exploiting the *demos* and gambling with other people's well-being while hedged by golden parachutes is its creed, even when half the U.S. population has been pushed below the government-stipulated low-income threshold.[51] Government capture may not be the only cause of the United States' degeneration, but it is the principal source of contemporary Americo-sclerosis and double arrhythmia.[52]

---

[51] The official "low income threshold – $45,000 for a family of four – should not be taken too seriously. It is set to justify politarchic social programming. Nonetheless, the headline shows that America's economic decline is not a mere annoyance. See Hope Yen, "Census Shows 1 in 2 People are Poor or Low-Income," Associated Press, December 15, 2011:

The latest census data depict a middle class that's shrinking as unemployment stays high and the government's safety net frays. The new numbers follow years of stagnating wages for the middle class that have hurt millions of workers and families.... "Safety net programs such as food stamps and tax credits kept poverty from rising even higher in 2010, but for many low-income families with work-related and medical expenses, they are considered too 'rich' to qualify," said Sheldon Danziger, a University of Michigan public policy professor who specializes in poverty.

[52] See Stacy Curtin, "3 Years After Lehman: Still No Solutions for 'Too Big to Fail' or Fannie & Freddie," Yahoo! News, December 8, 2011:

It's been three years since the financial crisis, which spurred the great recession. In that time little has been done to fix the 'too big to fail' banks or the government sponsored agencies – Fannie Mae and Freddie Mac – responsible for the global economic meltdown. Today U.S. banks are bigger than ever. The top four banks in the United States – J.P Morgan, Bank of America, Wells Fargo and Citigroup – control 62% of total commercial assets in this country, up 8% from five years ago, reports *The Wall Street Journal*. The Dodd-Frank bill was supposed to rein in the banks, but clearly has failed to do much to date, in part because the banks and many Republicans have been fighting to repeal the legislation. A big point of contention in the bill is the so-called Volcker rule, which would prevent firms from using customer deposits for trades made for the bank's own accounts. The banks have also been pushing back against calls to revamp debit card rules, as well as the outright breakup of the institutions. On the housing front, the government sponsored enterprises Fannie Mae and Freddie Mac have directly cost the U.S. taxpayer nearly $151 billion in the last three years; the indirect costs have been much higher. But again, little has been done to fix the problems surrounding those agencies. The Obama administration has really "dropped the ball" on this issue. "The Obama administration knows that the GSEs are a huge issue," says Swagel. "They were an important contributor to the crisis and they have done nothing but put forward a report that was just a menu of options."

SIX

Burden and Spoils

WHO PAYS?

The mission of true democratic governments is to provide the variety and quantity of public services (including charitable transfers) the people want, paid for by various groups at majority-approved tax rates, subject to the civil and property-rights protections set forth in the constitution. The methods used to fund programs variously financed through direct taxation, pass-through taxation (taxes levied on business passed through to purchasers), indirect taxation (inflation tax), stealthy taxation (military draft), and borrowing must express the people's will.

Contemporary U.S. politarchic government violates these principles by overspending, misspending, preferentially taxing groups in violation of Constitutional civil and property-rights protections, and by employing deceptive methods of financing. Excess federal spending attributable to overpaid and oversupplied factors of production is approximately $2 trillion (derived later in this chapter).

Privileges and excessive financial burdens are experienced individually in myriad ways that cannot be adequately evaluated with available statistics. Nonetheless, aggregate data in the public domain can be parsed to paint a composite picture that reveals the grand strategy of contemporary American politarchs. In a nutshell, politicians, big business and big social advocacy (including the poor, "deserving" minorities, and immigrants) are coddled. They pay less than their fair share. Most of the rest (workers, middle-class, and passive rich) are overtaxed.

This distribution is the consequence of politarchic optimization. Politarchs reward themselves and their allies and indulge those who for various reasons could rock the boat, (the underclass, the working poor, Hispanic immigrants, vocal minorities, and the state-private active rich), while pressuring those in the middle and affluent classes who receive little or none of the tangible public-service benefits that fund free riders. Once upon a time, workers were feared and appeased, but now they are mostly expected to cofinance politocracy. The course of least resistance within this framework appears to be relieving households with annual incomes less than $50,000 (adjusted gross income on IRS form 1040, line 37) of any federal income-tax obligation (47 percent of all households in 2009),[1] placing 73 percent of the federal income-tax burden on households earning at least $366,400 (top 10 percent of earners),[2] while dispersing the rest of the public expenditure burden helter-skelter across the social spectrum through corporate, social insurance (FICA, SECA, and Medicare), unemployment (paid by corporations), sales, excise, estate, property, and inflation taxes, plus sovereign borrowing (subject to "haircuts").[3] Total federal, state, and local taxes paid by persons (as distinct from corporations) in 2010 as a share of personal consumption was 26 percent.[4]

---

[1] Stephen Ohlemacher, "Nearly Half of US Households Escape Fed Income Tax," Yahoo! Finance, April 7, 2010: http:www.irs.gov, http://www.taxpolicycenter.org The number of households paying no taxes is business-cycle sensitive. The figure for 2007 was 38 percent, rising to 49 percent in 2008, and falling back to 47 percent in 2009. It was 46.4 in 2011. The issue gained media attention during the 2012 Presidential campaign. Many commentators tried to detoxify the facts by pointing out that the figure was actually 46.4 percent (2011), and observing that the statistic included some super rich. For example, see Daniel Bukszpan, "Where the 47 Percent Live," Yahoo! Finance, September 22, 2012:

"They're either paying payroll taxes or they're the elderly," Heather Boushey, senior economist at the Center for American Progress, said in an e-mail. "Only 7.9% of households do not pay any federal taxes, but that's because they're either students, on disability, or unemployed." These groups may not pay federal income tax, but that's different from paying no taxes whatsoever. "Everyone pays taxes of some sort," Boushey said. "If you have a job, you pay payroll taxes. If you buy things, you pay sales taxes. And people pay taxes to their state and local governments." Other groups who pay no federal income tax include retirees and people earning $20,000 a year or less. "The elderly don't have to pay income tax on their Social Security benefits (false statement), while low income workers qualify for the Earned Income Tax Credit or the Child Tax Credit," Boushey said.

[2] The bottom 40 percent, on average, gains from the federal income tax, meaning they get more money in tax credits than they would otherwise owe in taxes. The government sends these people a payment. Stephen Ohlemacher, "Nearly Half of US Households Escape Fed Income Tax," Yahoo! Finance, April 7, 2010: "President Obama signed the economic recovery law in 2009 that expanded some tax credits and created others, target mostly at low- and middle income families. His 'Making Work Pay' credit provides a 'guaranteed' income to 6 million households, with 15 million children at a cost of approximately $10 billion".

[3] A "haircut" is partial forfeiture of debt principal imposed on creditors. "Greece Says Investor Losses from Debt Swap May Top 70 Percent," Yahoo! Finance, January 31, 2012.

[4] www.bea.gov See National Income Accounts, Tables 3.1 (Government Current Receipts and Expenditures), and 1.1.5 (Gross Domestic Product). This is an underestimate, since

The scheme has some superficial resemblance to a Robin Hood model where the politicians soak the rich to underwrite a decent living standard for the underclass, working poor, immigrants, and lower middle class, but appearances are deceptive. The affluent do indeed pay the lion's share of income tax, regardless of the further issues of tax avoidance and evasion.[5] Mark Zuckerberg's 2010 federal tax bill was $2 billion.[6] However, ordinary people pay numerous taxes too. Worker households with unadjusted earned income from $1 to $106,800 pay for their own social security benefits.[7] Employees pay Medicare taxes as a percentage of income up to $107,523 of unadjusted earned income. Everyone, including the indigent, pays sales tax and excise taxes on products like gasoline and airline tickets. Everyone pays higher product prices as the pass-through effect of unemployment taxes paid by corporations. Alcohol and tobacco taxes are paid by rich and poor alike. People with medical-insurance plans and those with deep pockets pay hefty health-care inflation taxes through the federal government's medical-procedure-reimbursement price-rigging schemes (used to provide subsidized or free hospital services to the uninsured). Estate holders pay inheritance taxes one way or another, including state taxes and fees.[8] Home and real-estate owners, together with renters (except people living in public and rent-controlled lodgings), pay huge property taxes directly or via pass-throughs. The federal government doesn't directly levy local, state and property taxes, but much of these revenues are necessitated by the requirements of federal cost sharing schemes and mandates, and thus are part of the aggregate federally imposed tax burden.

some taxes are paid by corporations and passed in prices or fees to customers (individuals) so that individuals pay the taxes indirectly.

5 Julia Werdigier, "Tax Evaders Face Greater Scrutiny as National Debts Pile Up," November 2, 2011: "Assets held offshore by individuals worldwide have probably almost doubled from $11.5 trillion six years ago, according to the Tax Justice Network, a nongovernmental organization. Friedrich Schneider, a professor at Johannes Kepler University in Austria, said the shadow economy in 31 European countries was equivalent to 19.3 percent of gross domestic product."

6 Matt Nesto, "Facebook's Mark Zuckerberg Poised for Taxpayer Hall of Fame," Yahoo! Finance, February 8, 2012.

7 Social security, moreover, is treated improperly as new income instead of deferred compensation already taxed when earned, and therefore wrongly double taxed when paid out eventually as benefits. Working people must bear the burden for recipients who don't pay full freight. Unlike private pension plans, monies invested in the social security fund are not inheritable assets. If individuals and their spouses die the day before retirement, heirs receive nothing except a meager funeral benefit of $255.

8 But, of course there are ways to avoid a significant portion of estate tax through gifts to charity and trusts. Politarchs devote substantial energy to assisting friends through these deductions and tax credits.

The national debt and more than $10 trillion of unfunded promises will be paid with some combination of defaults on promises made to social security and Medicare recipients and bondholders, and intergenerational burden shifting to tomorrow's workers and other taxpayers. Importers and consumers of foreign goods will bear part of the cost of America's gargantuan sovereign debt in the form of rising foreign currency prices (depreciating U.S. dollar). The inflation tax will hit everyone, but the incidence will vary widely. Social security recipients and the poor will have their transfers partly protected by cost-of-living increases, but passive asset holders generally will suffer capital losses on bonds and negligible real interest, while speculators and many investors will reap capital-appreciation windfalls. Homeowners and renters will be assaulted with skyrocketing taxes tied to inflated real-estate assessments.[9]

Although the complexities of America's tax system make calibration of future net tax burdens difficult, it is easy to see that the middle class, including workers and the flatfooted affluent (passive wealth holders) will pay more than the indigent,[10] lower middle class, and nimble rich. The middle class in the annual income range of $50,000 to $366,400 will be most affected because inflation as in the past will be concentrated in the goods and services they intensely use: health care, education, child care, professional services (including lawyers and tax and financial advisors), food, entertainment, and imports. This is why majority resistance to tax increases is so intense at a time when 47 percent of households pay no federal income tax whatsoever. People do not know the intricacies, but they feel the pain and sense that the federal government is the culprit.[11]

The politicians are aware of this, and are trying to preempt a Tea Party-type revolt by reducing the number of citizens who pay federal income tax,[12] deferring tax obligations to future generations (increasing the national debt), fobbing off the liabilities on states and localities compelled to finance federal cost sharing and mandates, and fomenting high inflation (the inflation tax). Of course, they could always cut programs temporarily

---

[9] California, Florida, and some other states limit the impact of inflation-driven taxes on homeowners.

[10] James Stewart, "At 102%, His Tax Rate Takes the Cake," *New York Times*, February 4, 2012: Mitt Romney paid 102 percent of his taxable income in federal, state and local taxes for 2010. This was due to the fact that his business interest expenses were not deductible on New York City income tax.

[11] Cf. Raghuram Rajan, "The True Lessons of the Recession," *Foreign Affairs*, Vol. 91, Issue 3, May/June 2012, pp. 69–79. Rajan's narrative supports ours, but he emphasizes faulty policies.

[12] The Tea Party movement (TPM) is an American populist political movement that is generally recognized as conservative and libertarian and has sponsored protests and supported political candidates since 2009.

to alleviate middle-class resentment, but this is bad for politarchic business. Augmenting the total return to public-service enterprises not only inclines politarchs to adopt leveraged macromanagement and financial liberalization strategies that provide speculative capital gains, but also to employ the same practices to soak the middle class and passive rich. The approach is reprehensible in many ways, and would be shunned in a true democracy, but it suits contemporary U.S. politicians.

WHO BENEFITS FROM GOVERNMENT SPENDING?

Spoils to the Powerful

In a true democracy people acquire income and wealth from multiple sources and hire government as an agent to provide public services. Government does not deliver services as a private business for its own account and has no claim on the *demos's* income and assets, including inheritance beyond what is constitutionally approved. True democratic government serves the people; it does not treat them as its partners, subjects, tenants, servitors or mandate-slaves. In a politocracy, by contrast, everything is topsy-turvy. Politicians view themselves as masters and owners of the realm. Everything is theirs, except what they choose to leave to the people. This is the deep meaning of "tax-expenditure," an esoteric legal term for tax revenues that the government feels it ought to collect from taxpayers, but which law allows favorites to keep. The concept epitomizes the politocratic notion that the government is the ultimate owner of the people's income and arbiter of what, if anything, they should be permitted to retain.

The question of who gets the spoils cannot be conceptualized properly without grasping that in a politocracy what the people get is not just public services, but what politicians allow people to keep, including concealed incomes, capital gains, gifts, and inheritances. Some of these leavings, such as incomes from unreported informal labor activities in cash and kind and sundry capital gains, are uncollectible because monitoring and enforcement costs exceed likely tax receipts (for example, taxes on income earned by children selling lemonade). Other components, however, are individual and corporate tax concessions and disguised welfare transfers to politarchs, big business, big social advocates (including NGOs and charities), and social-service recipients,[13] as well as tolerated tax evasion.

---

[13] The term "tax expenditures" was coined by former Assistant Secretary of the Treasury Stanley Surrey in 1967 and represents estimated revenues "left" with individuals and companies through various tax breaks intended to stimulate specific consumption and investment activities. See Stanley Surrey, *Pathways to Tax Reform: The Concept of Tax Expenditures*, Cambridge, MA: Harvard University Press, 1974.

On one side of the spectrum, the IRS avoids auditing sensitive minorities, labor unions, and criminals in select localities. On the other, tax collectors either deliberately provide individuals with increased retained income by means of diverse exemptions and subsidies, or wink at income disguised as intermediate input costs (travel, catering, office furnishings for personal use, entertainment, escort services, etc.),[14] and somehow substantial parts of estates mysteriously disappear before becoming taxable on an immediate or intergenerational basis. Incomes of all sorts vanish abroad and are never traced. The Congressional Joint Committee on Taxation estimated that tax expenditures alone defined for more than 180 specific programs cost $1 trillion in off-budget revenues in 2009, before taking into account dubious deductions.[15] Although we do not know the full magnitude of these concessions, the figures could be staggering. For example, the value of untaxed intermediate goods and semi-fabricates used in producing final goods and services that can be siphoned off to personal consumption is equal to the entire GDP in U.S. national income accounting.[16] U.S. national wealth including derivatives runs close to $200 trillion,[17] but only peanuts are annually collected in federal inheritance taxes (approximately $35 billion). Needless to say, incomes from narcotics trade, prostitution, bootlegging, and illegal gambling go untaxed. Colossal amounts

[14] Kathy Kristof, "8 Outrageous Executive Perks," Yahoo! Finance, April 5, 2011: The scale of personal income disguised for tax purposes as "intermediate input costs" can be gleaned indirectly from the list of outrageous executive perks published by Kristof. These include Dennis Kozlowski, CEO of Tyco Corporation, who charged his company $2 million for his wife's 40th birthday party, likely as a "business expense," and Shaw Group, who paid $15 million plus interest to former CEO James Bernhard and his heirs to prevent him from competing two years after he died. The disguised "gift" can be treated as a factor cost and hence deductible to Shaw Corporation. Cf. Maria Newman, "Leona Helmsley," *New York Times*, August 20, 2007: "Leona Helmsley was indicted on charges that she had evaded more than $4 million in income taxes. Prosecutors charged that she fraudulently claimed personal luxuries as business expenses, including a $45,000 silver clock and a $210,000 mahogany card table for their Greenwich, Conn., mansion."

[15] The Congressional Joint Committee on Taxation estimates tax expenditures annually for more than 180 special programs listed in the U.S. tax code. The figure for 2009 was $1 trillion. The major recipient was wealthy homeowners. The majority of tax expenditures are targeted at individual social benefits and services. See Christopher Faricy, "The Politics of Social Policy in America: Indirect Versus Direct Social Spending," *The Journal of Publics*, Vol. 73, No. 1, January, 2011, pp. 74–83.

[16] See American input-output tables, www.bea.gov/industry/io

[17] John Rutledge, "Total Assets of the U.S. Economy $188 Trillion, 13.4x GDP," February 21, 2011. http://rutledgecapital.com/2009/05/24/total-assets-of-the-us-economy-188-trillion-134xgdp/ Rutledge provides a detailed breakdown of his estimates. He was unable to acquire information on various classes of tangible assets that could easily raise his total to $200 trillion.

of disputed assets that occasionally come to the public's attention turn out to be untraceable. The Soviet Communist Party had $90 billion stashed in New York, but Russia was unable to recover a dime. Bernard Madoff's Ponzi scheme allowed him to steal a fortune, but investigators still cannot find $10 billion. The government taxes too much, but it also takes too little from those with hidden incomes and assets, shifting the burden to the middle class.

From a democratic perspective, stolen and disputed assets should be returned to their rightful owners, and people should be taxed on a uniform basis (with special allowance made for the indigent). Hidden incomes should be uncovered and taxed, with tax rates lowered correspondingly so that government receives only the revenues needed to pay for legitimate public services. If the majority of the people decide that social justice requires confiscating extreme wealth when the rich die after dispassionate consideration of the Constitution's underlying property-right protections, then democracies can heavily tax their estates, reducing everyone else's income-tax liabilities in the process. There shouldn't be any general policy of estate-tax exemptions for selected groups beyond these general principles.

The politarchic pattern by contrast is mostly expedient and strongly biased toward protecting the income and assets of politically favored corporations, organized groups like trade unions,[18] big social advocates,[19] and individuals. Although politicians posture as guarantors of social justice, inclining them to be generous to have-nots, in the final analysis their

---

[18] The TARP bailout of General Motors privileged auto workers in the bankruptcy proceeding. See Justin Hyde, "Why a Millionaire Wants Trade Unions to Take a Pay Cut," Yahoo! Motor, December 17, 2011: "The former head of the Obama administration's auto task force says he should have pushed the United Auto Workers for steeper sacrifices in the General Motors bailout, including wage cuts."

[19] George Packer, in "The Broken Contract," *Foreign Affairs*, Nov/Dec 2011, Vol. 90, No. 6, p. 20, writes: "Over the past three decades, Washington has consistently favored the rich – and the more wealth accumulates in a few hands at the top, the more influence and favor the rich acquire, making it easier for them and their political allies to cast off restraint...." Scott Thurm, "For Big Companies, Life Is Good Large Corporations Emerge from Recession Leaner, Stronger – and Hiring Overseas," *Wall Street Journal*, April 9, 2012:

Big U.S. companies have emerged from the deepest recession since World War II more productive, more profitable, flush with cash and less burdened by debt. An analysis by *The Wall Street Journal* of corporate financial reports finds that cumulative sales, profits and employment last year among members of the Standard & Poor's 500-stock index exceeded the totals of 2007, before the recession and financial crisis. Deep cost cutting during the downturn and caution during the recovery put the companies on firmer financial footing, helping them to outperform the rest of the economy and gather a greater share of the nation's ...

actions are skewed toward helping themselves, big business, and big social advocacy.[20] This behavior is what politarchy is about.

The broad inference is confirmed by close scrutiny of current government expenditures (including state and local outlays: $5.3 trillion in 2010), mandates and insurance guarantees; what most people mean when they talk about the distribution of spoils. Ordinary people receive some portion of what they pay in taxes as transfers (social security, Medicare, etc.), public goods (national parks), together with inefficient collective services where costs far exceed their value, like border patrols, war on drugs, homeland security, national defense, the CIA, the State Department, the Department of Energy, the Environmental Protection Agency, the Agriculture Department, and the Department of Health, Education and Welfare. The government also provides some essential collective services like highway construction and maintenance, veterans' hospitals, federal courts, prisons, immigration facilities, the Internal Revenue Service, the Department of Commerce, labor departments, regulatory activities, macroeconomic management, and welfare transfers like unemployment compensation, food stamps, and housing subsidies, and transfers to the rest of the world (foreign aid totaled $76 billion in 2010), but it doesn't supply household services or goods to the majority. Such services are delivered by state and local governments supported in part by more than half a trillion dollars of grants-in-aid.

The value of these services, corrected for state price-fixing (including overpaying wages, vendor services, and boondoggles) and deleting social security ($700 billion FY2010) and Medicare ($250 billion FY2010, which for the most part could be provided better and cheaper through private sources) is a small fraction of the $5.3 trillion spent.[21] Let us assume for

---

[20] Hope Yen, "US Wealth Gap Between Young and Old Widest Ever," Associated Press, November 7, 2011:

The wealth gap between younger and older Americans has stretched to the widest on record, worsened by a prolonged economic downturn that has wiped out job opportunities for young adults and saddled them with housing and college debt. The typical U.S. household headed by a person age 65 or older has a net worth 47 times greater than a household headed by someone under 35, according to an analysis of census data released Monday.

Hope Yen, "US Poverty at New High: 16 Percent, 41.9 Million," Yahoo! Finance, November 7, 2011:

A record number of Americans – 49.1 million – are poor, based on a new census measure that for the first time takes into account rising medical costs and other expenses. The numbers released Monday are part of a first-ever supplemental poverty measure aimed at providing a fuller picture of poverty. Although considered experimental, they promise to stir fresh debate over Social Security, Medicare and programs to help the poor as a congressional supercommittee nears a Nov. 23 deadline to make more than $1 trillion in cuts to the federal budget.

[21] http://www.gpoaccess.gov/usbudget/fy10/hist.html

the sake of discussion that the actual market value of government services including welfare programs like Medicaid, less transfers (social security and Medicare), amounts to $2 trillion of legitimate collective services (approximately 14 percent of GDP), with the excess $2.3 trillion apportionable to overpaid and oversupplied factors of production.

Who are the beneficiaries of these $2 trillion of legitimate public-service value? Who receives $2.3 trillion in payments for fictive services (overpayments to employees, and vendors arising from overcharging and forced substitution)? How much income accrues to beneficiaries of preferential regulations, mandates and insurance guarantees?

There are four primary recipients of the $4.3 trillion of real and fictive services: civil service and military personnel (wages), contractors (sales and profits), collective beneficiaries (society), and designated benefices (business, welfare, and special-interest subsidies [TARP]). Federal employees and armed-forces personnel receive income whether or not their activities generate added value. If their competitive added value is zero, then they are welfare clients; if it is positive then their actions mostly assist the collective, with the residual going to various designated beneficiaries. Defense and civil-service wages in 2010 were $154.2 billion[22] and $190 billion, respectively;[23] approximately 8 percent of federal expenditure, excluding social security and Medicare transfers. This total understates federal personnel expenditures because it omits grants-in-aid funding to state and local positions. Washington spent $653 billion on these transfers in 2010,[24] a sum more than ample to cover a substantial portion of the more than $800 billion spent annually on state and local government wages.[25] Let us therefore conservatively assume that total direct plus indirect government personnel costs are 10 percent of all federal outlays, excluding social security and Medicare transfers.

The residual 90 percent ($3.9 trillion) is spent on programs that become incomes, grants, or transfers to final claimants. Individuals received $745 billion in 2010, 90 percent of which ($561 billion) were paid for income

---

[22] Wikipedia, Military Budget of the United States FY2010.

[23] U.S. Bureau of Labor Statistics, Employment and Wages Annual Averages, 2008, Bulletin 2718, January 2010, Table 645 (Employment and Wages: 2000 to 2008). See also http://www.bis.gov/cew/cewbultn08.htm

[24] U.S. Office of Management and Budget, *Budget of the United States Government, Historical Tables*, annual. See also http://www.whitehouse.gov/omb/budget

[25] U.S. Bureau of Labor Statistics, Employment and Wages Annual Averages, 2008, Bulletin 2718, January 2010, Table 645 (Employment and Wages: 2000 to 2008). See also http://www.bis.gov/cew/cewbult08.htm

security (welfare and unemployment compensation) and veterans' payments.[26] Other large categories include education, social services, and health. Interest on the national debt was $209 billion. Subtracting these amounts from total government expenditures (federal, state, and local) leaves $3 trillion for grants to state and local government excluding individuals ($259 billion), direct federal-contract services, and direct state and local outlays.

This sum represents the direct and indirect dependency of the private sector on government purchases (20 percent of GDP), excluding many social benefits like health care that wind up as subsidies to corporate and state programs.[27] These government purchases appear as private value-added services by sector of origin in national income accounts, but are paid for primarily by the federal government. Nongovernment employees capture a substantial portion of these monies, as do executives and shareholders via excess profits and personal consumption concealed as intermediate input costs. Insofar as these intermediate services add value, public services function as an engine diverting workers from productive occupations in the competitive private sector to provide excess compensation for corporate executives and investors, so that in the final analysis, consolidating results, the winners in the process are government employees, contract employees to the extent that they are overpaid, grantees, and a segment of the wealthy. The same conclusion holds if the value added by government services is negligible, but in this case, government becomes a gigantic grant-transfer operation costing $5.3 trillion with little or no benefit. Splitting the difference brings us closer to the truth (readers can adjust to their taste), underscoring the skewed distribution of benefits and the immense wastefulness of the public-service process.

The U.S. government and derivatively state and local governments in 2010 spent $3.6 trillion (excluding social security and Medicare and $745 billion paid to individuals) to create an estimated $1.5 trillion of legitimate

[26] Budget of the United States Government: Browse Fiscal Year 2011, Historical Tables, Section 3, Federal Outlays by Function, Table 11.2, p. 222. Payments to individuals in 2010 disbursed by agency in millions of current dollars were as follows: national defense (1,095), international affairs (583), agriculture (299), transportation (1,281), education and social services (44,633), health (20,696), Medicare (528,706), income security (560,788), social security (714,539), veterans (110,130), administration of justice (714), health reform (5,500). http:/www.gpoaccess.gov/usbudget/fy11/index.html

[27] Ricardo Alonso-Zaldivar, "Obama's Health Care Law Has Some Unexpected Beneficiaries," Yahoo! News, November 4, 2011: "Two Texas public employee programs are among the top 25 beneficiaries of a $5-billion fund to shore up employer coverage for early retirees." The story is based on a report by the Center for Public Policy Priorities.

collective services (mostly purchases from the private sector), grants and transfers (excluding $209 billion of interest payments on the national debt) that benefited a small fraction of the electorate, some poor, some middle class, and some rich. This broadly is the federal giveback to the politarchs' big business and big social-advocacy associates.

However, the story remains incomplete because it omits mandates,[28] (including those that impose stealthy taxes via medical reimbursement cost rigging to pay free hospital costs for the uninsured), forced substitution costs of less desirable goods (incandescent-light-bulb phase-out), tax-subsidy incentives, and regulatory windfalls excluded from the expenditure data – benefits that are highly skewed toward politarchs' private sector partners.

The compliance costs associated with federal mandates (non-negotiated, anticompetitive, and antidemocratic edicts imposed on the *demos*) broadly construed, including the ever-mounting complexity of income tax, pension, and employment reporting imposed on individuals and businesses are well known and intensely felt, making it easy to forget that the costs of unnecessary services borne by taxpayers generally are incomes to others. Mandates are a boon to accountants, lawyers, state hospitals, doctors, and miscellaneous vendors, especially outsourcing companies like Aon.[29] Vast sums are spent by state and local governments and corporations to implement, report, and monitor mandate compliance, while individuals, driven by a desire to tax avoid,[30] are compelled to waste their valuable time and purchase expensive accounting, legal, computing, and consultant services that could be reduced or eliminated entirely by tax and mandate simplification.

---

[28] Unfunded and unreimbursed regulations or conditions placed on grants imposing costs on state and local governments, and private entities. Mandates are commands akin to Soviet planning directives and product characteristic specifications. They are the antithesis of freely negotiated contracts and therefore anticompetitive and antidemocratic.

[29] Aon Corporation provides more insurance brokerage, reinsurance brokerage, and risk-management services than any other company in the world, and is a leader in human capital management. Its homepage describes the company as "No. 1 global employee benefits consultant." It is the outsourcing beneficiary of a Congressional mandate to assurance compliance with "cafeteria" plan pension and medical-tax-deduction benefits. Taxpayers can obtain extra medical deductions by prepaying medical costs, which are reimbursed to the client when medical expenses are incurred. The very same benefit could be achieved without any administrative cost merely by increasing the tax deductibility of medical expenses on Schedule A of the standard IRS 1040 form. From the politarch's viewpoint this waste is golden. Taxpayers enjoy the illusion of real benefit, while corporate allies earn fortunes for doing unnecessary administration..

[30] Tax evasion, that is, the concealment or falsification of information on income and deductions is criminal, but taking advantage of all that is legally allowed to reduce tax obligations is permissible tax avoidance.

Some mandates, like civil-rights enforcement and tax and administrative requirements, have some, albeit limited, merit, but most of the rest is forced substitution – disguised welfare transfers to lawyers, the finance and insurance industries, and the rich.

Tax-subsidy incentives function in the same way but rely on the carrot instead of the stick. The federal government partly or wholly compensates some taxpayers for making specific purchases rather than compelling them to do so. It induces businesses, including individuals filing 1040 Schedule C forms (business income) to hire labor or specific types of workers (like the handicapped) and purchase investor durables and services that were not justified by the competitive market test. As with mandates, these outlays may have some limited merit, but the government never finely calculates costs and benefits, is vulnerable to massive scamming, and mostly uses the device for politarchic gain. The Government Accountability Office (GAO) estimated that the federal government was improperly billed for $125.4 billion in 2010![31]

The total bill for politocratic waste, fraud, abuse, mandates, and tax-subsidy incentives probably approaches $3 trillion, but a precise figure cannot be calibrated.

Federal Regulation

The income restructuring and redistribution associated with tax subsidies and mandates, huge as they are (at least $1 trillion), pale in comparison with the consequences of business regulation (guidance as distinct from control) broadly construed,[32] which also imposes user costs that in effect are disguised taxes. All federal agencies and commissions regulate their own programs and thereby have the authority to affect contracting and competitiveness beyond the domains of mandates and tax-subsidies, but some regulatory missions span multiple constituencies and sectors. Government-sponsored enterprises (GSEs) also can be included in this category because of their immensely adverse effects on competiveness, transfers, and rents. The main microactivity-focused U.S. federal regulatory agencies are the Consumer Product Safety Commission (CPSC), the Environmental Protection Agency (EPA), the Equal Employment Opportunity Commissions (EEOC), the Federal Aviation Administration (FAA), the Federal Communications Commission (FCC), the Federal

---

[31] "US Government's 2010 Financial Report Shows Significant Financial Management and Fiscal Challenges," GAO, January 2011.

[32] The purpose of regulation is to guide rather than control. A mandate is a control because it prohibits or requires rather than guides. Regulations leave businessmen and consumers with degrees of decision-making freedom; mandates do not.

Trade Commission (FTC), the Food and Drug Administration (FDA), the Interstate Commerce Commission (ICC), the National Labor Relations Board (NLRB), the Nuclear Regulatory Commission (NRC), and the Occupational Safety and the Health Administration (OSHA). Government-sponsored enterprises (GSOs), designed intentionally to generate profits for shareholders, are Fannie Mae, Freddie Mac, and Farmer Mac.[33]

They all serve important social and collective purposes, protecting vulnerable elements in the private (CPSC, EPA, EEOC, FDA, NLRB, and OSHA) and collective good sectors (FAA, FTC, ICC, and NRC). However, these virtues do not obviate principal-agent moral hazards. It is too easy for appointees to use the regulatory powers vested in them by the people for their own private purposes as President Lyndon Baines Johnson did when he obtained lucrative broadcasting licenses in his wife's name.[34] Every regulation restrains the behavior of some and creates anticompetitive rents for others. The purpose of regulatory agencies is to correct private abuses of power, but in a politarchic world, more often than not the powers exercised by agencies result in rent granting (the issuance of contracts and grants that provide recipients with unearned incomes) to insiders and their associates.[35]

---

[33] Farmer Mac is an acronym for the Farm Credit System founded in 1916. Sallie Mae (student loans) and Federal Home Loan Banks were GSEs, but went private in the 1990s. The government also owns and chartered Amtrak, the TVA, the Corporation for Public Broadcasting, the Federal Deposit Insurance Corporation, the Millennium Challenge Corporation, St. Lawrence Seaway Development Corporation, Pension Benefit Guaranty Corporation, Americore, Overseas Private Investment Corporation, and Legal Services Corporation. In 2008 it acquired Citigroup, General Motors, AIG, Bank of America, JPMorgan Chase, Wells Fargo, GMAC Financial Services, Goldman Sachs, Morgan Stanley Capital One Financial, Regions Financial Corporation, American Express, Bank of New York Mellon Corp, State Street Corporation, and Discover Financial corporations. The stocks or assets of these corporations were purchased by the federal government because they were deemed "too big to fail," that is, their liquidation entailed "systemic risk." The Obama administration has declared its desire to eventually liquidate its stake in these companies.

[34] David Frum, *How We Got Here: The '70s*, New York, Basic Books, 2000. Robert Caro, "The Johnson Years: Buying and Selling, *The New Yorker*, December 18, 1989.

[35] *Wall Street Journal*, September 28, 2011: Ever since Congress passed the 2008 Consumer Product Safety Improvement Act in a rush to do something over lead content in toys, the Consumer Product Safety Commission has had to preside over a mess of nonsensical rules that needlessly burden small business. Today, the Commission will make an unpleasant splash of its own, with a vote that could force community and municipal pools to make unnecessary and expensive fixes to their drains. Under the 2008 law, the Commission was required to come up with a standard to make pool drains "unblockable," preventing paddling tots from getting their legs or arms stuck in the suction system. Last year, the commission voted 3–2 in favor of allowing pools to use a plastic mechanism that could be fastened over existing drains to avoid potential accidents. Problem solved. Or so it seemed until Commissioner Bob Adler, who voted in favor of the drain cover 18 months ago,

Savvy political observers know this and recognize that the subprime-loan scandal, which cost trillions of dollars, and the sort of regulations that bankrupted 747 U.S. savings and loan institutions in the late 1980s and early 1990s and cost taxpayers $150 billion, come with the territory (see Chapter 8).[36]

The main macroeconomic-focused U.S. federal regulatory agencies are the Federal Deposit Insurance Corporation (FDIC), the Federal Reserve System (FED), the Office of the Comptroller of the Currency (OCC), the Office of Thrift Supervision (OTS), and the Security and Exchange Commission (SEC). On the surface, they seem innocuous. The FDIC merely collects insurance premiums from member banks as a symbol of the government's commitment to protect ordinary depositors from bank runs and failures, currently up to $250 thousand per account per bank, and manages institutions in receivership. The OCC (established by the National Currency Act of 1863) charters, regulates, and supervises all private national banks and the federal branches and agencies of foreign banks operating in the United States. The OTS is a division of the Department of the Treasury created in 1989 as a successor to the infamous Federal Home Loan Bank Board. It is paid by the banks it regulates and has expanded its oversight to nonbank financial institutions like the American International Group (AIG), Washington Mutual, and IndyMac. The SEC (founded in 1934) is an independent quasi-judicial commission holding primary responsibility for enforcing federal laws and regulating the securities industry, including stock and options exchanges, in the United States. The Federal Reserve is the central banking system of the United States, created in 1913. Its duties

inexplicably changed his mind. Today, the Commission will hold a revote on the issue, which may now require all community pools to revamp their drainage systems, or padlock the gates. With many pools unable to afford the thousands of dollars in new equipment and retrofitting, the latter may be the only choice. Democrats like Henry Waxman and Florida's Debbie Wasserman Schultz have been in favor of requiring new safety mechanisms on drainage systems for a while, and one of the main potential beneficiaries of the change, Vac-Alert Industries President Paul Pennington, said in a CPSC hearing in April that he helped Ms. Wasserman Schultz write the original legislation. In a letter to the CPSC earlier this month, Mr. Pennington urged the CPSC to reconsider its requirements for an "unblockable" drain. Mr. Adler's sudden regulatory about-face is especially strange given that there have been no reported accidents in the interim. Mr. Adler was appointed by President Obama but he will be delivering one more loud public refutation of the President's promise of regulatory relief. While the more expensive remedy isn't expected to offer significant safety improvements over the drain covers, it will saddle plenty of small-town pools with unnecessary hassle and compliance costs. Taxpayers will be left to take the dive.

[36] Financial Audit, Resolution Trust Corporation's 1995 and 1994 Financial Statements, U.S. General Accounting Office, July 1996, pp. 8, 13.

are to conduct the nation's monetary policy, supervise and regulate banking institutions, maintain the stability of the financial system, and provide financial services to depository institutions, the U.S. government, and foreign official institutions. It is unusual among central banks because the United States Department of the Treasury creates the currency instead of the FED doing this itself.

The joint mission of these entities is to maintain a sound financial system in the people's and financial community's interests. The state is supposed to conduct its monetary policies for the general good while assuring that financiers are fairly compensated, but has chosen to delegate much of the task to self-regulating private organizations (SROs) like the Financial Industry Regulatory Authority (FINRA) tasked to oversee, regulate, and enforce the activities of member brokerage firms and exchange markets. The conflict of interest is obvious. Moral hazard inclines political appointees to indulgently regulate in return for diverse backdoor compensation, under the guise of protecting the public. Politarchs collude with the financial community in pursuing leveraged speculative gains that place the public at risk, hedged by the knowledge that when things go bad government partners will be bailed out on the pretext that the failure of major financial firms poses unacceptable systemic risks. It is not just a coincidence that the Office of Thrift Supervision, which under an earlier name gave the United States the savings and loan debacle, was complicit in the colossal financial bankruptcies of AIG, Washington Mutual, and IndyMac. It is the direct consequence of a regulatory strategy designed to enrich politicians and their big-business partners.

Politarchic regulation is win-win for insiders, and lose-lose for the people.[37] Regulators and the regulated enjoy expanded opportunities for ill-gotten gain, and lawyers reap bonanzas protecting participants from occasional prosecution. When misdeeds cannot be concealed, or politarchs need scapegoats, all regulatory punishments are subject to legal challenge. Malfeasance and recklessness are not riskless, but the benefit-cost ratio is skewed heavily against the public interest. The people pay twice

---

[37] Marcy Gordon, "Watchdog: Regulators Bowed to Banks on Bailouts," Associated Press, September 30, 2011:

Federal regulators bowed to pressure from big banks seeking a quick exit from the financial bailout program and did not uniformly apply the government's own conditions set for repaying the taxpayer funds, a new watchdog report says. The report was issued Friday by the office of Christy Romero, the acting special inspector general for the $400 billion taxpayer bailout of the financial industry and automakers. It found that regulators, to varying degrees, "bent" to pressure from the banks in late 2009 and relaxed the requirements put in only weeks earlier.

for politarchic regulation, first bearing the cost of regulatory services, and second shouldering the anticompetitive burden. No wonder Wall Street trumps the SEC's, OTC's, OCC's, FDIC's, and FED's declared purpose of fostering macroeconomic stability. Politarchs doubtlessly want to have their cake and eat it too (financial stability and payoffs), and when push comes to shove, their true priorities are transparent.

Macroeconomic Policy

The United States' core macroeconomic policymaking agencies charged with assuring bank solvency, [38] restraining financial leverage, and providing just enough money to achieve wage, price, and business activity equilibrium primarily serve the interests of politicians, the financial sector, asset speculators, and big social advocacy. They set the overnight money-borrowing rate and other fed fund rates low enough so that member banks can always turn a profit doing nothing more than lending deposits to the government. This effectively transfers income from the public which receives a pittance on its deposits to financial institutions, encouraging imprudence. Permitting banks to gouge retailers for debit-card clearing has the same effect.[39] Fed and treasury interest and monetary policies likewise create inflationary windfall-gain opportunities in commodities, stocks, and business by creating bank reserves (under the euphemism "quantitative easing"), excess stimulus compounded by congressional deficit spending, which some openly laud as a way in which the rich can lighten their burden of assisting the poor.[40]

The perpetual excess aggregate effective demand generated in these and other ways is defended in the professional literature by appeals to concepts like sticky wages, liquidity traps, Phillip's curves, full employment, systemic risk, too big to fail, and accelerated GDP growth, all of which may occasionally have some merit, but for the most part are just arcane excuses for pursuing politocratic policies. The SEC's, OTC's, OCC's, FDIC's, FED's and Congress's declaratory macroeconomic stabilization missions might be achievable in a true democracy, but not in a politocracy that has transformed public service into a private business for elite enrichment.

The United States' economic malfunctioning thus is not the consequence of unfettered free enterprise. It is not attributable to scientific incompetence,

[38] A policy is a set of principles guiding both regulation and control.
[39] Simon Johnson, "Big Banks Have a Powerful New Opponent," Yahoo! Finance, April 7, 2011.
[40] Mark Faber, interview, CNBC, April 8, 2011.

inadvertent regulatory flaws, partisan strife, or a rudimentary system of political spoils. It is the intentional result of politarchic priorities, comprehensively implemented through the instruments of politocratic governance with a fixed cast of winners and losers, skewed toward politicians, big business and big social advocacy, with ordinary people serving as the sheep most likely to be fleeced. It is fundamentally anti-*demos*cratic, or as Bernard Madoff recently put it, "the government is a Ponzi scheme"[41] that claims to provide members with prodigious investment gains while actually transferring money from one pocket to another until the pyramid collapses. It takes a crook to know a crook, and Madoff is not wrong. Apparently, he grasps how paltry his own Ponzi operation was compared with Washington's sophisticated antics (e.g., infinitely deferred sovereign debt repayment).

Ponzi federal governance, like Madoff's scam, is not rocket science. It only requires maintaining public trust in Washington's good intentions, without any effort at optimizing net benefits. Easy pickings are sufficient (satisficing). Wall Street and other lobbies (including foreign governments) pay both Democrats and Republicans lavishly for their ears, regulatory access, and the opportunity to participate in writing programs and statute. Politicians merely press their staffs to give the appearance of contesting rival staffs in crafting legislative content. They also exert pressure for clever new forms of stealthy taxation, appoint federal reserve chairpersons, treasury secretaries, SEC commissioners, and other key regulators from the Wall Street-Washington power nexus,[42] pump more than half a trillion dollars of grants-in-aid to states, localities, and individuals, and mandate

---

[41] "Madoff to NY Magazine: Government a Ponzi Scheme," Yahoo! Finance, February 27, 2011: "The new regulatory reform enacted after the recent national financial crisis is laughable and the federal government is a Ponzi scheme." Linda Sandler, "Madoff Cost Surpass Victims' Pay-Offs As Strategy Lies in Ruins," Yahoo! Finance, May 1, 2012: "Irving Picard, the liquidator of Madoff's Ponzi scheme thus far, has disbursed $330 million to victims while billing the estate $554 million. It appears that at the end of the day, victims will receive very little."

[42] See Simon Johnson, "Is the New York Fed Making a Big Mistake?," Yahoo! Finance, March 3, 2011. Johnson reports that despite the 2008 financial crisis, the New York Federal Reserve is

incredibly working hard to enable big banks actually to reduce their capital ratios (in the first instance by allowing them to pay increased dividends).... Without any substance on its side, the New York Fed is increasingly creating the perception that it is just doing what its key shareholder – the Wall Street Banks – want.... The Dodd-Frank legislation reduced the power of big banks slightly... so that the president of the New York Fed is no longer picked by Wall Street's board representatives (as was Timothy Geithner, who was president of the New York Fed until being named Treasury secretary, and William Dudley, the current president and former Goldman Sachs executive).... The top leadership of the New York Fed has a responsibility to engage constructively and openly in the technical

and continuously increase the national debt, deferring the day of reckoning so that the United States' children can bear the full brunt of politicians' avarice. Ponzi federal governance is probably more the result of adverse learning than a premeditated master plot. Nonetheless, it is user hostile, and potently toxic for workers, the vulnerable middle class, and passive wealthy that pay the bills first, and is left holding the bag later.

debate. Yet some Federal Reserve officials act as if they have a constitutional right to run an independent central bank. This is not the case: Congress created the Fed, and Congress can amend how the Fed operates.

Johnson lucidly describes politocracy at work, but misses the connection that Congress will approve anything the Fed wants, if Wall Street pays the politarchs to do it.

SEVEN

Treadmill of Reform

Politocracy is sapping U.S. economic vitality with exorbitant and wasteful government spending and stultifying bureaucratic and regulatory compliance obligations. It is overtaxing workers and the middle class, widening income and wealth inequalities, adulterating public services including health, education, transport, and security, and spawning social discord. Macro-stimulation policies and lax regulation aimed at giving a hand up to politicians, big business, and big social advocacy are warping the system further, diminishing competitiveness,[1] and making the United States increasingly crisis-prone.

---

[1] For most of the twentieth century U.S. business operated without much regard to the federal government. Top executives were selected for business acumen and focused on the marketplace. But as the federal government expanded its scope (a process led by politicians and endorsed by the courts), business had to direct more attention to Washington (the same is true of state and local government officials). As the federal government became the source of ever more regulation, taxation, subsidies, and so forth, business executives had to spend more time and money dealing with Washington. Slowly, with the growth of federal government intrusion, responsibility in business for government relations moved up the hierarchy from association executive (like those of the National Association of Manufacturers), to public relations people, to government-affairs people assisted by lobbyists, to the CEO assisted by legal counsel and lobbyists. As government became ever more important (both in what it was doing and as importantly, in what it threatened to do) boards of directors began to elect candidates for top executive positions based on their sophistication about politics and government. The performance-driven CEO focused on the marketplace was replaced by the smooth political operative who spends more than half his or her time on government relations. Business operations were delegated to chief operating officers. The political operative CEO supported others of his or her type to succeed him. More and more attorneys made their way into corner offices because they thought like and interrelated well with the lawyers who came to dominate politics almost to the exclusion of politicians of other backgrounds. By this process of evolution the leadership of American business has both joined the politarchy and lost much of its competitive edge. In the process of this evolution the politarchy has expanded and entrenched itself so that

Fragments of these essentials are well understood, but the public continues hoping against hope that the curative powers of the true democratic icon will somehow set things right. Big government and politocracy however are not self-healing and cannot make good on their promises partly because they do not want to change and have the power to resist, but also because they cannot fulfill their promises even if they try (see Chapter 4). Politocracy offers only a treadmill of futile reform.[2]

IMPOSSIBILITY OF WELFARE IMPROVING POLITOCRATIC REFORM

Big government and politocracy are inherently inefficient:

1. Kenneth Arrow mathematically proved sixty years ago that voting cannot convey people's preferences to agents with the precision of markets.[3] *Ceteris paribus*, as the U.S. Constitution suggests, individuals should pursue their own well-being without deferring to inadequately informed federal officials.

2. Buchanan and Tullock have shown by extension that supplementary sources of information don't resolve "Arrow's Paradox."[4] Furthermore, agents and bureaucrats are usually unqualified, even if they somehow were accurately informed. These insights led Buchanan and Tullock to claim that government programs should be undertaken only when approved by unanimous workable public consent. The Soviet Union's collapse underscores the danger of relying too heavily on bureaucrats to determine production and ration supplies. Citizens in the USSR were prohibited from countermanding planners' preferences, assuring that buyers' demands were seldom satisfied. Forced substitution ruled, and the people suffered.

3. Social-welfare losses caused by forced substitution are a direct function of scale. The more government usurps economic rights that

it is now almost impregnable. It fully dominates the political scene and largely dominates that of business.

[2] Gertrude Schroeder, "The Soviet Economy on a Treadmill of Reforms," in *Soviet Economy in a Time of Change*, Washington, D.C.: Joint Economic Committee of Congress, 1979, pp. 312–66.

[3] Kenneth Arrow, *Social Choice and Individual Values*, New York: Wiley, 2nd ed., 1963.

[4] James Buchanan and Robert Tollison, *The Limits of Liberty Between Anarchy and Leviathan*, Chicago: University of Chicago Press, 1975. James Buchanan, *Democracy in Deficit: The Political Legacy of Lord Keynes*, Indianapolis, IN: Liberty Fund, 1999.

should be reserved to the people (and so are reserved in the U.S. Constitution), the worse off they are. Bigness matters. This should be obvious, but is widely overlooked. Again the Soviet experience confirms the deduction.

4. These problems cannot be eliminated by substituting incentives for directives because administrators do not have enough information, or the capability of making best choices, even if optimal incentives schemes could be devised.

5. Adding market elements to the mix cannot redress the deficiencies of command- and incentive-guided bureaucratic choice making unless markets are competitive enough to eradicate government-created distortion. They never are because the concept of substituting state for individual choice requires market subordination.

6. Tax-transfer schemes that redistribute money instead of providing programs and goods fall afoul of the same problem. Grants-in-aid from the federal to state governments merely shift programming responsibility from one set of incompetent hands to another, while wastefully adding layers of bureaucracy. Likewise, administrators cannot precisely determine needs. They transfer funds helter-skelter using broad, often misleading rules of thumb.

7. Government macro-policymakers do not have the knowledge, skills, or power to keep excess aggregate demand regimes on track and out of politocratic clutches.

8. All these deficiencies apply even if federal officials are not politocrats and strive to act as honest agents of the people. Politocracy makes matters much worse and cannot be reformed.[5]

These eight principles illuminate the wisdom of the founding fathers in assigning a limited role to government in economic affairs.[6] The state should provide some essential public services, discipline would-be Ponzi-scheme speculators, and moderate business cycles but should not assume

---

[5]   Steven Rosefielde, "The Impossibility of Russian Economic Reform: Waiting for Godot," in Stephen Blank, ed., *Russian Reform*, Carlisle Barracks: US Army War College, 2012. Stefan Hedlund, *Invisible Hands, Russian Experience, and Social Science: Approaches to Understanding Systemic Failure*, Cambridge University Press: Cambridge, 2011. See this work for a discussion of the distinction between good and bad greed.

[6]   All of these disorders were grasped in their essentials by Enlightenment democrats like John Locke and America's founding fathers, and the safeguards they recommended remain valid. Solutions for the West and the rest therefore can be readily found by returning to basics (including an appreciation of minority property rights) and purging what purports to be superior modern democracy of its antidemocratic accretions.

the role of master economic puppeteer. The politarchic state should be constrained by the same rules but placed on a shorter leash. There always is room for debate on the optimal scale of true democratic federal government. However, in the politarchic case, erring on the side of smaller government is the wisest course. If government is too big, then it must be rolled back.

PART II

HOW POLITOCRACY DRIVES U.S. POLICY

EIGHT

Subprime Mortgage Crisis

Politocracy's *modus operandi* in formulating and executing American domestic policy can be illustrated with a single, complex, but nonetheless compelling, example connected with the 2008 global financial crisis: subprime mortgage loans. This case study shows how politicians in the Clinton, Bush, and Obama administrations used the government-sponsored Enterprises (GSE) Fannie Mae to provide subsidized loans to anyone claiming to be disadvantaged as a vehicle for enriching themselves, big business, and big social advocacy, and in the process not only contributed to the 2006–2007 real-estate crisis and the 2008 global financial crisis but continued the operation thereafter with bailouts and new schemes at the people's expense instead of responsibly protecting the true democratic interest.

THE SUBPRIME MORTGAGE POLITARCH ENRICHMENT SCHEME

The adjective subprime refers to mortgages issued to borrowers with poor credit credentials who normally wouldn't qualify for loans at the competitive rate because their income prospects are poor or uncertain or their credit histories unsatisfactory.[1] Many prospective borrowers in this category are minorities, immigrants, young, indigent, low income, unemployed, imposters, speculators, or deadbeats. Most either live with relatives or friends or in traditional public housing but desire to improve their living standard by owning their own homes or to make quick profits from flipping properties in an appreciating real-estate market.

---

[1] It might seem then that subprime loans would have always been widely available, but this ignores federal requirements that prohibit discriminatory lending under the fair housing act enforced by the Department of Housing and Urban Development (HUD), and may therefore require lenders to prove that their subprime loan premiums are fair.

These individuals aren't directly excluded from homeownership because of their age, gender, sexual orientation, race, ethnicity, religion, nationality, or immigration status.[2] They cannot buy homes under normal competitive, nondiscriminatory conditions because statistically they cannot be expected to fully repay their obligations independently or with the assistance of co-signers (family, friends, and benefactors).[3] This means that if non-creditworthy borrowers receive mortgage loans at subsidized rates and terms as they did,[4] the funds must come as transfers from taxpayers (workers, the middle-class, and passive rich) through federal intermediation.

It is unlikely that the people would support subprime mortgage loan subsidies (in lieu of traditional public housing) in a true democracy based on a full cost-benefit analysis. Nonetheless subprime mortgages for those claiming to be disadvantaged have many advocates in the politarchic United States. The non-creditworthy and those posing as non-creditworthy (and therefore needy) seeking subsidies want the people to supplement their income. Some humanitarians favor reducing income inequality, guaranteeing a good life (minimum middle-class living standards) for everyone or giving a head start to minorities with low average creditworthiness records that have been left behind.[5] Professional social advocates relish the chance

---

[2] Some social advocates contest this tenuously equating denial of subsidized loans to the disadvantaged as racial redlining.

[3] The probability of default is at least six times higher for nonprime loans than prime loans. See Souphala Chomsisengphet and Anthony Pennington-Cross, "The Evolution of the Subprime Mortgage Market," *Federal Reserve Bank of St. Louis Review*, Vol. 88, No. 1, January/February 2006, pp. 31–56. Anthony Pennington-Cross, "Credit History and the Performance of Prime and Nonprime Mortgages," *Journal of Real Estate Finance and Economics*, Vol.27, No. 3, November 2003, pp. 270–301.

[4] The literature on this subject is contradictory. Authors go out of their way to assert that subprime borrowers in principle pay above prime interest rates and must comply with stringent down payment and other repayment requirements, before going on to complain that prime borrowers tapped the subprime market to obtain cheaper loans on better terms. These ostensibly contradictory claims are easily reconciled by distinguishing loans made under the HUD/Fannie Mae informal quota system to those applying as disadvantaged that were subsidized de facto, from those made by commercial banks catering to high-risk borrowers. It became common practice at the start of the new millennium to permit subprime and prime borrowers to obtain loans without any down payment, making home purchase risk-free to them because if obligations couldn't be fulfilled, borrowers could simply walk away from homes, leaving mortgage owners holding the bag. See Stan Liebowitz, "New Evidence on the Foreclosure Crisis: Zero Money Down, Not Subprime Loans, Led to the Mortgage Meltdown," *Wall Street Journal*, July 3, 2009: "Although only 12% of homes had negative equity, they comprised 47% of all foreclosures."

[5] See Austin Goolsby, "'Irresponsible' Mortgages Have Opened Doors to Many of the Excluded," *New York Times*, March 29, 2007: As Professor Rosen (Harvey Rosen, Council of Economic Advisors, 2003–2005) explains, "The main thing that innovations in the

to expand federal institutions that further their causes and pay them dividends. Residential real-estate developers welcome disguised federal subsidies for new homes. Real-estate agents encourage politicians to subsidize the commissions that they make selling old units. Mortgage lenders are willing to offer loans to non-creditworthy borrowers in return for roundabout federal compensation, including regulatory authorization to sell these mortgages to third-party investors. Wall Street is delighted to make immense underwriting profits from packaging an ever-expanding supply of high-risk subprime mortgages, sprinkled with a few sound ones, and is glad to have the government stoke a real-estate bubble that allows the financially nimble to make windfall gains. Federal housing bureaucrats enjoy expanding their supervisory, administrative, and regulatory empires,[6] and politicians receive laundered compensation in multiple forms for providing subsidies,[7] supplemented with the electoral benefits of claiming to have devised cost-free assistance to the disadvantaged.

All parties, including non-creditworthy borrowers at some point, come to realize that someone, someday will have to pay the piper, but they are more than willing to get what they can while they can and worry about acquiring bailout assistance later. Subprime mortgages offer an opportunity for all participants to feather their nests by setting aside differences, a chance that was not overlooked.

mortgage market have done over the past 30 years is to let in the excluded: the young, the discriminated against, the people without a lot of money in the bank to use for a down payment." It has allowed them access to mortgages whereas lenders would have once just turned them away. The Center for Responsible Lending estimated that in 2005, a majority of home loans to African Americans and 40 percent of home loans to Hispanics were subprime loans. The existence and spread of subprime lending helps explain the drastic growth of homeownership for these same groups. Since 1995, for example, the number of African-American households has risen by about 20 percent, but the number of African-American homeowners has risen almost twice that rate, by about 35 percent. For Hispanics, the number of households is up about 45 percent, and the number of home-owning households is up by almost 70 percent.

[6] See Margaret Chadbourn, "Fannie, Freddie Faulted for Spending on Conference," Reuters, March 22, 2012: "Almost half of the $600,000 that the two companies spent for a conference held by the Mortgage Bankers Association in October 'was of questionable value,' the inspector general for the companies' federal regulator said."

[7] See Conor Friedersdorf, "Did Newt Gingrich Play a Part in Freddie Mac's Fundraising Scandal?," *The Atlantic Monthly*, November 17, 2011: "Freddie Mac was accused of illegally using corporate resources between 2000 and 2003 for 85 fundraisers that collected about $1.7 million for federal candidates. Much of the fundraising benefited members of the House Financial Services Committee, a panel whose decisions can affect Freddie Mac." Gingrich is on record advocating abolishing HUD. Politarchs do not mind playing all sides. Cf. Jeff Jacoby, "(Barney) Frank's Fingerprints Are all Over the Financial Fiasco," *Boston Globe*, September 28, 2008.

The non-creditworthy, big social advocacy, big business, federal bureaucrats, and politicians forged an unwritten strategic partnership in the 1990s using subprime mortgages as a vehicle for increasing their slice of the federal pie.[8] They hatched what was purported to be a noble scheme to provide individual homeownership for millions of non-creditworthy people, with a hidden agenda aimed at (1) expanding big social advocacy's income and influence, (2) increasing the size of the federal housing bureaucracy's domains, (3) generating windfall gains to non-creditworthy borrowers (as well as imposters) and all homeowners by fueling real-estate appreciation, (4) providing subsidies to real-estate developers and brokers, (5) diminishing mortgage lenders' risk and increasing their profits through subprime loan mortgage securitization, (6) enriching Wall Street underwriters of mortgage-backed securities (MBS) and collateralized debt obligations (CDOs), (7) providing windfall profits to other financial and real-estate speculators (including some of the non-creditworthy recipients of subprime loans), and (8) lining the pockets of politicians selling these favors. Moreover, real-estate developers, mortgage lenders, Wall Street underwriters, financial and real-estate speculators, and politicians all attempted to leverage the direct gains by capitalizing on the goodwill associated with assisting the disadvantaged.[9]

The scheme was shrewdly designed to conceal costs by funding them with insurance guarantees and indirect inflation taxes and by shifting the remaining burden to those ultimately stuck with massive financial losses, including future generations obligated to pay for the ever-mounting federal debt and forego retirement.[10] It also ignored catastrophic national risk, placing insider gain above the people's will and welfare. The results were predictable and were predicted,[11] but few participants were chastened

---

[8] Unwritten strategic partnerships are commonplace among oligopolists seeking to evade the Sherman Antitrust Act.

[9] Goodwill in business and economics is defined as market asset value created when buyers and communities look favorably on sellers' commercial activities.

[10] See Anne Kadet, "Working 9 to 5 – at 75: How the Fastest Growing Group in the American Workforce is Changing What it Means to be 'Retired,'" *Wall Street Journal*, March 21, 2012: "The number of working people over age 65 reached an all-time low in 2001, when just 13 percent held a job. Now that rate is rebounding, and fast; last summer, it hit 18 percent, a level not seen since Kennedy faced the Cuban Missile Crisis."

[11] Robert Shiller, *Irrational Exuberance*, Princeton, NJ: Princeton University Press, 2005. James R. Barth, Tong Li, Triphon Phumiwasana, and Glenn Yago, *A Short History of the Subprime Mortgage Market Meltdown*, Santa Monica CA: Milken Institute, January 2008. Souphala Chomsisengphet and Anthony Pennington-Cross, "The Evolution of the Subprime Mortgage Market," *Federal Reserve Bank of St. Louis Review*, Vol. 88, No. 1, January/February 2006, pp. 31–56.

because they bet correctly on winning themselves, and leaving the debt baby to others.[12]

IMPLEMENTATION

There have always been subprime mortgages in the strict sense that some borrowers paid above prime interest rates for their loans. There is nothing disreputable in the practice, and a private market gradually developed during the postwar years. The potential for political mischief arose only after the establishment of the Federal National Mortgage Association (FNMA) in 1938, which created a secondary market for mortgages, and didn't become significant until the 1990s under the administration at FNMA (Fannie Mae) of Franklin Raines, a Clinton administration appointee.[13] He inaugurated a pilot program in 1999 to issue subprime loans to moderate-income, minority, and low-income borrowers,[14] and to ease credit requirements on mortgages Fannie Mae purchased from commercial banks.

Fannie Mae began requiring commercial lending institutions to prove that they were not redlining (refusing loans to creditworthy minority applicants in desirable neighborhoods), which as a practical matter forced them to accept many non-creditworthy minority mortgage applicants on a quota basis (the majority of blacks and 40 percent of Hispanics). The initiative did not favor all the non-creditworthy, just those linked to alleged redlining. Private banks were reluctant to issue these high-risk loans, but were mollified in part by Fannie Mae's willingness to hedge their risk by purchasing their

---

[12] Robert Shiller and George Akerlof, *Animal Spirits: How Human Psychology Drives the Economy and Why It Matters for Global Capitalism*, Princeton, NJ: Princeton University Press, 2009.

[13] Raines was Fannie Mae's vice chairman from 1991 until 1996. He returned to Fannie Mae in 1999 as CEO. The Office of Federal Housing Enterprise Oversight (OFHEO), the regulating body of Fannie Mae, accused Raines of abetting widespread accounting errors, which included the shifting of losses so senior executives including Raines could earn large bonuses. The OFHEO sued in 2006 to recover $90 million paid Raines attributable to overstated earnings. A settlement was reached in 2008 fining Raines several millions of dollars, which allowed him to retain most of the alleged ill-gotten gains. *The Wall Street Journal* reported that he was the beneficiary of below-market real-estate loans from Countrywide Financial, a firm financing 20 percent of the mortgage market in 2006, taken over by the Bank of America in 2008, shortly before the global financial crisis erupted in September 2008. See "Charles Whitaker, Franklin Raines: First Black Head of a Fortune 500 Corporation – Fannie Mae," *Ebony*, April 2001; "Senior Fannie Mae Boss Resigns," BBC News, December 22, 2004; "Scandal to Cost Ex-Fannie Mae Officials Millions," *New York Times*, September 23, 2008.

[14] Steven Holmes, "Fannie Mae Eases Credit to Aid Mortgage Lending," *New York Times*, September 30, 1999.

subprime paper. This put politicians squarely in the business of giving the title to assets that many non-creditworthy borrowers ultimately would be unable to afford, with the implicit promise of covering bad-loans losses variously with future tax revenues, increased national indebtedness, and inflations taxes. Big commercial banking quickly grasped the unwritten rules flooding the market with subprime loans including adjustable-rate "balloon" mortgages, often with no down payment even though they knew that these mortgages could not be repaid in hard times.[15] Subprime balloon mortgages were touted as socially responsible but primarily served as a device to swell residential housing demand and generate windfall gains to politicians, their big social advocacy and big business allies with an implicit promise to partly or wholly cover windfall losses should they occur at the public's expense. Fannie Mae's promotion of subprime mortgages achieved this purpose initially by stoking the housing bubble, and then later with emergency deficit spending and diverse bailouts that were an integral part of the tax-transfer process from the public to politocracy. The process was not driven by good intentions gone wrong as supporters contend, but by bad intentions gone more or less as planned, obscured by finger pointing.[16]

The impact of Fannie Mae's drive to promote subprime loans, at least initially as a remedy for redlining is etched into the record. The subprime share of total originations was less than 5 percent in 1994. It jumped to 13 percent in 2000 and then catapulted to 20 percent in 2005 and 2006, just before the U.S. real-estate market collapsed. A total of 653,000 subprime loans originated in 2000, and this figure soared to 4.13 million in 2004 before it crashed to 472,000 in 2007.[17] Balloon loan originations skyrocketed from 50,000 at the start of the new millennium to 800,000 in 2006.[18] The share of subprime originations packaged as mortgage-backed securities (MBS) more than doubled from 31.6 percent to 80.5 percent during the same period.[19] These trends were not entirely Fannie Mae's doing, but an appreciation of the fact that it and Freddie Mac stood ready to purchase all originators' bad mortgage loans was decisive.

[15] Stan Liebowitz, "New Evidence on the Foreclosure Crisis: Zero Money Down, Not Subprime Loans, Led to the Mortgage Meltdown," *Wall Street Journal*, July 3, 2009.

[16] The distinction here is analogous to the difference between manslaughter and murder in criminal law.

[17] Souphala Chomsisengphet and Anthony Pennington-Cross, "A Look at Subprime Mortgage Originations: 2000–2007," http://www.ftc.gov/be/workshops/mortgage/presentations/Cross_Chomsisengphet_Subprime_2008.pdf

[18] *Ibid.*

[19] James R. Barth, Tong Li, Triphon Phumiwasana, and Glenn Yago, *A Short History of the Subprime Mortgage Market Meltdown*, Santa Monica CA: Milken Institute, January 2008.

The key point to grasp here is not the unsustainable claim that subprime loans alone caused the residential housing crisis of 2006–2007, but the demonstration that the federal government via Fannie Mae could and did collude with big social advocacy and big business to provide subsidies and rig the real-estate market for their collective advantage without finely calibrating insider benefits or the public's liabilities.[20]

THE 2006–2007 RESIDENTIAL HOUSING CRISIS AND BEYOND

There is no reason to doubt that Fannie Mae would have continued pressing subprime loans if the real-estate boom had persisted, but the speculative fillip provided by its subprime campaign lost its potency in 2006 when experts, investors, and other real-estate participants became wary, fearing that the price appreciation, capital gains, and ordinary profit growth trends 2000–2006 couldn't be sustained. Home prices, which had risen nearly 9 percent per annum during these years (compared to 3 percent in the preceding decade) began dropping moderately,[21] raising the specter of capital losses on new real-estate purchases. Interest rates began to rise, setting off alarm bells that homeowners could not pay the higher costs stipulated in their adjustable-rate balloon mortgages,[22] and the parlous state of over-indebted consumers made it plain that new market entrants were not going to pick up the slack. These factors depressed sales and profits, and price appreciation expectations soured. Suddenly, speculative demand for real-estate properties plummeted, homebuilding stocks collapsed, and the real-estate market was flooded with subprime and prime property foreclosures. The number

---

[20] Some observers argue that the role of subprime mortgages in the real-estate and financial crises is exaggerated because subprime loans at the end of the day did not perform materially worse than prime loans. This may not be true because most federal mortgage relief assistance went to subprime loans creating the false impression of creditworthiness. Nonetheless, and be this as it may, the MBS shadow bank run that triggered the global financial crisis was based on the expectation that subprime mortgages at the end of the day would prove to be junk.

[21] James R. Barth, Tong Li, Triphon Phumiwasana, and Glenn Yago, *A Short History of the Subprime Mortgage Market Meltdown*, Santa Monica CA: Milken Institute, January 2008.

[22] Subprime borrowers' diminished ability to pay their monthly mortgage bills was exacerbated by the practice encouraged by Fannie Mae and other lenders of taking out second mortgages based on the appreciation of their homes and using the money for current consumption. When the housing market crashed, subprime mortgagees (and prime mortgagees) not only had to make first mortgage payments but second mortgage payments as well.

of foreclosures jumped 42 percent in 2006 and 75 percent the following year to 2.2 million.[23]

The value of U.S. subprime loans in 2007 was $1.3 trillion, with more than 7.5 million first-lien subprime mortgages outstanding.[24] Total home equity in the United States, which was valued at $13 trillion at its peak in 2006, dropped to $8.8 trillion by mid-2008. Total retirement assets, Americans' second-largest household asset, dropped by 22 percent, from $10.3 trillion in 2006 to $8 trillion in mid-2008. During the same period, savings and investment assets (apart from retirement savings) lost $1.2 trillion, and pension assets lost $1.3 trillion. Taken together, these losses total $8.3 trillion.[25]

This however merely proved to be the tip of the iceberg because the real-estate sector was indirectly hard hit by the delayed toxic effects of subprime mortgages in the global credit market during the 2008 financial crisis. As previously mentioned, mortgage lenders and Wall Street financial firms reaped enormous profits from Fannie Mae's decision to serve as a deep-pocketed buyer in the secondary mortgage market. Savings and loans and other commercial mortgage originators used the Fannie Mae option to reduce their subprime risk exposure while Wall Street turned the underwriting and trading of subprime mortgage-backed securities into what seemed to be a one-way street bonanza that did not survive the 2006–2007 real-estate crisis. Demand for subprime mortgage-backed securities (MBS and related CDO) began to weaken in 2007 and quickly evaporated in 2008 as investors began scrutinizing the risks of subprime mortgage default that might culminate in a run on shadow banks (nonbank financial institutions operating as credit-creating quasi banks),[26] and a severe depression.

---

[23] Realty Trac Staff, "More than 1.2 Million Foreclosure Filings Report in 2006," Realty Trac, February 8, 2007. Realty Trac Staff, "U.S. Foreclosure Activity increase 75 Percent in 2007," Realty Trac, January 29, 2008.

[24] "How Severe is the Subprime Mess?," Associated Press, March 13, 2007. Ben Bernanke, "The Subprime Mortgage Market," Speech, Chicago, Illinois, May 17, 2007.

[25] Roger Altman, "The Great Crash, 2008," *Foreign Affairs*, Vol.88, No. 1, January/February 2009, pp. 2–14. http://www.foreignaffairs.org/20090101faessay88101/roger-c-altman/the-great-crash-2008.html

[26] The term includes hedge funds. In a June 2008 speech, President of the New York Federal Reserve Bank Timothy Geithner, who later became secretary of the treasury, placed significant blame for the freezing of credit markets on a "run" on the entities in the "parallel" banking system, also called the shadow banking system. These entities became critical to the credit markets underpinning the financial system, but were not subject to the same regulatory controls as depository banks. Paul Krugman described the run on the shadow banking system as the "core of what happened" to cause the crisis. Paul Krugman, *The Return of Depression Economics and the Crisis of 2008*, New York: W.W. Norton Company, 2009.

Subprime mortgages were not the only cause of the global financial crisis, but they played a major role.

Their defaults contributed to the start of the global financial crisis when HSBC wrote down its holding of MBS by $10.5 billion on February 27, 2007[27] and continued to play a key role thereafter.[28] The timeline below covering both the Bush and Obama administrations highlights the essentials, underscoring Fannie Mae's and Freddie Mac's centrality, and illuminating aspects of trans-partisan politocracy's machinations:[29]

August 6, 2007: American Home Mortgage Investment Corporation (AHMI) files Chapter 11 bankruptcy.

August 16: Countrywide Financial Corporation, the biggest U.S. mortgage lender, narrowly avoids bankruptcy by taking out an emergency loan of $11 billion from a group of banks.

October 15–17: A consortium of U.S. banks backed by the U.S. government announces a "super fund" of $100 billion to purchase mortgage-backed securities whose mark-to-market value plummeted in the subprime collapse. Both Federal Reserve Chairman Ben Bernanke and Treasury Secretary Hank Paulson express alarm about the dangers posed by the bursting housing bubble; Paulson says "the housing decline is still unfolding and I view it as the most significant risk to our economy.... The longer housing prices remain stagnant or fall, the greater the penalty to our future economic growth."

December 6: President Bush announces a plan to voluntarily and temporarily freeze the mortgages of a limited number of mortgage debtors holding adjustable rate mortgages (more than 1.2 million foreclosure filings reported in ARM). He also asks members of Congress to: 1) pass legislation to modernize the FHA, 2) temporarily reform the tax code to help homeowners refinance during this time of housing market stress, 3) pass funding to support mortgage counseling, and 4) pass legislation to reform government-sponsored enterprises (GSEs) like Freddie Mac and Fannie Mae.

January 24, 2008: The National Association of Realtors (NAR) announces that 2007 had the largest drop in existing home sales in 25 years, and "the first price decline in many, many years and possibly going back to the Great Depression."

June 18: Connecticut's Christopher Dodd proposes a housing bailout to the Senate floor that would assist troubled subprime mortgage lenders such as Countrywide Bank. Dodd admitted that he received special treatment, perks, and campaign donations from Countrywide, who regarded Dodd as a "special" customer and a "friend of Angelo." Dodd received a $75,000 reduction in mortgage payments from Countrywide. Chairman of the Senate Finance

---

27 "Timeline: Subprime Loses," BBC News, 2008.
28 HSBC was the world's largest bank in 2008.
29 "Subprime Timeline Impact," Wiki.

Committee Kent Conrad and head of Fannie Mae Jim Johnson also received mortgages on favorable terms due to their association with Countrywide CEO Angelo R. Mozilo.

July 11 Indymac Bank, a subsidiary of Independent National Mortgage Corporation (Indymac), is placed into the receivership of the Federal Deposit Insurance Corporation by the Office of Thrift Supervision. It was the fourth-largest bank failure in U.S. history and the second-largest failure of a regulated thrift. Before its failure, IndyMac Bank was the largest savings and loan association in the Los Angeles area and the seventh-largest mortgage originator in the United States.

July 30: President Bush signs into law the Housing and Economic Recovery Act of 2008, which authorizes the Federal Housing Administration to guarantee up to $300 billion in new 30-year fixed-rate mortgages for subprime borrowers if lenders write down principal loan balances to 90 percent of current appraisal value.

September 7: Federal takeover of Fannie Mae and Freddie Mac, which at that point owned or guaranteed about half of the United States' $12 trillion mortgage market, effectively nationalizing them. This causes panic because almost every home-mortgage lender and Wall Street bank relied on them to facilitate the mortgage market, and investors worldwide owned $5.2 trillion of debt securities backed by them.

September 17: The U.S. Federal Reserve lends $85 billion to American International Group (AIG) to avoid bankruptcy.

September 23: The Federal Bureau of Investigation discloses that it had been investigating the possibility of fraud by mortgage financing companies Fannie Mae and Freddie Mac, Lehman Brothers, and insurer American International Group, bringing the number of corporate lenders under investigation to 26.

September 25: Washington Mutual is seized by the Federal Deposit Insurance Corporation, and its banking assets are sold to JP MorganChase for $1.9 billion.

September 29: The Emergency Economic Stabilization Act is defeated 228–205 in the United States House of Representatives; Federal Deposit Insurance Corporation announces that Citigroup Inc. would acquire banking operations of Wachovia.

September 30: The U.S. Treasury changes the tax law to allow a bank acquiring another to write off all of the acquired bank's losses for tax purposes.

October 3: President George W. Bush signs the Emergency Economic Stabilization Act, creating a $700 billion Troubled Assets Relief Program to purchase failing bank assets. It contains easing of the accounting rules that forced companies to collapse because of the existence of toxic mortgage-related investments. Also key to winning GOP support was a decision by the Securities and Exchange Commission to ease mark-to-market accounting rules that require financial institutions to show the deflated value of assets on their balance sheets.

November 25: The U.S. Federal Reserve pledges $800 billion more to help revive the financial system. Some $600 billion will be used to buy mortgage bonds issued or guaranteed by Fannie Mae, Freddie Mac, and the Federal Home Loan Banks.

April 16, 2010: The Securities and Exchange Commission sues Goldman Sachs for fraud, for allegedly having failed to disclose vital information to investors in one of its "Abacus" mortgage-backed CDOs in 2007. The CDO was allegedly "designed to fail" by the hedge fund of John Paulson, so that Paulson could make large profits betting against it. Allegedly this was not disclosed to investors by Goldman, and they lost roughly a billion dollars while Paulson and company profited.

October: A foreclosures crisis occurs due to many foreclosures being carried out without the necessary paperwork, instead relying on "robo-signing" of the legal documents. Many demand that all foreclosures be halted nationwide until the systemic issues of extrajudicial practices have come under control.

January 2011: The U.S. Financial Crisis Inquiry Commission reported its findings in January 2011. It concluded that "the crisis was avoidable and was caused by: Widespread failures in financial regulation, including the Federal Reserve's failure to stem the tide of toxic mortgages; dramatic breakdowns in corporate governance including too many financial firms acting recklessly and taking on too much risk; An explosive mix of excessive borrowing and risk by households and Wall Street that put the financial system on a collision course with crisis; Key policy makers ill prepared for the crisis, lacking a full understanding of the financial system they oversaw; and systemic breaches in accountability and ethics at all levels."

April, 2011: The U.S. Senate Permanent Committee on Investigations releases the Levin-Coburn report "Wall Street and the Financial Crisis: Anatomy of a Financial Collapse." It presents new details about the activities of Goldman Sachs, Deutsche Bank, Moody's, and other companies preceding the financial crisis. Former New York governor Eliot Spitzer says that if the attorney general cannot bring a case against Goldman Sachs, after the revelations of the Levin-Coburn report, then he should resign.

DAMAGES

Total losses from the politarchic subprime prime mortgage gambit cannot be finely calibrated because they depend on the timeframe chosen and cannot be precisely separated from other contributing factors. Nonetheless, the figures in the real-estate sector run well into the trillions and continue to mount in terms of foreclosures, cumulative unemployment, deficit spending, and national indebtedness.

Between 2007 and 2009, 4.2 million properties were foreclosed in the United States at an average cost of $225,000 (the average home-mortgage cost during the real-estate boom), summing to nearly $1 trillion, with 10 million more foreclosures forecast through 2012.[30] The disadvantaged minorities and the poor that Fannie Mae claimed it was serving have been disproportionately harmed because of their large presence in the subprime mortgage market.

The subprime mortgage and MSB crises also contributed substantially to collateral damage in the wider national economy. Unemployment has run about 5 million above normal for more than four years since 2008 with no clear end in sight, the interest income earned by retirees has dwindled to almost nothing, and the national debt has more than doubled. No matter how the bottom line is tallied, the public as intended all along has been stuck with an astonishing bill brought about by politarchic "reckless endangerment" for the enrichment of a relative handful of politicians, big business, and big social advocacy.[31]

UNWRITTEN LAW

The unwritten law of politocracy is to limit damage to politicians, big business, and big social advocacy and never retreat so that benefits and costs are always asymmetrically in favor of the politocracy. The people always lose. Most of the principals in the subprime mortgage scheme were winners before the real-estate and financial crashes, took hits during the crashes, but had their winning or losses cushioned immediately thereafter, and then resumed the tax-transfer subsidy game from the public to themselves in ways suitable to new conditions. They are doing well today. Others – workers, the middle class, and passive rich – are bearing the losses.

Washington's response to both the subprime mortgage and MBS debacles was not to let the market punish those who created the bubble, but insofar as politically possible to deny culpability, to selectively bail out key allies including big social advocacy,[32] save its GSEs (Fannie Mae and Freddie Mac), and generate grand new opportunities for politarchic enrichment

---

[30] Mike Colpitts, "Housing Predictor: 10 Million Foreclosures Through 2012," June 16, 2009, www.realtrac.com The forecast is realistic. There were 2.8 million foreclosures in 2009 and 3.8 million in 2010.

[31] Reckless endangerment in law is defined as the crime of knowingly and wantonly creating a substantial risk of serious bodily or material injury to another person. "Reckless" conduct involves the culpable disregard of foreseeable consequences to others from the act or omission involved. The accused need not intentionally cause the resulting harm. The ultimate question is whether under the circumstances, the accused's (here politocracy's) conduct was of that heedless nature that made it actually or imminently dangerous to the rights or safety of others.

[32] See "U.S. Regulator Feels Pressure Over Freddie, Fannie: Report," Yahoo! Finance, March 26, 2012: "Some officials in the Obama administration, the Federal Reserve and Congress

with a quantum trillion dollar jump in annual deficit spending, and an easy money policy that provides windfall profits to financial institutions at savers' expense. All these actions are given a heroic spin and justified by appeals to Keynesian macroeconomic theory; however, as shown in Chapter 5, the rationale is not hard science.

Congressional Budget Office (CBO) statistics as of November 2009 provide an illuminating overview of new federal commitments and expenditures intended to bail out real-estate, financial concerns, and others directly and indirectly connected to the subprime mortgage and MBS crises. These data reveal that Washington committed $11 trillion and spent $3 trillion specifically for these purposes,[33] with trillions more in emergency spending going to other purposes like extended unemployment relief and healthcare. Although big businesses like AIG, Citibank, and Bear Stearns are primary beneficiaries, there also are ample transfers granted to big social advocacy including $25 billion to help the Treasury Department launch its $75 billion multipronged foreclosure prevention plan. That plan, as should now be expected by the reader, benefits the banks far more than homeowners.

Regulatory responses have followed the same pattern. The federal government made a small gesture to restrict executive pay and diminish systemic risk. It expanded consumer protection, increased oversight over the shadow banking system and derivatives and enhanced the Federal Reserve's authority to wind down some failing institutions. The Dodd-Frank Wall Street Reform and Consumer Protection Act signed into law in July 2010 addresses some of the causes of the crises, but also predictably makes provisions to increase subprime mortgage lending to those claiming to be disadvantaged. The bottom line thus is more of the same: trans-partisan back scratching among politicians, big business, and big social advocacy.

POLITOCRACY UNSCATHED AND UNCHASTENED

The U.S. Financial Crisis Inquiry commission reported its findings in January 2011 (see the timeline earlier in the chapter).[34]

---

have called on Fannie Mae and Freddie Mac to write down the value of mortgages they own or guarantee as part of an effort to help the U.S. housing market recover from a deep slump that saw one third of property values wiped out since 2006."

[33] David Goldman, "CNNMoney.com Bailout Tracker," http://money.cnn.com/news/story-supplement/economy/bailouttracker/index.html The subcomponents of these totals are: Troubled Asset Relief Program, Federal Reserve Rescue Efforts, Federal Stimulus Program, American International Group, FDIC Bank Takeovers, Other Financial Initiatives, and Other Housing Initiatives

[34] Financial Crisis Inquiry Commission Press Release, January 27, 2011.

The summary judgment is true as far as it goes, but it also airbrushes federal politocracy out of the picture. Both the subprime mortgage and MBS crises were avoidable, but there was a principal culprit – politocracy both in its direct pursuit of self-enrichment and its collateral refusal to regulate in the public interest.

Much of the professional economics literature similarly glosses the federal government's responsibility for these disasters by contending that the objectives of Fannie Mae, the real-estate, and financial communities were progressive, but those responsible hadn't adequately worked out the glitches. Economic commentators thereby are innocently or knowingly complicit in the crime – justifying the cover given to the theft. The solution recommended is more and better.[35] This rationalization ignores the fact that under politocracy, more will never be better.

What is required is true democratic regulation that is minimalist and focused on preventing conspiracies against market competition and the people. If this is our policy, then another subprime scandal will not happen.

Politocracy's virulence and persistence in domestic policy is easily understood. It has come away from the subprime mortgage and MBS crises largely unscathed and undaunted. The only lesson it plausibly can have learned is that it can expect to win in nearly all circumstances and that it never need retreat. This is the reality of domestic politarchic policymaking in action.[36] The consequence of the subprime crisis is not punishment of the offenders and effective reform, but a green light for the next great crisis.[37]

---

[35] Robert Shiller, *The Subprime Solution: How Today's Global Financial Crisis Happened, and What to Do about It*. Princeton, NJ: Princeton University Press, 2009.

[36] Aaron Task, "Fannie and Freddie Employees Rake in the Big Bucks," Yahoo! Finance, December 10, 2012: "More than 2,000 non-executive senior managers at Fannie and Freddie were paid over $200,000 in 2011, *the Wall Street Journal* reports, citing a new report from the Federal Housing Finance Agency. Among those senior managers, the median pay of vice presidents was $388,000 while 1,650 'directors' had a median income of $205,300." The median pay of 23 vice-presidents was $1.7 million.

[37] See "Huntsman's Good Economic Plan," *Wall Street Journal*, September 2, 2011:

Today, the United States has the most troubled housing market in the developed world. It's also the only developed country with a major government role in housing policy. In less than twenty-five years, "affordable housing" and other housing policies have turned a healthy market into a financial ruin. In 1989, for example, only 1 in 230 homebuyers made a down payment of 3 percent or less; by 2007, it was 1 in 3. Meanwhile, average home equity plunged from 45 percent to 7 percent. The policies that caused the financial crisis are still in force. Until they and the government's role in housing are eliminated, the US housing market will not return to health.

NINE

Foreign Imbroglios

A TRULY DEMOCRATIC FOREIGN POLICY

A truly democratic foreign policy flows directly from first principles. It must be of the people (citizens only), by the people, and for the people as stipulated in the Constitution, subject to Bill of Rights minority and property protections, and supported by inter-branch federal checks and balances. Its primary purpose is to prudently defend and promote the *demos*'s welfare vis-à-vis foreigners and their governments, not to globally advance politarchic agendas at the expense of American workers, the middle class, and passive rich. There is no policy for all seasons. Pragmatic, realist, and idealist approaches each may be best in specific circumstances, and nothing in the Constitution obligates citizens to proselytize, forcibly convert the benighted, or assume the role of *salvator mundi*. Few Americans are prepared to squander their own treasure for these purposes, but are susceptible to cajolement by foreign-affairs advocates invoking the national interest or human rights.

People broadly prefer peace to war and prosperity to indigence. They appreciate the wisdom of some collective spending on defense, diplomacy, immigration control, alliances, environmental protection, trade facilitation, international monetary, financial and banking institutions, and foreign assistance to secure these ends to the extent that benefits exceed costs. However, as previously explained, fundamental principal-agent problems preclude the attainment of reliably effective international security, political and economic regimes, even before taking account of politocracy.

Small therefore is beautiful. True democratic foreign policy should focus on immediate rather than remote, worst-case threats. U.S. war fighting and alliance participation should be stringently restricted within this framework. Impractical nation-building adventures like the ones in Iraq and Afghanistan should be eschewed. Obsolete organizations like NATO should be pared down or abandoned. Oversized forums like the Group of Eight (G8) should be trimmed.[1] Participation in transatlantic, transpacific, and trans-global partnerships should be pragmatic, and supranational entanglements shunned. Immigration should be limited (contrary to the demand of most globalizers).[2] The nation should protect itself against destructive currency imbalances (China), and vigorously press for trade and property-rights reciprocity.

The guiding principle throughout the economic sphere should be the promotion of a level international playing field for all market participants, in sharp contrast to the special pleadings of self-seekers looking for public trade subsidies, globalizers, and politocrats. An ideal democratic foreign policy must inevitably be national in a universe where Enlightenment democratic world government is the pie in the sky (see Chapter 10), and also must be austere to avert economic sclerosis and bipolar arrhythmia (see Chapter 5).[3] It is compatible with free trade, Heckscher-Ohlin and Stolper-Samuelson equilibria,[4] individual liberty, Pareto optimality,[5] Arrow optimality,[6] and even limited Meadean and Rawlsian social justice,[7] but draws the line at antidemocratic politocracy.

---

[1] The G8 began as the G7. It was initiated by France in 1975 and was comprised of Canada, France, Germany, Italy, Japan, the United Kingdom, and the United States. Russia was added in 1997. Brazil, the People's Republic of China, India, Mexico, and South Africa have participated as guests. The forum expanded to the G20 after 2009.

[2] "France's Sarkozy Defies Europe with Protectionist Push," Yahoo! News, March 12, 2012. http://news.yahoo.com/french-sarkozy-wants-europe-trade-border-protection-141252760.html. French president Nicolas Sarkozy advocates EU action to restrict immigration. If this does not materialize, he asserts that France should withdraw from the Schengen Agreement and restrict immigration on its own.

[3] See macroeconomics section in Chapter 5.

[4] Heckscher-Ohlin and Stolper-Samuelson equilibria are two ideal competitive free-trade outcomes referring respectively to the role of factor endowments and global product price adjustments. See Steven Rosefielde, *Soviet International Trade in Heckscher-Ohlin Perspective*, Heath-Lexington, 1973.

[5] Pareto optimality is a condition that defines the outcome of individual competitive utility searches that makes any individual and, by extension, all individuals as well-off as they can possibly be without exerting market power or benefiting from preferential government transfers. Vilfredo Pareto, *Cours d'économie politique professe a l'universite de Lausanne*, Vol. I, 1896.

[6] Kenneth Arrow identified the conditions setting the boundaries on efficient democratic voting. Kenneth Arrow, *Social Choice and Individual Values*, New York: Wiley, 1951.

[7] James Meade extended the core competitive model to incorporate efficient wealth and income transfers. James Meade, *Liberty, Equality and Efficiency*, New York: New York University Press, 1993. John Rawls developed a set of legal principles that provide a foundation for some forms of government action on society's behalf. John Rawls, *A Theory of Justice*, Cambridge MA: The Belknap Press of Harvard University Press, 1971.

Contemporary U.S. foreign policy unsurprisingly uses the vocabulary of true democracy, but is politocratic through and through, ensnaring the nation in destructive foreign imbroglios.

BIG SOCIAL ADVOCACY'S AND BIG BUSINESS'S FOREIGN-POLICY AGENDA

Big social advocacy and big business both employ true democratic rhetoric that conceals their hidden agendas. Big social advocacy nominally pushes causes that include world government, multilateral global power sharing, nuclear nonproliferation, open migration, minority empowerment (including women's and homosexual rights), social justice (egalitarianism and reparations), environmental protection, and energy security. It insists that the nation's *demos* ought to desire these missions, while lobbying for lucrative government programs behind drawn curtains. Big business, especially Wall Street, rhetorically champions free enterprise and international competition, while primarily seeking government-backed rent and profit-enhancing economic power. Big business and big social advocacy cross swords, but partner too in using government as a tool for self-enrichment abroad. [8]

COMMON GROUND

Big social advocacy and big business are prepared to engage each other and foreigners on multiple levels, grabbing and conceding as circumstances dictate. However, to do so effectively, they require common declaratory ideals and ground rules,[9] including consensus about the limits of noncompliance (cheating). The professed ideals are laudable: national interest, prosperity, equal opportunity, peace, friendship, security, harmony,[10] human rights,

---

[8] Cf. Benabou, Roland, and Jean Tirole, "Individual and Corporate Social Responsibility," *Economica*, 2010, Vol. 77, pp. 1–19.

[9] Charles Kupchan, "NATO's Final Frontier: Why Russia Should Join the Atlantic Alliance," *Foreign Affairs*, Vol. 89, No. 3, May 2010, pp. 100–12. Richard Rosecrance," Bigger is Better: The Case for a Transatlantic Economic Union," *Foreign Affairs*, Vol. 89, No. 3, May 2010, pp. 42–50.

[10] Thomas Fleming, *The New Dealers' War*, New York: Basic Books, 2001, p.308. Cordell Hull, the first secretary of state to address a joint session of Congress, spoke for the president, Franklin Roosevelt. He stated that the global war (World War II) had transformed international relations: "There will no longer be need for spheres of influence, for alliances, for balances of power or any of the other special arrangements through which, in the unhappy past, nations strove to safeguard their security and promote their interests." At another joint session of Congress more than a year later, FDR echoed the same theme. "He said that there would be no more unilateral action by governments, exclusive alliances, balances of power, spheres of influence, and all the other expedients that have been tried for centuries – and have always failed." Ibid., p. 498.

justice, fairness, gender equality, egalitarianism, and empowerment. Lenin and Stalin said all the same things.

The rules also are unobjectionable, ostensibly committing participants to equal opportunity, reciprocity, mutual support, affirmative action, cooperation, transparency, impartial mediation, and conflict resolution. The particulars do not matter. Any set of common goals that deflect attention from ulterior motives is sufficient for the politocracy's purposes.

POSTWAR GLOBALIST PROJECT

The ideals, rules, and institutions in force today shaping U.S. foreign policy are the result of a protracted process that began with the founding of the League of Nations,[11] evolving with twists and turns through the depression, World War II, Cold War,[12] and post-Bretton Woods globalist resurgence.[13]

---

[11] America's foreign policy today bears little resemblance to its isolationist past when elected officials heeded the people's will by rejecting the Versailles Peace Treaty (1919) and the League of Nations with it because they didn't want to bear the burden of saving the world from itself. Until Pearl Harbor (December 7, 1941) foreign policy was mostly routine consular and diplomatic activity. There were no extensive military, political, economic alliances, intergovernmental or transgovernmental entanglements, only treaties on special issues like naval arms control (Washington Treaty 1920–1922, London Naval Treaties 1930, 1936). The State Department didn't oversee assistance programs for promoting democracy, human rights, development, or coalition building. The United States was neither the world's patriarch nor policeman. It minded its own business and encouraged others to do the same. Ralph Stone, ed., *Wilson and the League of Nations: Why America's Rejection*, New York: Krieger Publishing Company, 1978. John Maynard Keynes, *The Economic Consequences of the Peace*, New York: Harcourt, Brace and Howe, 1920.

[12] The colossal expansion of America's foreign-policy mission coincides with the emergence of politocracy but also is the by-product of multiple factors including the lessons of World War II, the outbreak of the Cold War, revival of Wilson idealism, restored post-depression national confidence, narcissism, liberal and socialist politics, pacifism, visionary longing for world government, altruism, and bureaucratic empire building. The case for the new world order includes various win-win claims like spreading democratic free enterprise, spurring global economic growth, surmounting economic protectionism, especially beggar-thy-neighbor policies, installing a dependable international monetary and financial order, preventing economic crises, diminishing income disparities, enhancing social justice, and insuring perpetual peace. The term Wilsonian idealism is used here to indicate both Woodrow Wilson's own foreign-policy principles as well as the Enlightenment, twentieth-century socialist and religious currents shaping his aspirations

[13] The Bretton Woods monetary management system stabilized rules for commercial relations among the world's major industrial states in 1945. It was based on the fixed exchange-rate principle. The International Monetary Fund and International Bank for Reconstruction and Development (IBRD) were created to support the fixed

They retain many features of the first globalization wave 1870–1913,[14] but substitute universal material and social goals for pre-World War I imperial-racist objectives. Hegemony and cheap labor exploitation no longer can be publically espoused. They are taboo and have been replaced by the concepts of leadership and mutually beneficial global development. Colonization (China's subjugation of Tibet notwithstanding) mostly has been eschewed in practice, with low-cost workers migrating instead to the West.

Soft power has replaced imperial coercion.[15] The United States' globalist project thus is less nefarious than Hitler's, Stalin's, Hirohito's, or those of their nineteenth-century predecessors but still is a far cry from anything that can be considered an Enlightenment democratic ideal.[16]

---

exchange-rate regime. The IBRD was transformed later into the World Bank Group. Members were supposed to use monetary policy to assume foreign currency parities. The Bretton Wood system was scuttled on August 15, 1971, when the United States unilaterally terminated convertibility of the dollar into gold. The dollar then became a fiat currency, backed by nothing but the federal government's good faith. The international monetary system then gravitated toward flexible exchange rates. The Plaza accord, signed in September 1985 by the United States, West Germany, France, Britain, and Japan to appreciate the yen and deutsche mark, was another watershed event. It led to the expectation of a continuously appreciating yen that attracted hot money from abroad, fueling rising asset price appreciation, and paving the way for the eurozone crisis.

[14] Niall Ferguson, 2008, *The Ascent of Money: A Financial History of the World*, New York: Penguin, 2008. Niall Ferguson, "Complexity and Collapse," *Foreign Affairs*, March/April 2010, Vol. 89, No. 2, pp. 18–32.

[15] Joseph Nye coined the term "soft power" in the late 1980s. It is now used frequently – and often incorrectly – by political leaders, editorial writers, and academics around the world. So what is soft power? Soft power lies in the ability to attract and persuade. Whereas hard power, the ability to coerce, grows out of a country's military or economic might, soft power arises from the attractiveness of a country's culture, political ideals, and policies. Joseph Nye, *Soft Power: The Means to Success in World Politics*, Public Affairs, 2004. Cf. Joseph Nye, "The Decline of America's Soft Power," *Foreign Affairs*, May/June 2004, pp. 16–20.

[16] The move from hard power to soft power gradually reduced the importance of communist deterrence in favor of coexistence, detente, post-Soviet partnership, multilateralism, and aspects of supranational government. The progression was partly a rational accommodation to changing realities. The Soviet threat restricted the United States' room for maneuver, but as Kremlin prospects for immediate conquest dimmed, options expanded. When the USSR disbanded, champions of other causes rushed into the breach to plead their cases and capture the "peace dividend" before taxpayers received the refund. China, Brazil, Russia, and India, transition states, the developing world, nation building, democratization, globalization, Islamic interests, environmentalism, and crime fighting (against drug dealers, sex traffickers, nuclear proliferators, and female and homosexual repression) were upgraded, while nuclear deterrence, core conventional war-fighting capabilities, and nuclear nonproliferation were downgraded.

STRATEGY AND TACTICS

The politocratic ideal is reflected in the Department of State's (DoS) mission statement:[17] "Advancing freedom for the benefit of the American people and the international community by helping to build and sustain a more democratic, secure, and prosperous world composed of well-governed states that respond to the needs of their people, reduce widespread poverty and act responsibly within the international system."[18]

The DoS promotes and protects the interests of American citizens by 1) fostering peace and stability in regions of vital interest, 2) creating jobs at home and by opening markets abroad, 3) helping developing nations establish investment and export opportunities, and 4) bringing nations together and forging partnerships to address global problems such as terrorism, the spread of communicable diseases, cross-border pollution, humanitarian crises, nuclear smuggling and narcotics trafficking.

It has tried to realize these goals by establishing 250 posts in 180 nations and intergovernmental institutions, with an alphabet soup of departments, and spends $51.7 billion annually (including USAID), with negligible success.

The charter is formulated as a framework rather than a fully elaborated blueprint for the ideal global order,[19] allowing bureaucrats to avoid premature battles, while forging consensus for ever-expanding international governmental operations.[20] The process occurs simultaneously on four separate, but often overlapping planes: (1) bilateral diplomacy, (2) multilateral regional consultation, (3) supranational organization building, and (4) global institutional action. Nation-states play pivotal roles in bilateral, multilateral, and most global institutions like the United Nations, but there are incessant calls to subordinate and even eradicate national governments in favor of supranational organizations like the European Union, and more ambitiously a World Nation, where representatives are directly elected

---

[17] At http://www.state.gov: The United States Department of State (often referred to as the State Department or DoS, is the executive department responsible for international relations of the United States, equivalent to the foreign ministries of other countries. The department was created in 1789 and was the first executive department established. The secretary of state is the first Cabinet official in the order of precedence and in the presidential line of succession.

[18] United States Department of State FY2010 Agency Financial Report.

[19] The policy link provides a sweeping inventory of the topics under its jurisdiction from climate change to sex trafficking and women's issues.

[20] Samuel Huntington, "The West: Unique, Not Universal," *Foreign Affairs*, November/ December 1996, Vol. 75, No. 6, pp. 28–46.

by all the planet's citizens. The politocratic motive, as always, is building more and more layers of government. Bigness has been achieved in the European Union where government organizations have grown like Topsy,[21] and doubtlessly would continue apace in a World Nation. Wiser heads tutored by recent EU woes ultimately may check the drive for ever-bigger government, but if common sense fails, the drift toward increased Western supranationalism (ASEAN) and a World Nation will persist.

Both the grand vision and substantive detail of this globalist project are compatible with true democracy in principle, but devoid of Enlightenment democratic content because they make no pretense of tailoring the supply of DoS services to the U.S. *demos*'s aggregate and specific demand. The State Department will spend as much money as it can get, growing as big as federal revenues and borrowings permit, and has broad discretion within shifting parameters imposed by diverse politarchic handlers.

Moreover, the United States', and more broadly the West's, rules-based globalist project is an ongoing disaster for another reason. It marries politocracy with antidemocratic forces abroad (expediently dubbed "emerging democracies"). Politarchs conflate their own interest with the nation's, while China, Russia, and a host of other inveterate authoritarian states across the globe reject the rule of law, preferring the rule of men.[22] This is an unholy marriage. Neither side is likely to ever act in accordance with a true democratic social contract, essential for achieving satisfactory results from a universal rules and institutions strategy. This would not be

---

[21] *Uncle Tom's Cabin, or Life among the Lowly* by Harriet Beecher Stowe. SparkNotes.com describes the character:

Topsy – A wild and uncivilized slave girl whom Miss Ophelia tries to reform, Topsy gradually learns to love and respect others by following the example of Eva. "Have you ever heard anything about God, Topsy?" The child looked bewildered, but grinned as usual. "Do you know who made you?" "Nobody, as I knows on," said the child, with a short laugh. The idea appeared to amuse her considerably; for her eyes twinkled, and she added, "I spect I grow'd. Don't think nobody never made me."

Given the astounding popularity of *Uncle Tom's Cabin* (at the time of its publication it outsold every book previously published in the United States except the Bible), it seems that legions of readers were charmed by Topsy's declaration that she just "grow'd."

[22] Walter Russell Meade, "The Myth of America's Decline," *Wall Street Journal,* April 9, 2012:

For American foreign policy, the key now is to enter deep strategic conversations with our new partners – without forgetting or neglecting the old. The U.S. needs to build a similar network of relationships and institutional linkages that we built in postwar Europe and Japan and deepened in the trilateral years. Think tanks, scholars, students, artists, bankers, diplomats and military officers need to engage their counterparts in each of these countries as we work out a vision for shared prosperity in the new century.

a problem, if Western leaders were "Masters of Illusion,"[23] but politarchs and big business are preoccupied with self-seeking, big social advocacy is too myopic, and executive-branch officials are too absorbed with their politarchic agenda to outplay Russia's and China's Machiavellians in the national interest.[24]

Advocating universal ideals like open markets, free competition, democracy, multilateral cooperation, equal opportunity, and social justice are innocuous enough, but the devil is in the details of the dense network of procedural rules and institutions that allow politocrats, big business, and big social advocacy to arrogate popular sovereignty.

U.S. foreign policy has both politarchic rhyme and reason, but this has little to do with the DoS mission statement. The State Department touts the link between opening foreign markets and domestic job creation as big business requires, but politarchs do little to curtail China's protectionism, which destroys jobs in the United States.[25] The State Department promotes U.S. prosperity by fostering constructive dialogue among well-governed states while simultaneously ensnaring the nation in foreign imbroglios by fomenting color revolutions,[26] urging military adventures, and pressing for supranational partnerships and world government. Tests can be constructed to evaluate the success or failure of each initiative in terms of declaratory purpose, with depressing results. Russia, China, Iraq, and Afghanistan, as the White House and the State Department insisted in various statements, were all supposed to have transitioned to democratic free enterprise, but failed. Nuclear proliferation was supposed to have been prevented, and terrorism and drug trafficking eradicated, but were not.[27] These

---

[23] Steven Rosefielde and Quinn Mills, *Masters of Illusion: American Leadership in a New Age*, Cambridge: Cambridge University Press, 2007.

[24] John Bolton, "The Innocents Abroad," *National Review*, September 6, 2011:

> But it is folly to look for rhyme and reason when there is neither. For better or worse, there is no single dispositive flaw in Obama's doctrine, since there is little that resembles a doctrine. His saunter through world affairs is unstructured. Instead, the explanation for his policy's failure, and its well-deserved collapse now unfolding before us, lies in a jumbled mix of philosophy, political priorities and personal inadequacy.

> If American foreign policymakers were not absorbed in politocratic gains they might be able to effectively engage China and Russia.

[25] Steven Rosefielde, "China's Perplexing Foreign Trade Policy: Causes, Consequences and a Tit for Tat Solution," *American Foreign Policy Interests*, Vol. 33, No. 1, January/February 20, 2011, pp. 10–16.

[26] The Ukraine (orange), Georgia (rose), Kyrgyzstan (tulip), Lebanon (cedar), Kuwait (blue), Iraq (purple), Iran (green), Tunisia (jasmine), Egypt (lotus), Burma (saffron), Libya, Syria.

[27] Kishore Mahbubani, "The Case Against the West," *Foreign Affairs*, May/June 2008, Vol. 87, No. 3, pp. 111–24. Daniel Blumenthal, "How Many Nuclear-Armed Countries Does Obama

failures and myriads of others, however, never are interpreted as evidence for retrenchment.[28] They are spun instead as reminders of the difficulty of defending freedom and the imperative of redoubling efforts to sustain the politocratic merry-go-round.

The United States has squandered more than a trillion dollars in the new millennium to enrich nation-building contractors (domestic and foreign), big business, and big social advocacy alike, saddling the people with an oppressive national debt, and degrading the nation's power and security in most respects. No one is contrite because true democratic foreign policy never was the real game. Big business, big social advocacy, and politocrats got what they wanted most, and unashamedly insist that what is best for them is good for the country. This, more than any learned disquisition on the national interest and universal well-being, is the key to accurately forecasting the effectiveness and content of U.S. foreign policy. Although programmatic and rhetorical details will change, the politocratic substance and patchwork outcomes of the nation's foreign imbroglios will remain the same.[29]

Want in Asia?," *Foreign Policy*, November 29, 2011: http://shadow.foreignpolicy.com/posts/2011/11/29/how_many_nuclear_armed_countries_does_obama_want_in_asia

Of course President Obama does not want any more nuclear powers in Asia. But his policies are hastening that reality. Why? First, "global zero" and deep cuts in conventional forces are both tempting Beijing to up its nuclear arsenal and giving allies pause about our "extended deterrent." Second, Obama has continued the Bush and Clinton policies that have allowed North Korea to become a nuclear power.... South Korea, Japan, Taiwan, Australia are all quite capable of acquiring nuclear weapons but chose (sometimes with U.S. prodding) not to do so. Now South Korea and Japan have at least two reasons to reconsider – North Korea is a nuclear weapons state and China may be a growing one. Taiwan is less confident that it will get the conventional arms it needs from the U.S., and we would do well to remember that it sought nuclear weapons when it was previously abandoned by the U.S.

[28] Joseph M. Parent and Paul K. MacDonald, "The Wisdom of Retrenchment," *Foreign Affairs*, November/December 2011, Vol. 90, No. 6, pp. 32–47: "The United States can no longer afford a world-spanning foreign policy. Retrenchment – cutting military spending, redefining foreign priorities, and shifting more of the defense burden to allies – is the only sensible course."

"At the same time that progressives (liberals) argue for retrenchment, they assert a new obligation: Western progressives now attempt to legitimize armed intervention for humanitarian purposes (if it really occurs for those purposes) as 'the responsibility to Protect.'" Cf. Jon Western and Josh.ua S. Goldstein, "Humanitarian Intervention Comes of Age," *Foreign Affairs*, Vol. 90, No. 6, Nov/Dec 2011, pp. 48–59, in summary statement, "...as Libya has shown – the international community has... grown much more adept at using military force to save lives."

[29] Niall Ferguson, "Complexity and Collapse," *Foreign Affairs*, March/April 2010, Vol. 89, No.2, pp.18–32.

DEFENSE

Defense of the realm is a fundamental aspect of foreign policy in all systems, together with commerce and diplomacy. It has many aspects, one of the most important of which is protecting the people from armed external attack using diverse defensive techniques including arms control, preemption, deterrence, and compellence.[30] In the United States this task is assigned primarily to three executive entities: the Department of Defense (DOD), the Central Intelligence Agency (CIA), and the U.S. Arms Control and Disarmament Agency (ACDA).[31] They are instruments of the president and act under his/her authority, advised by the National Security Council (NSC),[32] ultimately with the consent of Congress. Defense policy is also part of the State Department portfolio,[33] and it routinely counsels the NSC

[30] Thomas Schelling, *Strategy of Conflict*, Cambridge MA: Harvard University Press, 1981.

[31] The U.S. Arms Control and Disarmament Agency (ACDA) was established as an independent agency of the United States government by the Arms Control and Disarmament Act (75 Stat. 631) on September 26, 1961. Its mission is to strengthen U.S. national security by "formulating, advocating, negotiating, implementing and verifying effective arms control, nonproliferation and disarmament policies, strategies, and agreements." ACDA ensures that arms control is fully integrated into the development and conduct of United States national-security policy. ACDA also conducts, supports, and coordinates research for arms-control and disarmament policy formulation, prepared for and managed U.S. participation in international arms-control and disarmament negotiations, and prepared, operated, and directed U.S. participation in international arms-control and disarmament systems. ACDA was merged into the Department of State in April 1999.

[32] The National Security Council (NSC) is the president's principal forum for considering national security and foreign-policy matters with his senior national-security advisors and cabinet officials. Since its inception under President Truman, the council's function has been to advise and assist the president on national-security and foreign policies. The council also serves as the president's principal arm for coordinating these policies among various government agencies. The NSC is chaired by the president. Its regular attendees (both statutory and nonstatutory) are the vice president, the secretary of state, the secretary of the treasury, the secretary of defense, and the assistant to the president for national-security affairs. The chairman of the joint chiefs of staff is the statutory military advisor to the council, and the director of national intelligence is the intelligence advisor. The chief of staff to the president, counsel to the president, and the assistant to the president for economic policy are invited to attend any NSC meeting. The attorney general and the director of the office of management and budget are invited to attend meetings pertaining to their responsibilities. The heads of other executive departments and agencies, as well as other senior officials, are invited to attend meetings of the NSC when appropriate.

[33] The executive branch and the U.S. Congress have constitutional responsibilities for U.S. foreign policy. Within the executive branch, the Department of State is the lead U.S. foreign affairs agency, and its head, the secretary of state, is the president's principal foreign-policy advisor, though other officials or individuals may have more influence on their foreign-policy decisions. All foreign-affairs activities – U.S. representation abroad, foreign-assistance programs, countering international crime, foreign military training programs, the services the department provides, and more – are paid for by the foreign-affairs budget, which represents little more than 1 percent of the total federal budget.

and president on its views about arms control, preemption, deterrence, and compellence. The Department of Commerce (DOC), the Department of Homeland Security (DHS), and the U.S. Agency for International Development (USAID) from time to time may also offer advice on defense issues that affect their operations.

This chain of command and consultation means that none of the defense power organizations (DOD, CIA, ACDA) has the power to make defense policy on its own. Political authorities are in command (civilian control), and in politarchic America this means that big government, big business, and big social advocacy make defense policy rather than the people's national-security concerns.[34]

Their collective interests lie in expanding the size and scope of most foreign-policy operations, while downsizing programs offering low net politocratic gain. The people's national-security priorities are extraneous. It suffices for politarchs to crow about U.S. superpower, and then embark on profitable crusades even when this degrades deterrence and national welfare.

A clear picture of how politocracy has warped U.S. defense policy can be constructed by comparing U.S. strategy during the last two decades with the realist alternative occasioned by the collapse of the Soviet Union.

On December 25, 1991 the USSR stunned the U.S. national-security community by disbanding itself,[35] leaving the United States as the world's only military and economic superpower. The chaos that ensued temporarily eliminated the threat of a Russian conventional attack on Europe and quickly led to the widespread abandonment of command communism across the globe including China, Vietnam, Cambodia, and Laos. The United States found itself with no imminent vital military threats and capable of deterring future potential adversaries (Russia and China) merely by preserving its nuclear arsenal and building an effective ballistic missile defense. This "strategic independence" policy offered a low-cost, low-risk approach to durable peace.[36] It provided a peace dividend from drastically downsizing conventional forces, without increasing existing nuclear stockpiles.

---

[34] It is commonplace to find assertions that U.S. defense policy is made by the "military-industrial complex," meaning the Defense Department and big business. This concept is too narrow. It erroneously excludes the rest of the U.S. national-security policymaking community and the politarchs, including the president and Congress.

[35] Steven Rosefielde, *Russia in the 21st Century: The Prodigal Superpower*, New York: Cambridge University Press, 2005.

[36] New START (Strategic Arms Reduction Treaty), called Measures for the Further Reduction and Limitation of Strategic Offensive Arms, was signed in Prague, the Czech Republic, on April 8, 2010, and is expected to last until at least 2021. Under the terms of the treaty, the

Politocrats, big business, and big social advocacy, however, pressed American defense policy in the opposite direction. Social advocates (particularly those championing unilateral disarmament) successfully persuaded President Obama to cut the United States' strategic nuclear arsenal to near parity with China, under the guise of an ill-advised bilateral agreement (New START) with Russia.[37] During the Clinton, Bush, and Obama years, the United States redesigned, modernized, and expanded conventional forces for peripheral deployments in the Middle East, and to a lesser extent naval engagements in the Asia Pacific, and greatly reduced ground-based combat capabilities against major powers like Russia and China.

This restructuring of the United States' conventional armed forces, combined with the Iraqi War and postwar nation building proved to be more than a trillion-dollar bonanza for big business that accomplished little, while greatly degrading land-based capabilities against major powers, even though Russia and China rapidly modernized and revved up their own conventional forces.[38] Big business also has prospered from the United States' ongoing ballistic missile defense development, which although technically sound is nonetheless a de facto boondoggle because big social advocacy

number of strategic nuclear launchers will be reduced by 50 percent, and a new inspection and verification regime established. It does not limit the number of operationally inactive stockpiled nuclear warheads. See Steven Rosefielde and Quinn Mills, *Masters of Illusion: America Leadership in a Media Age*, New York: Cambridge University Press, 2007. Steven Rosefielde, *Russia in the 21st Century: The Prodigal Superpower*, New York: Cambridge University Press, 2005. The New START agreement is ill-advised because the probable outcome of Russia's military modernization remains unclear; Russia has the right under the accord to increase its launcher stockpiles (while the United States won't), and indirectly gives China strategic nuclear parity.

[37]   Steven Blank, ed., *Russian Nuclear Weapons: Past, Present and Future*, Carlisle Barracks, PA: Strategic Studies Institute, U.S. Army War College, 2012.

[38]   Steven Rosefielde, "Economics of the Military-Industrial Complex," in Michael Alexeev and Shlomo Weber, eds., *The Oxford Handbook of Russian Economy*, Oxford: Oxford University Press, 2013. Steven Rosefielde, *Russia in the 21st Century: The Prodigal Superpower*, Cambridge University Press, 2005. U.S. Department of Defense, *Military and Security Developments Involving the People's Republic of China 2011, Annual Report to Congress*, 2011:

Nuclear Forces. China's nuclear arsenal currently consists of approximately 55–65 intercontinental ballistic missiles (ICBMs), including the silo-based CSS-4 (DF-5); the solid-fueled, road-mobile CSS-10 Mods 1 and 2 (DF-31 and DF-31A); and the more limited range CSS-3 (DF-3). This force is complemented by liquid-fueled CSS-2 intermediate-range ballistic missiles and road-mobile, solid-fueled CSS-5 (DF-21D) MRBMs for regional deterrence missions. The operational status of China's single XIA-class ballistic missile submarine (SSBN) and medium-range JL-1 submarine-launched ballistic missiles (SLBM) remain questionable. By 2015, China's nuclear forces will include additional CSS-10 Mod 2s and enhanced CSS-4s. The first of the new JIN-class (Type 094) SSBN appears ready, but the associated JL-2 SLBM has faced a number of problems and will likely continue flight tests.

considers the system strategically destabilizing.[39] The shield will never be comprehensively deployed.

Big social advocacy is content with the compromise because it reduces public concern about further nuclear cuts and facilitates the achievement of other aspects of its agenda, particularly the use of conventional armed forces to change regimes it finds abhorrent, and increased funding for soft power.[40] Big politarchic social advocacy's goal at the end of the day is to make the world free for its enrichment; that is, prospering while advancing what it considers worthy causes. It can claim a few successes in the latter regard in mitigating ethnic cleansing (Serbia and Sudan), promoting economic development, encouraging balloting, combating sex trafficking, and championing gender, sexual, and social equality, but most of the material benefits have accrued to the politarchs themselves and their allies.

In a nutshell, the demise of the Soviet Union, which should have enhanced U.S. security in ensuing years, prompted a series of politarchic policies that degraded its nuclear shield and conventional deterrence against major powers,[41] while simultaneously transforming what should have been a generous peace dividend into an enormous politarchic tax.

The date when the JIN-class SSBN/JL-2 SLBM combination will be fully operational is uncertain. China is also currently working on a range of technologies to attempt to counter U.S. and other countries' ballistic missile defense systems, including maneuvering re-entry vehicles, MIRVs, decoys, chaff, jamming, thermal shielding, and anti-satellite (ASAT) weapons. PRC official media also cites numerous Second Artillery Corps training exercises featuring maneuver, camouflage, and launch operations under simulated combat conditions, which are intended to increase survivability. Together with the increased mobility and survivability of the new generation of missiles, these technologies and training enhancements strengthen China's nuclear force and enhance its strategic strike capabilities.

The introduction of more mobile systems will create new command and control challenges for China's leadership, which now confronts a different set of variables related to deployment and release authorities.

[39] Most big social advocates in international affairs adhere to the doctrine of mutually assured destruction (MAD). They believe that if the major powers including Russia, China, and India have immense equivalent nuclear arsenals, this will deter aggression among them, the European Union, and the United States. As a corollary, it is contended that U.S. strategic independence is destabilizing because the doctrine encourages the United States to employ conventional forces anywhere it chooses throughout the world under its superior nuclear umbrella. Big social advocates recognize that Russia's and China's closed societies make it possible for them to violate their pledges of nuclear parity, but they consider this a risk worth taking for the semblance of mutually assured destruction.

[40] Soft power is the use of economic, educational, and social development projects as well as moral suasion as a tool for achieving objectives without military means (hard power).

[41] Mackenzie Eaglen and Douglas Birkey, "Nearing Coffin Corner: US Air Power on the Edge," *American Enterprise Institute*, March 21, 2012: "After two decades of deferred programs and curtailed buys in key platforms, America's combat air assets are worn out and spread too thin."

These actions might have had some tenuous justification if elected officials had a coherent, cost-effective plan for suppressing oil-price gouging (which the government now admits was possible),[42] enhancing energy security, and containing Russia and China, but the facts belie the rationalizations. The United States never billed Iraq, Libya, or Afghanistan for its nation-building assistance, as it did Kuwait and Saudi Arabia in the first Gulf War. It failed to create a stable, democratic Islamic order, and acquiesced to OPEC's oil-price gouging. Putin's Russia, operating with a weak hand, has outplayed the United States at every turn in Central Asia, the Baltic and Black Seas, Georgia, Moldova, many former Soviet satellites, and Syria, while China is on the fast track to overtake U.S. nuclear and conventional war-fighting capabilities and hold the West in thrall with its financial power. All of these adverse outcomes were unnecessary in a true democracy, but they were written in the stars for the United States' politocracy, where the core security agenda is set by big business and big social advocacy.[43]

The extension of the mutually assured destruction doctrine to China, the subordination of conventional force deterrence to peripheral theater concerns, and the decision to spend trillions on nation-building adventures is epochal, sharply dividing Cold War from post-Cold War U.S. foreign policy.[44] The Western international affairs community today places little weight on nuclear advantage, a conventional war-fighting edge against rival great powers, and nuclear nonproliferation.[45] Once upon a time preserving

---

[42] Stacy Curtin, "$4 Gas: 'There is no Justification' for High Prices, Says Fmr. Senator Dorgan," Yahoo! Finance, March 31, 2012. Senator Byron Dorgan asserted that "We could shutdown excess speculation in commodity markets. This government should do that." The CEO of ExxonMobil (XOM) believes speculation could be driving up oil prices by as much as 40 percent a barrel.

[43] G. John Ikenberry, "The Rise of China and the Future of the West," *Foreign Affairs*, January/February 2008, Vol. 87, No. 1, pp. 23–37. Ikenberry, *Liberal Leviathan: The Origins, Crisis, and Transformation of the American System*, Princeton, NJ: Princeton University Press, 2011.

[44] The United States had the opportunity to take a better course by adopting a policy of strategic independence, but declined. See Steven Rosefielde and Quinn Mills, *Masters of Illusion: America Leadership in a Media Age*, New York: Cambridge University Press, 2007.

[45] The foreign-policy community in addition to the DoS includes the Department of Defense (DoD), the Central Intelligence Agency (CIA), the Defense Intelligence Agency (DIA), the National Intelligence Council (NIC), the Bureau of International Security and Nonproliferation, the Bureau of Verification, Compliance, and Implementation, the International Monetary Fund (IMF), and the World Bank. The White House is interested in nuclear nonproliferation, but has accommodated itself to failure in part by reducing the verification staff of the Bureau of Verification, Compliance, and Implementation.

the United States' superpower status was sacrosanct;[46] the foreign-policy community fretted about rouges with nukes including Iran and Pakistan, and was willing to aggressively defend the status quo, while hawking U.S. jobs, and the rest of its global financial and Wilsonian agenda. Now, however, core hard-power deterrence priorities have faded, and the White House's energies have been channeled into new agendas like coercing weak states into nation building as a platform for "pretend" democratization and liberalization.

The approach discounts catastrophic risk in order to concentrate on advancing a politarchic agenda with expedient means.[47] Like the sovereign-debt problem, foreign policymakers increasingly leverage the nation's nuclear deterrent, while using multiple instruments (including soft power) to purportedly advance an international social agenda (global entitlements) only obliquely tied to national security. Democratization, liberalization, poverty reduction, equal opportunity, affirmative gender action, social justice, and universal prosperity are all virtuous goals, but the U.S. foreign-policy community's ability to recoup the trillions of dollars spent pursuing these chimera is unproven.[48] By contrast, the long list of the United States' international security fiascos and dubious meddling, including the unfolding Egyptian, Syrian, and Libyan stories, is stark. The failures include North Korean,[49] Iranian, Pakistani, and Indian nuclear proliferation, China's protectionism and regional bullying, natural-resource cartel price gouging, and frozen conflicts (Trans-Dneister, Nagorno-Karabakh, Chechnya, and Georgia's Abkhazia and South Ossetia).

Likewise, the Obama administration has encouraged and heralded "color revolutions" and other regional unrest as harbingers of global democratization. Its efforts, driven by a big business and big social-advocacy agenda rather than a quest for true democracy and the ensuing turmoil,

---

[46] The United States could have been the sole superpower, but the foreign-policy community decided that nuclear "parity" with the Soviet Union was sufficient.

[47] Margherita Stancati, "India's Missile Launch Puts China in Range," *Wall Street Journal*, April 19, 2012: "India test launched a new nuclear-capable missile that would give it, for the first time, the capability of striking the major Chinese cities of Beijing and Shanghai." The government has hailed the Agni-V missile, with a range of 5,000 kilometers, or 3,100 miles, as a major boost to its efforts to counter China's regional dominance and become an Asian power in its own right.

[48] The figure includes nation building in Iraq and Afghanistan, as well as direct war costs there and in Libya.

[49] "North Korea Says It Will Launch Long-Range Rocket," Associated Press, March 16, 2012: "The North agreed to a moratorium on long-range launches as part of the deal with Washington, but it argues that its satellite launches are part of a peaceful space program that is exempt from any international disarmament agreements."

occasionally resulted in regime change, but more often than not the new cast of characters is just as unsavory as its predecessor in the Ukraine (orange), Georgia (rose), Kyrgyzstan (tulip), Lebanon (cedar), Kuwait (blue), Iraq (purple), Iran (green), Tunisia (jasmine), Egypt (lotus), Burma (saffron), Libya, and Syria.[50]

Nor can it be seriously said that the Obama administration's Russia "reset" has made the Kremlin a stable partner,[51] despite baseless claims that Putin wouldn't be reelected in March 2012 or that his days as an effective autocrat have passed.[52] The United States' core security has not been advanced by the reset.[53] The White House surrendered to Putin's pressure by withdrawing

---

[50] The Middle Eastern "democratic revolutions" were precipitated in part by food riots caused derivatively by the United States' Iraqi adventures, the consequent petro bubble, and explosion in food prices. See Robert McNally, and Michael Levi, "A Crude Predicament," *Foreign Affairs*, July/August 2011, Vol. 90, No. 4, pp.100–11. Instead of acknowledging that nation building was a fiasco, the DoS has chosen to glorify the unintended consequences.

[51] Lilia Shevtsova, "Russia's Choice: Change or Degradation?" in Stephen Blank, ed., *Can Russia Reform? Economic, Political and Military Perspectives*, U.S. Army War College, Carlisle Barracks, 2012, pp.1–36: "The Kremlin's offensive worked. The Russian elite succeeded in forming a fairly broad range of instruments of influence in the West that continues to work today. They include co-opting Western business and intellectual representatives into their own network, playing on the contradictions between Western countries, imitating the West and making use of Western double-speak to justify Russian double standards." Bradley Klapper, "Kremlin Halts US AID Work in Russia," Yahoo! News, September 18, 2012: "The United States said Tuesday it is ending the U.S. Agency for International Development's operations in Russia after a Kremlin demand that the aid organization leave the country, dealing a blow to President Barack Obama's policy of 'resetting' relations between Washington and Moscow."

[52] Anders Aslund, group e-mail, December 12, 2011: "Has Putin Come to the End of His Regime?":

On Saturday December 10, the spell of the Vladimir Putin regime was broken. Today, the key questions that many are asking are how fast he will lose power and what will come in his place. Peaceful mass demonstrations took place all over Russia. In Moscow, probably 80,000 gathered on Bolotnaya Ploshchad near the Kremlin to protest against Putin and what they and most observers say were the stolen elections of December 4. I had argued before these protests that if more than 50,000 came, the regime would be seen as finished. This was the biggest and most important demonstration in Russia since August 1991. Demonstrations took place in at least 15 Russian cities throughout the country, so this is a national phenomenon and not limited to Moscow.

[53] The term "reset" applied to Russia refers to the Obama administration's policy of restoring the Clinton-era strategy of transforming the Kremlin from an adversary to a trustworthy partner worth of munificent assistance (Grand Bargain) after the Bush administration shifted to a "containment" strategy from 2002–2008 to counter increased Russian geopolitical aggressiveness. U.S. policymakers bent over backward to accommodate the Kremlin with nothing positive to show for it. See "Our Friends the Russians: The Kremlin Picks a Fight with America in Time for Elections," *The Wall Street Journal*, Review and Outlook, December 2, 2011:

ground-based missile defense forces from Poland and the Czech Republic in September 2009[54] and crafted a 2011 Strategic Arms Limitation treaty with Russia (appropriately signed in Munich) that makes China a de facto co-equal nuclear superpower with the United States and the Russian Federation.[55] Likewise, the reset has left Foggy Bottom flatfooted in dealing

One of the foreign policy priorities of the Obama Administration was to "reset" relations with Russia. How's that working out? Dmitry Medvedev, the placeholder for Vladimir Putin in the presidency, gave one indication last week. He declared that Russia may deploy "strike forces" and aim mid-range Iskander missiles at Europe. He also threatened to pull out of the 2010 New Start arms accord, which is supposed to be the hallmark achievement of the "reset." The excuse for Mr. Medvedev's tantrum is the long-planned missile defense shield for Europe. Once deployed in 2020, it's designed to stop a limited number of missiles from Iran and doesn't diminish Russia's nuclear deterrent. The Obama Administration scaled back the shield to please Russia in 2009, and with Russian agreement in return for the U.S. signing up to New Start, but now apparently that's not enough. On Tuesday Mr. Medvedev opened a new Russian early-warning radar in the Kaliningrad enclave between Poland and Lithuania and said: "When they tell us – 'It's not against you' – I would like to say the following: 'Dear friends, the radar launched today isn't against you either. But it's for you and for fulfilling the tasks we have set.'" Moscow's ambassador to NATO this week amplified this message by threatening to close the transport route through Russia that the U.S. and its allies use to supply troops in Afghanistan. This so-called northern corridor was another touted achievement of the "reset." Then there's Russia's veto of a Security Council resolution to sanction Syria and its continuing arms sales to the regime of Bashar Assad. Moscow also resists putting any new pressure on Iran's nuclear bomb makers .But the lesson for the U.S. concerns the limits of friendship with an authoritarian government that has no interest in being a strategic partner with the West.

[54] "New Missile Defences in Europe: Shooting Down a Plan," *The Economist*, September 24, 2009: The Obama administration saved face (or achieved its unstated goal) by substituting an inferior Aegis sea-based ballistic missile defense for proven ground-based missiles. Putin however was not placated. Russian Foreign Minister Sergei Lavrov is now pressing for a guarantee that the Aegis system won't be used against the Federation. The goal is to degrade the Aegis defense. See "U.S. Could Threaten Russian Strategic Nuclear Forces – Foreign Minister Lavrov," *RIA Novosti*, September 1, 2011. Cf. John Bolton, "Innocents Abroad," *National Review*, September 6, 2011:

With Russia, naivete is Obama's dominant flaw. He believed incredibly, that by canceling planned missile defense facilities in Poland and the Czech Republic, and broadly scaling back plans for national missile defense; agreeing to the ill-advised New START arms-control treaty; and turning a blind eye to Moscow's ongoing reassertion of hegemony in the former Soviet Union, he could persuade Russia to look kindly on American interests elsewhere. But appeasement, needless to say, has brought nothing but scorn from Moscow.

The U.S. announced that it would have an ABM defense system in place in 2012 in Europe and the United States capable against the Middle East. "NATO declares European Missile Shield Up and Running," Yahoo! News, May 21, 2012. Cf. Frank Rose, Deputy Assistant Secretary, Bureau of Arms Control, Verification and Compliance, National Defense University Congressional Breakfast Seminar, Washington D.C., May 11, 2012. (State Department Web site).

[55] The agreement, a cornerstone of Barack Obama's efforts to 'reset' US relations with Russia, came into effect as Secretary of State Hillary Clinton exchanged ratification papers with Russian Foreign Minister Sergey Lavrov in Munich February 5, 2011. The New START treaty limits

with the festering Sino-Russian enmities and the larger dangers entailed by the scramble for natural-resource rights in the Arctic.[56]

Foreign-policy politocrats have grown so complacent that they can barely rouse themselves to pen a coherent statement, justification, and cost-benefit assessment of their foreign imbroglios, assuming that the White House actually has a grand strategy.[57] Despite widespread recognition that the United States is a sclerotic superpower with waning economic, political, and military clout, the DoS, the Pentagon, the CIA, and the White House are content to stonewall embarrassments like its fruitless nation-building exercises across the globe or to declare that this or that regime-change policy is imperative; the United States' position in Asia is stronger than ever,[58] and that failures like nuclear nonproliferation are successes.[59]

Big business and big social advocacy have had their ways. Big business got a scaled-down core defense, with high-tech, peripheral theater war-fighting capabilities and ample support for defense contractors,[60] international assistance and trade, while big social advocacy obtained strategic

each side to 1,550 strategic warheads, down from 2,200, and reestablishes a monitoring system that ended in 2009. The Pentagon keeps a tight lid on its inside perception of China's nukes, but a figure of 1,500 strategic warheads, now or soon, is well within the realm of feasibility.

[56] Stephen Blank, "The Chinese and Asian Impact o Russian Nuclear Policy," paper delivered at the American Association for Slavic, East European, and Eurasian Studies, 43rd Annual Convention, Washington, D.C., November 18, 2011.

[57] Matthew Rojansky, Nikolas Gvosdev, "Keep the 'Reset' Moving," *International Herald Tribune*, December 15, 2011. Matthew Rojansky, "Congress Can Stand Up for U.S. Interests in Russia," Carnegie Endowment for International Peace, March 15, 2012. The article urges Congress to capitulate to Russia by abolishing the Jackson-Vanik amendment and replacing it with a binational consultative council as a spur to trade.

[58] Obama described himself as the United States' first "pacific president," trying to make it seems as if the United States is not being displaced by China. See "'Pacific President' Obama Behind Diplomatic Push," Associated Press, September 7, 2011. Cf. Michael Austin, "The End of Japan's China Optimism," *Wall Street Journal Asia*, September 8, 2011. Japan Prime Minister Yoshihiko Noda recently observed that China's rapid military buildup was of great concern, not only for Japan, but for the entire region.

[59] It can be counterargued that today's foreign policy is the best the White House can devise and that Obama is a "master of illusions," playing the game to maximize national welfare. We wish that this were so and do not exclude the possibility that foreign policymakers could be more sensible than they seem, but have concluded that if there are masters of illusion, they are politocrats looking out solely for themselves.

[60] Dick Cheney was CEO of Halliburton Corporation, a major recipient of Iraq War

"nation building contracts, before becoming Vice President of the United States. The association has been a source of intense controversy, and in this instance smoke undoubtedly was caused at least in part by fire. Cheney retired from the company during the 2000 U.S election campaign with a severance package worth $36 million. In the run-up to the Iraq war, Halliburton was awarded a $7 billion contract for which 'unusually' only Halliburton was allowed to bid." See Dan Brody, *The Haliburton Agenda: The Politics of Oil and Money*, New York: John Wiley and Sons, 2004.

arms reduction, the marginalization of ballistic missile defense, and international social-entitlement crusading.

Everyone, it seems, should be satisfied. Citizens should be comforted by their unfounded hope that its leaders are doing the right thing. Big business and big social advocacy are winners. But still, many suspect that something is amiss. The public dimly discerns the connection between the sovereign-debt crisis, mass involuntary unemployment, vanished prosperity, and the United States' politarchic foreign policy. Proponents of soft power complain that George Bush, Jr.'s neoconservative interventionist strategies have been foisted on them in Libya, while some hard-power advocates recognize that the substitution of peripheral for core-defense capabilities could be catastrophically shortsighted, but few adequately grasp the larger picture because of the politocratic fog.

Politarchs use every trick at their disposal, including manipulating the media, educational institutions, charitable organizations, NGOs, partners, outsourcers, contractors, and executive bureaucracies to muster support for big business's and social advocacy's agendas. The contemporary politarchic globalist project consequently cannot be reformed. Politocracy cannot be beaten at its own game by potshot criticism, special interest political action, the invisible hand, or the cunning of historical reason.[61] Politocrats are self-assured and will stay the course until public consciousness is heightened.

WHAT SHOULD BE DONE?

The right thing to do faced with chronic annual trillion-dollar budget deficits and globally destabilizing sovereign debts is to pare the politocratic foreign-policy mission.[62] After all, this is a post-Cold War age, and there is supposed to be a peace dividend that can be applied to assuring global economic security. The NIC, DoS, DOD, CIA, DIA, ACDA, World Bank, IMF, and UN can be slashed in half without sacrificing any fat if their big business and big social-advocacy missions are purged and their residual activities are funded strictly on a cost-benefit basis.[63]

---

[61] Robert Tucker, *The Cunning of Reason in Hegel and Marx*, Cambridge: Cambridge University Press, 1956.

[62] Slashing foreign-policy funding won't eliminate politocracy or legitimate constituent requests for state assistance. The representative system will continue to operate with its pluses and minuses but should provide higher net benefit.

[63] The U.S. defense industry is now reported to be spending twice as much annually on legal services (lawyers, litigation, etc) than on research. Arthur Herman, *Commentary*, Vol. 132, No. 5, December 2, 2011, p. 19. Sanjeev Gupta, Benedict Clements, Rina Bhattacharya, and Shamit Chakravarti, "The Elusive Peace Dividend," *Finance & Development*, 2002.

TEN

Transnationalism

MULTILATERALISM

The United States Constitution divides responsibility for formulating, nego-tiating, funding and overseeing foreign policy between the president and Congress.[1] Both play important, often overlapping roles in devising and monitoring bi- and multinational treaties of diverse types, covering peace, arms control, environmental, health, trade and finance.[2] Treaties (and alli-ances), as distinct from commercial contracts, are concluded with sovereign institutions and address broad issues. In true democracies they provide the people via their elected agents with tools for enhancing national wel-fare and should not be devices for transferring U.S. sovereignty to foreign potentates. International cooperation is fine; forfeited sovereignty is not unless the Constitution is formally amended. The same principle applies to informal state-to-state understandings.

---

[1] The president or the executive branch can make foreign policy by responding to for-eign events, proposing legislation, negotiating international agreements, issuing policy statement, and implementing policy and independent action. Congress can make for-eign policy through resolutions and policy statements, legislative directives, legislative pressure, legislative restrictions/funding denials, informal advice, and congressional oversight.

[2] The power of negotiation gives the executive branch a dominant role in making foreign policy through international agreements, but the president must take into account con-gressional opinion because often agreements must be approved by the Senate or Congress. Most international agreements, however, have some form of congressional participation

There is no fundamental difference between bilateral and multilateral treaties in these regards other than the number of participants. Any terms fixed in multinational agreements should be achievable through a series of bilateral treaties, although a larger multinational pie could induce bilateral participants to make especially generous concessions (commitments), or lead to deleterious foreign entanglements.[3] The choice between frameworks is a technical matter,[4] not one of high principle for a true democracy. Politocracy, however, changes the game because politarchs have no compunction flouting the Constitution. They can and do use multilateralism (collusive insider multinational networks) as a vehicle for widening their public-service trafficking at the country's expense, claiming that the United States as leader of the free world has a sacred obligation to create a democratic multinational global order.

The duty had a valid national-security justification after World War II and through much of the Cold War, but as time passed, the politocratic motive gradually became ascendant. Over the past six decades, the United States initiated a succession of military alliances and pioneered an alphabet soup of globalist political and economic institutions with independent quasi-sovereign policymaking powers. It led the charge for the North Atlantic Treaty Organization (NATO) and the Southeast Asian Treaty Organization (SEATO). It joined the United Nations and immersed itself in postwar European economic reconstruction (the Marshall Plan). It forged the Bretton Woods Agreement, creating the World Bank (WB) and the International Monetary Fund (IMF). The United States organized the General Agreement on Trade and Tariffs (GATT), superseded later by the World Trade Organization (WTO). It participated in the customs union movement by orchestrating the North American Free Trade Agreement

---

[3] George Washington cautioned the American people in his Farewell Address that "It is our true policy to steer clear of permanent alliance with any portion of the foreign world." See David Fromkin, "Entangling Alliances," *Foreign Affairs*, Vol. 48, No. 4, July 1970, p. 688.

[4] This is why it is misleading to suggest as many do that collective security preserves the peace better than alternative arrangements, that multilateralism can stop the violence in Syria with certainty, or prevent Iran from developing nuclear weapons.

and has continued apace pushing transpacific (TPP)[5] and transatlantic partnerships.[6]

None of these organizations is inherently detrimental, but all eventually had two adverse politocratic consequences. First, they enlarged the scale of big government by committing vast sums to foreign projects and international institutions. Second, they began a process of transferring *de jure* constitutional sovereignty from the American people to multinational entities, allowing politicians greater latitude in horse trading for their private benefit. The influence of multinational authorities in the United States' domestic and foreign policy moreover was strengthened by foreign stakeholder claims (globalist entitlements). Many people across the globe and their governments contend that U.S. elections are too important to be left to Americans. The United States as they see it is morally and legally obligated to transfer its treasure to them and heed their stakeholder demands, a view partly supported by the jurisdictional overreaching of international tribunals.

Big social advocacy, big business, and a multitude of politicians energetically promote these tendencies. New institutions are continually being created, but national well-being would be far greater if their activities were

---

[5] Vikram Nehru, *Southeast Asia: Will Markets and Geography Trump the TPP?* Carnegie Endowment for International Peace, July 9, 2012:

Born to modest parents (Singapore, Chile, and New Zealand) in 2002, the TPP has grown to include eleven countries, of which two (Mexico and Canada) were just invited to join at the mid-June G20 meeting in Los Cabos, Mexico. Japan and Korea are also considering participation – and if they do join, the TPP countries together would account for 40 percent of global GDP and 28 percent of world trade. The hope is that the TPP will eventually expand to include all members of the Asia-Pacific Economic Cooperation and become the Free Trade Agreement of the Asia Pacific. What makes the TPP unusual is its ambitious scope. It aims to confront barriers to trade and investment that operate at – and behind – national borders, not just by tackling tariff, non-tariff, and technical barriers but also by addressing intellectual property rights, the policy environment for state enterprises, investor-state dispute settlement arrangements, labor rights, and environmental protection, to name a few. The only trade agreement of such scope is the one recently concluded by South Korea and the United States, which, no doubt, serves as an important reference point for the TPP negotiators. The TPP is expected to cover over twenty trade- and investment-related topics. While much progress has been made in some of these areas, virtually all the difficult issues remain unresolved. The thirteenth round of discussions started on July 2 in San Diego, and the general consensus is that the spring of 2013 is the earliest an agreement could be reached – not the end of 2012, the deadline set by TPP leaders. China is conspicuous by its absence in the TPP. True, the TPP's open architecture allows entry of any country willing to sign up to its high standards, and it is possible that at some point China may do so. But that is unlikely to be soon.

[6] *Toward a Euro-Atlantic Security Community*, Carnegie Endowment for International Peace, Euro-Atlantic Security, Euro-Atlantic Security Initiative EASI Final Report, February 2012.

curtailed and well established multinational organization like the United Nations and NATO were rolled back.

Multinationalism of course is not the root of all evil, nor is it the principal danger confronting U.S. foreign policy, but it is a serious source of domestic resource misallocation and dangerous foreign entanglements, and it forms a bridge to more complex schemes afoot aimed at diluting the United States' sovereign powers.

SUPRANATIONALITY

Many voices today consider multinational sovereignty sharing to be a good first step, but no more. They advocate the formation of multinational coalitions that explicitly transfer important aspects of national political, defense, judicial, and economic sovereignty to higher entities with governing boards appointed and /or elected by community members. The new communities are interchangeably called transnational or supranational communities or unions. Advocates, idealists, and politocrats alike contend that supranational governments are better than traditional national regimes, including unitary federations like the United States, and provide viable pathways to harmonious world government. The vision has struck a responsive chord across the globe resulting in a profusion of supranational initiatives that have enabled America's politocrats to successfully extend their foreign reach by enlarging the scale and scope of Washington's international operations.

The European Union was and remains the poster child for supranationalists and U.S. politocrats pursuing their private internationalist agendas. [7]

---

[7] Nation states before World War II never voluntarily surrendered their control over fiscal and monetary policy as part of a package to achieve political goals, even though they participated in international institutions like the League of Nations. The horrors of WWII, combined with Cold War politics and the welfare state tide, however, propelled Europe along a novel supranational trajectory with unintended consequences. On September 19, 1946 Winston Churchill gave a speech in Zurich not only advocating Franco-German *rapproachement*, but a kind of United States of Europe, called a European "Third Way." He also advocated a "Council of Europe," formed soon thereafter with the assistance of French Foreign Minister Robert Schuman, mandated to create supranational communities on the path to a fully democratic, integrated Union. The Schuman Declaration on May 9, 1950 reaffirmed the concept in conjunction with the formation of the European Coal and Steel Community (ESCS). It proclaimed the community as the world's first supranational institution, marking the "birth of modern Europe," and initiating an epoch where intra-European wars were impossible. The Soviet Bloc formed a rival economic community, the CMEA (Council for Mutual Economic Cooperation) in 1949, but Comecon, as it is sometimes called, was more like the OECD (Organization for Economic Cooperation and Development), rather than a supranational economic governance mechanism superior to national authorities. Schuman's utopian vision, which can be traced back to

However, the EU experiment has recently fallen on hard times, providing insight into the vulnerabilities of supranational organizations,[8] and a clinic on the dangers of politarchically motivated foreign entanglements.

EUROPEAN UNION

The EU was designed to be the showcase for supranational theory,[9] and behind lace curtains it served as a proving ground for transnational politocracy. It is a federation of twenty-seven independent West, Central, and East European states (with ambitions in Eurasia and the Islamic Mediterranean region) that retains many sovereign powers,[10] but cedes others to the

France's first socialist, Claude Henri de Rouvroy, the comte de Saint-Simon (1760–1825) [*On the Reorganization of European Industry*, 1814], was the prelude to a succession of developments culminating in today's European Union including the European Economic Community (EEC), known as the Common Market (1958), the European Community (1967) [together with the European Commission and the European Council of Ministers], the single market act (1986), the European Council (1974), the European Monetary System (1979), the European Parliament (1979), the Schengen Agreement (1985), the Single Market Act (1986), the Maastricht Treaty (1993), which founded the European Union (EU), and the European Monetary Union (2002), which inaugurated the euro.

[8] Steven Rosefielde and Assaf Razin, "PIIGS," in Steven Rosefielde, Masaaki Kuboniwa, and Satoshi Mizobata, eds., *Prevention and Crisis Management: Lessons for Asia from the 2008 Crisis*, Singapore: World Scientific 2012. Rosefielde and Razin, "What Really Ails the Eurozone?: Faulty Supranational Architecture," *Contemporary Economics*, Vol. 6, No. 4, December 2012, pp. 10–18. Rosefielde and Razin, "A Tale of a Politically-Failing Single-Currency Area," *Israel Economic Review*, Vol. 10, No. 1, 2012, pp. 125–38.

[9] EU ideologists contend that the European Union was designed to promote "social" priorities among member states at the expense of individual economic rights. These priorities include: the scale and character of public programs, tax transfers, regulation, the rule of contract law, civic and worker participation, economic, civic and public liberty, income and wealth distribution, and the propensity to deficit spend.

[10] The EU has twenty-seven members: Germany, France, Britain, Italy, Denmark, Netherlands, Belgium, Luxembourg, Ireland, Greece, Spain, Portugal, Austria, Sweden, Finland, Estonia, Latvia, Lithuania, Poland, Czech Republic, Hungary, Romania, Bulgaria, Slovakia, Slovenia, Cyprus, and Malta. Croatia, Macedonia, Iceland, Montenegro, and Turkey are official candidate members. It is an "organization" supervising more than 500 million people, rather than a supranational sovereign government because it lacks power to adequately tax, transfer, and compel member compliance. The key treaties governing the European common space are the Paris Treaty of 1952, the Rome Treaty of 1958, the Maastricht Treaty of 1993, and the Lisbon Treaty of 2009. The EU's political headquarters are located in Brussels, Luxembourg, and Strasbourg. Each EU country controls its own legislation (parliament), fiscal policy and programs, courts, internal security and defense. Some members – Great Britain, Sweden, Denmark, and Norway – determine their own monetary policy (independent currencies), while others, like Germany, France, and Italy, have delegated this responsibility to the European Central Bank which governs the euro. The EU government has seven institutions. The European Parliament, the Council of the European Union, the European Commission, and the European Council (made up

European Union Council. Members who chose to join the eurozone after the adoption of the Maastricht Treaty in 1993 agreed to abandon their own currencies for a common unit (the euro),[11] and ipso facto surrendered their independent control over monetary and foreign exchange-rate policy, which saves intraregional foreign-exchange transaction costs and is thus needed for efficient macroeconomic regulation.[12] They did so purportedly in the inclusionist spirit of the EU's founders Jean Monnet and Robert Schuman[13] but also acted as politocrats seeking to kill four birds with one

of the president of the European Council, the president of the European Commission, and one representative per member state, either its head of state, or head of government), the European Central Bank, the Court of Justice of the European Union, and the European Court of Auditors guides the EU. It is the supreme political authority, negotiating treaty changes and defining union policies and strategies. It convenes at least four times a year. Both the European Parliament and the Council of the European Union have legislative oversight and amendment responsibilities. The European Commission is the EU executive arm, assisted by the European Council. The interpretation and application of EU law and treaties is the responsibility of the Court of Justice of the European Union. The Common Foreign and Security Policy Committee discusses and coordinates external relations.

[11] The eurozone is a subcomponent of the twenty-seven member EU. It contains seventeen member states: Austria, Belgium, Cyprus, Estonia, Finland, France, Germany, Greece, Ireland, Italy, Luxembourg, Malta, Netherlands, Portugal, Slovakia, Slovenia, and Spain with a combined population of 330 million people.

[12] The four main practical accomplishments of the EU, beyond cultivating a common identity intended to forestall another intra-European and world war are (1) the formation of the European Common Market in 1957 (renamed the European Economic Community or EEC in 1993) to promote intraregional trade by eliminating tariff and quota barriers; (2) the European Council's decision to permit unimpeded tourist travel within the common space for EU citizens and foreigners (Schengen Agreement, 1985), although work permits remain strictly controlled, hampering labor mobility; (3) the transunion standardization of product characteristics, labor, business, and human rights regulations promoting liberalization and competitiveness (mostly under the aegis of the European Commission); and (4) the creation of the euro to facilitate pan-union business and travel, and earn international seigniorage.

[13] Jean Omer Marie Gabriel Monnet (1888–1979) was a French political economist and diplomat. He is regarded by many as a chief architect of European Unity and is regarded as one of its founding fathers. Never elected to public office, Monnet worked behind the scenes of U.S. and European governments as a well connected pragmatic internationalist. As the head of France's General Planning Commission, Monnet was the real author of what has become known as the 1950 Schuman Plan to create the European Coal and Steel Community (ECSC), forerunner of the Common Market. In 1955, Monnet founded the Action Committee for the United States of Europe in order to revive European construction following the failure of the European Defense Community (EDC). It brought political parties and European trade unions together to become a driving force behind the initiatives which laid the foundation for the European Union as it eventually emerged: first the European Economic Community (EEC, 1958, widely known as the "Common Market"), which was established by the Treaty of Rome of 1957; later the European Community (1967) with its corresponding bodies, the European Commission and the European Council of Ministers, British membership in the Community (1973), the European

stone by expanding opportunities for trafficking in public services, deepening supranationality, stimulating catch-up among low per-capita income members and spurring collective EEC economic growth with implicit creditworthiness guarantees. Foreign direct investors from within the EU and others around the globe sensed an investment bonanza in the eurozone's low productivity economies (Portugal, Ireland, Italy, Greece, and Spain (PIIGS, or the now more politically correct GIIPS) due to implicit credit guarantees from Germany and France after the Maastricht Treaty came into force. These investors began speculatively outsourcing there, triggering an artificial upsurge analogous to America's subprime mortgage bubble (see Chapter 8).

The EU's bubble caused labor and other factor costs to soar without corresponding productivity gains vis-à-vis other member states, particularly Germany, discouraging further outsourcing, and making it extraordinarily difficult for the PIIGS to cope with deficient postcrisis aggregate effective demand.[14] Portugal, Ireland, Italy, Greece, Spain, and now Cyprus cannot rely on the ECB (European Central Bank) to work efficiently as a lender of last recourse to their floundering commercial banks or to purchase their sovereign debt. Other burden-sharing schemes continue to be vetted, as yet to no avail. The only residual instrument available to PIIGS and Cyprus is fiscal

---

Council (1974), the European Monetary System (1979), and the European Parliament (1979). Robert Schuman (June 29, 1886–September 4, 1963) was a noted Luxembourg-born French statesman. Schuman was a Christian Democrat (M.R.P.) and an independent political thinker and activist. Two-time prime minister of France, a reformist minister of finance, and a foreign minister, he was instrumental in building postwar European and transatlantic institutions and is regarded as one of the founders of the European Union, the Council of Europe, and NATO. On May 9, 1950, his principles of supranational democracy were announced in what has become known as the Schuman Declaration. The text was jointly prepared by Paul Reuter, the legal adviser at the Foreign Ministry, his chef-de Cabinet, Bernard Clappier and Jean Monnet, and two of his team, Pierre Uri and Etienne Hirsch. The French government agreed to the Schuman Declaration, which invited the Germans and all other European countries to manage their coal and steel industries jointly and democratically in Europe's first supranational community with its five foundational institutions. On April 18, 1951 six founder members signed the Treaty of Paris, which formed the basis of the European Coal and Steel Community. They declared this date and the corresponding democratic, supranational principles to be the "real foundation of Europe." Three communities have been created so far. The Treaties of Rome in 1957 created the economic community and the nuclear nonproliferation community, Euratom. Together with intergovernmental machinery of later treaties, these eventually evolved into the European Union. The Schuman Declaration was made on May 9, 1950, and to this day May 9 is designated Europe Day.

[14] PIIGS is an acronym for Portugal, Ireland, Italy, Greece, and Spain. They are the European Union members with the largest debt-to-GDP ratios. Cyprus's debt to GDP ratio is 81, which puts it in the same category as the PIIGS.

policy, but decades of excess public spending have placed tight constraints on further debt accumulation, forcing them to shoulder the quadruple burdens of high debt service, depression, mass unemployment, and vanishing social services. PIIGS and Cyprus cannot depend on yet-to-be-developed EU financial institutions, yet-to-be-implemented ECB expanded credit lines, or government-facilitated debt restructuring. Generous EU government financial credits might have mitigated the sovereign-debt problem if they had been provided in a timely manner with appropriate conditionality. High unemployment likewise could have been ameliorated by stronger EU labor mobility,[15] but none of these options were implemented. The euro is impoverishing the PIIGS and Cyrpus sparking widespread rioting, and the politarchs do not care enough to do anything fundamental about it.

The EU's ongoing sovereign-debt crisis, central to any assessment of Europe's malfunctioning supranational social democracy, thus is more than a matter of faulty policy, or easily rectified organizational misdesign. EU Saint Simonians and those inspired by the vision campaigned for federation as a stepping stone to one-world social democracy and tried to construct it through piecemeal negotiation, but thanks to politocratic hijacking (politarchs' venal preference for the eurozone as it is currently structured) wound up with a dysfunctional mechanism resistant to consensus reform. Once upon a time, when Europeans were misled into believing that union vouchsafed perpetual prosperity, it was relatively easy for people to invest in the dream, but Eurosclerosis and the sovereign-debt crisis have revealed that while there always are free riders, there are no free lunches for the people.[16]

---

[15] Free movement of labor is one of the four basic freedoms enshrined in the Acquis Communautaire, and EU leaders frequently reiterate their adherence to the principle. However, a task force headed by Walter Nonneman found that despite good intentions, substantial and perhaps increasing barriers to labor mobility remain. There is "pronounced immobility of the European workforce that despite high unemployment in the local area is disinclined to resettle in areas with more job opportunities. Less than 0.5 percent of European workers move to a different region every year. This is very little, compared, for example, with the 2.5 percent of Americans who take up residence in a different state every year." Nonneman identifies a host of institutional factors that contribute to this outcome. See Walter Nonneman, *European Immigration and the Labor Market*, The Transatlantic Task Force on Immigration and Integration, Migration Policy Institute, Bertelsmann Stiftung, July 2007, available from http://www.migrationinformation.org/transatlantic2006/ImmigrationEULaborMarket_72507.pdfCf. "Class of 2012: EU Labor Market Largely Immobile as Young Find Themselves Trapped by Language," Associate Press, December 5, 2012.

[16] "German Faith in Euro and EU Lags Behind French: Poll," Yahoo! Finance, September 17, 2012: "Almost two thirds of Germans think their country would be better off without

Politocratic sacrifices for expected gain are one thing; for expected losses something entirely different. It will take a Herculean effort for the EU to extricate itself from this morass. EU leaders are going to be reluctant to confront the organization's flawed design, eradicate dysfunctional dependences, and slenderize government programs and regulation. The Soviet Union's demise proved that planned socialism (where private property, business, and entrepreneurship are criminalized) failed the competitive systems test. It seems that the EU now is on a path to demonstrate that politocratically co-opted social democracy is similarly inferior.[17]

This is not what Schuman expected. He expressed confidence that communitarians would be considerate, fair, self-restrained, and altruistic or could be tutored to act responsibly, but this proved to be the triumph of hope over

the euro, according to a poll published on Monday which highlighted growing unease in Europe's largest economy about the costs of the euro crisis."

[17] The saga has daily twists and turns, some of which seem desperate. Seventeen members agreed to negotiate a side agreement circumventing the EU constitution to bolster fiscal discipline, but in doing so are making a mockery of the constitution and exposing leaders' antidemocratic expediency. See Michael Greve. "New Eurozone 'Fiscal Rule' Is Absurd and Illegal," *The American* (AEI), December 12, 2011:

As if to illustrate the depths to which it has sunk, the European Union picked December 8, the day of the Feast of the Immaculate Conception, to produce an agreement that is rotten to its core. Its proposed creation of "a new fiscal rule" – that is, "automatic" sanctions for eurozone countries that run up excessive deficits – is both absurd and manifestly illegal. Prohibitions against debts exceeding 3 percent of GDP were introduced along with the euro. They are to be enforced by the European Council. Because that body consists of member states' leaders, the injunctions have been routinely ignored and no sanctions have ever been imposed. Thus, the Brussels agreement shifts enforcement authority to the European Commission and the European Court of Justice unless a qualified majority of the Council intervenes. Message to Athens, Rome, Paris, and Berlin: if you can't balance your budget, the justices in Luxembourg will fine you. Good luck with that. The enforcement mechanisms at issue are contained in the Maastricht and Lisbon Treaties, which can be amended only by unanimous consent of all EU members. Because in Brussels, Britain said "no," the eurozone states decided to adopt the reforms through an international agreement, to be signed by March 2012. That cannot be done, at least not lawfully. While the Treaties provide for a few limited derogations and side agreements among member states, wholesale treaty revisions are not among those exceptions. The Brussels communique's Eurospeak barely disguises the fact. The heads of state "consider" that their plan "should be contained in primary legislation." In English: they know that their plan must be enacted by treaty amendments – they just chose to do otherwise. Similarly, the eurozone states "recognize the jurisdiction of the Court of Justice to verify the transposition of [balanced budget requirements] at [the] national level." The operative verb should be "create," because there's nothing to "recognize": the Treaties specifically enjoin the ECJ from exercising this jurisdiction. The ECJ's budget oversight, should it ever enter into effect, will join the European Stability Mechanism, which was likewise stick-built outside and in contravention of the Treaties. This Monday, as the markets re-open and the sordid Brussels deal begins to disintegrate, is the Feast of the Virgin of Guadalupe. Europe needs all the divine assistance it can get.

experience. On one hand, the supranational deck was stacked in favor of over-borrowing by the PIIGS, East Europeans and Cyprus. On the other hand, the PIIGS misled themselves into prematurely surrendering control over their monetary and foreign exchange-rate policy without receiving fiscal quid pro quos. As a result, the transnational EU finds itself in an ideological quandary, where the gap between rich and poor members is widening, at a time when supranational institutional arrangements are forcing the PIIGS to extricate themselves from their predicament with painful and problematic deflationary tactics necessary to regain their competitive strength.

The contradictory EU mandate to bring ever more relatively poor countries into the fold, bolstering their creditworthiness with implicit guarantees, pressuring them to adopt the euro, and straitjacketing their fiscal options while undermining fiscal discipline with sympathetic approval of entitlements and leveling has solutions within a nation-state framework (a true democratic United States of Europe) that could be simulated by a supranational organization. However, this is difficult to accomplish because Schuman's communitarian optimism was misplaced. The EU has yet to find a supranational architecture that reconciles its politocratically hijacked idealism with optimal macroeconomic regulation, to say nothing about designing a viable world government.[18]

It is in this sense that the 2008 financial crisis's aftermath is more than a relatively simple matter of conventional macroeconomic management. It is partly a crisis of politocracy and supranationality, and as such of overlooked elements in the half-century-long debate on optimal economic union and communities. The supranational aspect is the logical consequence of ideologically infused politocracy. If the EU does eventually go the way of the CMEA over the PIIGS and Cyprus sovereign-debt crisis, it won't be because economists failed to grasp the theory of unions and communities,[19] but because the European Union, like the United States, does not operate on the rules of true democracy.[20]

---

[18] The supranational entitlement and moral-hazard problem mirrors domestic disorders often said to cause Eurosclerosis, but is potentially more pernicious because governments can borrow more than individuals.

[19] See Razin, Assaf and Rosefielde, Steven . "PIIGS," in Steven Rosefielde, Masaaki Kuboniwa and Satoshi Mizobata, eds., *Prevention and Crisis Management: Lessons for Asia from the 2008 Crisis*, Singapore: World Scientific, 2012.

[20] Even the Schengen accord that permits border-free travel inside the EU is under assault from French Prime Minister Nicolas Sarkozy, who wants to curb illegal migration. Angelique Chrisafis, "Nicolas Sarkozy Courts Rightwing Voters with Schengen Zone Threat," *The Guardian*, March 11, 2012.

WORLD GOVERNMENT

Politarchs across the globe are not ready to abandon supranationality, hoping that the benefits of their bigger and bigger transnational trafficking in public services won't be outweighed by economic sclerosis, sovereign-debt crises, and other related financial disasters. They can be expected to persevere both in their economic and foreign-policy missions,[21] despite significant disaffection, causing ever-increasing harm because EU leaders refuse to allow the people's welfare to constrain their zealotry and avarice. The same fate awaits the United States as it slips ever closer to the supranational abyss.

Most contemporary politarchic advocates of supranationality harbor even greater ambitions for world government. They fulsomely claim that planet-wide government of all the people, by and for them is better than nationally based true democracy and believe that any costs of getting there from here will be dwarfed by future benefits. This party line explains why politarchs embrace global warming – because any solution to it seems to call for supranational institutions.

True democracy requires that the people not be separated by huge distances from the seat of their government, but world-governance advocates belittle the danger. They also are insensitive to the dysfunctional effects of culture clashes among contending groups trying to shape the interpretation of minority rights and entitlements. Idealist world government supporters likewise hold a jaundiced attitude toward national social contracts and are oblivious to the danger of politocratic and authoritarian capture. They espouse universal human goodness and harmonism (the unfounded conviction that everyone must inevitably live together in perfect harmony), and

---

[21] Britain and Denmark have bolstered their resolves to avoid eurozone entanglements and have been wary of side agreements that rewrite the EU Constitution. The Czech Republic has postponed joining the eurozone, and the foreign-policy mandates that emerged from the Lisbon Treaty are in disarray. See Stefan Lehne, "How to Strengthen the European External Action Service," Carnegie Foundation, December 16, 2011:

The European Union is currently going through one of the most difficult periods of its existence. While the focus is on the efforts to save the euro, its foreign-policy arm, the European External Action Service (EEAS), is struggling as well. Originally conceived in a more optimistic era, the foreign-policy reforms of the Treaty of Lisbon are being implemented against this backdrop of crisis and loss of confidence. Roughly one year after its establishment, the EEAS still suffers from a number of design flaws. It has an insufficient resource base and there is a lack of genuine buy-in on the parts of both the member states and the European Commission.

if these premises fail, they place their faith in the virtue and competence of elected officials.[22]

World government's intellectual pedigree is mixed and often woolly headed. Enlightenment thinkers before the nineteenth century preoccupied themselves with elaborating the principles of national republican democracy,[23] avoiding utopian distractions. Nonetheless, a few thinkers reflected on natural international law and the universal moral principles essential for obviating war. Hugo Grotius's treatise on the international status of war in *De jure belli ac pacis (On the Law of War and Peace)*, regarded today as the foundation of modern international law, made a case for the idea that there were some transnational commons, like the seas, that are amenable to international governance based on the verities of natural law.[24] His theorizing created a presumption for the possibility of a universal standard of just international governance. Immanuel Kant, more than a century-and-a-half later, introduced the concept of world citizenship in *Zum ewigen Frieden: Ein philosophischer Entwurf (Perpetual Peace: A Philosophical*

---

[22] Critics have long alleged that advocates of world government have hidden authoritarian (e.g., Soviet communist) agendas. This chapter assumes that they are either sincere or support politarchic as distinct from open or conspiratorial authoritarian orders. Politocratic control is softer than Soviet or Nazi authoritarianism. Large literatures exist on authoritarian world governance, including computopia (perfect planning), totalitarianism, and conspiratorial authoritarianism. Some world government advocates dismiss critics as paranoid and cranks. In many cases, when conspiracies are alleged their diagnosis is correct, but this does not establish the feasibility of Enlightenment democratic world government, or the merit of global, authoritarian computopia. Critics emphasizing the conspiratorial dimension of world government or Wilsonian New World Order advocacy include H. G. Wells (*Open Conspiracy*, 1928; *The New World Order*, 1940), some opponents of the international communist movement, some opponents of the Council on Foreign Relations and the Trilateral Commission (Pat Robertson, *The New World Order*), and the authors of the Protocols of the Elders of Zion, written in 1903 and claiming the existence of a Jewish-Masonic cabal to achieve world domination. The latter was probably a disinformation operation by the tsarist Okhrana (secret police). Some "New Age" advocates contend that flower power themes have been conspiratorially usurped for Machiavellian ends.

[23] Immanuel Kant stressed the importance of a federation of independent republican states, each with its own constitution. See Immanuel Kant, *Zum ewigen Frieden: Ein philosophischer Entwurf (Perpetual Peace: A Philosophical Sketch)*.

[24] Hugo Grotius, *De jure belli ac pacis (On the Law of War and Peace)*, 1625. Grotius, a jurist in the Dutch Republic, advanced a system of principles of natural law, which are held to be binding on all people and nations regardless of local custom. He argued that war was justifiable in some cases involving self-defense, reparation of injury and punishment, and investigated "legitimate rules of conduct." The arguments constitute a theory of just war, including justice in resorting to war, and in its conduct.

Sketch), [25] but the possibility of abolishing nations and substituting comprehensive democratic world governance was not broached until the beginning of the nineteenth century, when numerous thinkers began pondering whether society should take precedence over the *demos*, nationally and across the planet. Saint-Simon expressed the view and Karl Krause elaborated it in *The Archetype of Humanity*,[26] where he championed the amalgamation of five regional federations (Europe, Asia, Africa, America, and Australia) into a world republic. Karl Marx, other socialists, and various pacifists after the First World War carried the torch without burdening themselves with particulars.[27] The sentiment became intertwined with notions of the universal rights of humankind,[28] women's liberation, antiimperialism, and strong government that kept capitalism on a short leash. It was encouraged by the founding of the League of Nations, the United Nations, the proliferation of globalist institutions like the IMF, and the emergence of supranationalism, particularly the European Union, while the universal rationalist style of utopian theorizing that dominated postwar social science created an aura of plausibility.

This habit of reasoning is naïve. If everyone were rational, moral, and wise with a shared concept of the good, and democratic world government were deemed best, why has humanity dithered and historical dialectic faltered? Is it because, rationality, morality, wisdom, and concepts of the good are relative and therefore do not support a consensus-based, planet-wide social contract? Is it because politarchic national potentates have proven stronger than the forces of history? These questions have two broad answers: one accepting the assumption that people everywhere are rational, moral, and wise; the other assuming that they are not clever enough to outwit authoritarians and their elected enemies.

---

[25] Kant believed that institutions could be devised that deterred nations from scheming against one another, thereby ensuring perpetual peace. His book was published in 1785.

[26] Karl Krause, *The Archetype of Humanity*, 1811. Echos of this sort of universalist humanitarians can be found in Karl Jung's psychological archetypes and in various religious doctrines. See Karl Jung, *The Structure of Pysche, Collected Works*, Vol. 8, 1927.

[27] The nationalist phenomenon arose gradually after the American and French revolutions becoming a dominate force in shaping political control. Nationalist sentiment played an important role in mobilizing citizens to fight in the First World War, and was blamed for the carnage by pacifists after 1918 under the slogan "Never Again!" They preached internationalism during the interwar period and continued the struggle after the Second World War, arguing that if there were no nations, then there couldn't be wars among them.

[28] Wendell Wilkie and Emery Reves pressed a world federalist vision. See Wendell Wilkie, *One World* (1943) and Emery Reves, *The Anatomy of Peace* (1945).

In the first instance, world government may be thwarted even though people are rational, moral, and wise because citizens disagree about constitutional content and the meanings of rights and entitlements.[29] Bigness is important here because it compounds the problem by implausibly requiring people from disparate, often hostile cultures to negotiate a democratic constitution that vouchsafes minority rights sufficiently to eliminate micro and macroeconomic disorders. The more some limit the freedom of others, the greater the anticompetitive loss, and the higher the risks of macroeconomic malfunction and social injustice. Achieving a true democratic world government consensus in relatively homogeneous cultures is difficult, and almost inconceivable as a practical matter in the world we inhabit. People residing in national democracies accordingly are justifiably apprehensive. They prefer a bird in the hand that preserves their assets, economic, religious, social, and political rights to two chimerical birds in the bush, and it follows directly that assumptions of rationality, morality, and wisdom, even if valid, do not make ideal world governance ineluctable.

If one already lives in a well-functioning national democracy, what possible grounds exist for supposing that a worldwide variant would be sufficiently better to justify the high risk of something far worse?

This deduction holds doubly if the assumption that all nations are true democracies is dropped, acknowledging as one must that most countries today are governed by authoritarians, oligarchs, and politocrats. World government under these conditions is tantamount to making the *demos* even more vulnerable than it already is to the machinations of predators. It can be counterargued that the process of building true democratic world government will eradicate politocrats, authoritarians, and oligarchs, but this is wishful thinking. When and if the nations of the world become true democracies, there will be ample time to experiment with supranationality and ultimately world government. The woes besetting the contemporary West haven't arisen because government is too small. They have arisen because politocratic governments are too big, and leaders are intent upon making them bigger.[30] There is no popular ground swell for

---

[29] Many Western intellectuals find it rational, wise, and morally imperative to rationalize Stalin's mass murders as "necessary." See Alec Nove, *Was Stalin Really Necessary?* Routledge: London, 1964 and Paul Gregory, "Was Stalin Really Necessary?" paper presented to the International Conference on Stalinism, Moscow, December 5, 2008. Cf. Steven Rosefielde, *Red Holocaust*, New York: Routledge, 2010; Athanasius D. McVay and Lubomyr Y. Luciuk, eds., *The Holy See and the Holodomor*, Toronto: Kastan Press, 2011.

[30] G. John Ikenberry, "The Rise of China and the Future of the West," *Foreign Affairs*, Vol. 87, No. 1, January–February 2008, pp. 23–37; Ikenberry, *Liberal Leviathan: The*

world government; only special interests seeking opportunities through enlargement.[31]

Foreign policies built on the premise that multilateralism, supranationality, and world government are panaceas are delusionary. They harm ordinary citizens in the United States and the European Union, serving true democracy's enemies, including some big social advocates who believe that the West is morally obliged to finance and subject itself to the majority rule of former third-world colonial people.[32] America's globalist project (multilateralism, supranationalism, and world government) has no redeeming value. National security, prosperity, and economic stability all can be enhanced by paring the State Department's declaratory mission and cutting spending to the bone. [33]

Origins, Crisis, and Transformation of the American System, Princeton, NJ: Princeton University Press, 2011; Richard Rosecrance, "Bigger is Better: The Case for a Transatlantic Economic Union," *Foreign Affairs*, Vol. 89, No. 3, May 2010, pp. 42–50; Charles Kupchan, "NATO'S Final Frontier: Why Russia Should Join the Atlantic Alliance," *Foreign Affairs*, Vol. 89, No. 3, May 2010, pp. 100–12; Ken Morita and Yun Chen, "Toward an East Asian Economic Community," in Steven Rosefielde, Masaaki Kuboniwa, and Satoshi Mizobata, eds., *Prevention and Crisis Management: Lessons for Asia from the 2008 Crisis*, Singapore: World Scientific Publishers, 2012.

[31] For a survey of contemporary scholarly world-governance advocacy rooted in legal and international relations communities, see John Fonte, "Sovereignty or Submission: Liberal Democracy or Global Governance?" http://www.fpri.org/enotes/2011/201110.fonte.sovereignty.html; T. Harold Koh, "Why Transnational Law Matters," *Penn State International Law Review* Vol. 24, 2006, p. 745; Anne-Marie Slaughter, "The Real New World Order," *Foreign Affairs*, September/October 1997, pp. 184–87; Robert Cooper, *The Breaking of Nations: Order and Chaos in the Twenty-First Century*, New York: Atlantic Monthly Press, 2003; Linda K. Kerber, "The Meanings of Citizenship," *Journal of American History*, Vol. 84, No. 3, December 1997, pp. 833–54; John Fonte, *Sovereignty or Submission: Will Americans Rule Themselves or be Ruled by Others?*, New York: Encounter Books, 2011.

[32] The claim is twofold. First, "democracy" is universal, requiring global one-person, one-vote rule. The national principle from this perspective is inherently antidemocratic. Second, the West owes the East reparations for its nineteenth- and twentieth-century imperialism. The claim disregards minority-rights protections and the intrinsically local characters of legitimate social contracts.

[33] Cf. Dani Rodrik, *The Globalization Paradox: Democracy and the Future of the World Economy*, New York and London: W. W. Norton, 2011.

PART III

DEMOCRATIC RETREAT AND REVIVAL

ELEVEN

Global Retreat

DOUBLE JEOPARDY

The United States' foreign policy is harmful to U.S. workers, the middle class, and the cause of universal true democracy. The benefits are slight relative to the costs, and the ratio is likely to deteriorate as Washington's bargaining power diminishes with its waning global stature. The planet is becoming increasingly multipolar as large countries like China, India, and Brazil rapidly modernize and the United States loses leverage in key international institutions like the United Nations, the International Monetary Fund, the World Bank, and the World Trade Organization. Many claim to welcome these changes[1] and we would agree if advancing nations like China were not authoritarian and protectionist. Bad as things are, they could get worse.

It is premature to write the United States' obituary as a great power and perform funeral rites for true democracy and those beleaguered by politocracy, but a sketch of the dominant trend is sobering. The United States and true democracy are falling on hard times.[2]

RECONFIGURATION OF GLOBAL WEALTH AND POWER

The diminishing effectiveness of U.S. economic and foreign policy over the course of the last decade echoes the pattern between the First and Second World Wars. The analogy is partial for various reasons. The lingering effects of the 2008 depression have been comparatively mild judged by the standard

---

[1] Ivan Tselichtchev, *China versus the West: The Global Power Shift of the 21st Century*, Singapore: John Wiley & Sons, 2012. World Bank, *China 2030: Building a Modern, Harmonious, and Creative High-Income Society*, 2012.

[2] Cf. Francis Fukuyama, *The End of History and the Last Man*, New York: Free Press, 1992.

of the 1930s,[3] and potential foreign adversaries today are less belligerent than they were eight decades ago. Perhaps it would be best to ride out the storm without seeking fundamental governmental change, erroneously assuming balloting makes the United States immune to secular decay.[4]

This would be unwise. The politarchic cancer enfeebling the U.S. government domestically and throughout the globe suggests that there may not be a happy ending this time around. The United States may be not only economically and diplomatically eclipsed by emerging great powers but overburdened to boot by foreign entanglements.[5] The United States' foreign and defense policies are part of this destructive vortex. More is being spent for less, degrading the United States' ability to influence, deter, and self-protect. [6]

---

[3] See "Prechter: Market Is Reliving Late Stages of 1930's Depression," Yahoo! News, December 6, 2011: "Don't get too comfortable with the relatively flat markets of 2011, there's a big storm coming our way. This is the view of Robert Prechter. He compares the current phase of the market to the late stages of the 1929–1933 period in U.S. history; a time marked by extreme volatility eventually ending in tears."

[4] All great nations rise in their own individual manner; all decay in the same way. How do powers decay? The answer is that governments get captured for private gain and cease to contribute to public advance. Sometimes it happens very quickly, especially when the elite gets very wealthy very fast – Alexander's empire; Hitler's. Sometimes it happens more slowly – the USSR; even more slowly, the United States. Government capture is both a cause and a symptom of decay. Patriotism has eroded. Political participation among the masses declines because the politarchy controls all. Leadership collapses in quality because private interests do not want strong leadership. In this formulation, politarchy is a general phenomenon (historically, globally), though it takes different specific forms in each era and country.

[5] Aaron Task, "As D.C. Deliberates Europe's Impact, Goldman Warns of Big Risks to U.S.," Yahoo Daily Ticker, December 15, 2011:

According to Goldman Sachs, further upheaval in the eurozone could cut as much as 1 percent from the U.S. GDP in 2012. A separate but related factor: Goldman estimates U.S. banks are exposed to $1.8 trillion of counterparty risk from European banks, which is equal to 3.3% of all U.S. debt outstanding. In a related but separate development, the OECD this week warned of a potential... funding crisis in 2012 for developed countries, where borrowing is expected to exceed $10.5 trillion next year. Much of that borrowing is to refinance or rollover outstanding debt, a normally smooth process that could very much become difficult if the European banking system goes into cardiac arrest. As we saw in 2008 with subprime and this year with Greece, the idea that a crisis in Europe could be "contained" is very much wishful – and foolish – thinking."

[6] Marie B. Hecht, *John Quincy Adams*, New York: The Macmillan Company, 1972, pp. 330–31. Speaking on the 4th of July in 1821 President John Quincy Adams addressed the dilemma of American interventionism: "America would involve herself... in all the wars of interest and intrigue, of individual avarice, envy and ambition which assume the colors... of freedom. The fundamental maxims of our policy would insensibly change from liberty to force." This is almost exactly what has happened. By attempting to intervene with force to promote liberty, we have instead become a dominate sponsor of force in the world. It was Adams's great insight that conflicts over interest and intrigue, avarice, envy, and ambition can and will be portrayed as in pursuit of liberty, to entice our intervention.

The die is cast, providing rivals with a golden opportunity to overtake and surpass the United States in all important dimensions: wealth, living standards, well-being, and power, and in the process more effectively press their interests to the United States' detriment under the guise of multinationalism, supranationalism, and world government. Will newcomers seize the day, compounding the United States' woes?

Systems and development theory suggest that the answer will be yes. It won't happen tomorrow, nor by 2020, but as these things go, if the United States' ship of state is not righted, it will happen soon. While a persuasive scientific case can be made for the economic superiority of true democratic free enterprise, the same arguments do not apply to degenerate elected regimes. Politocracy affords rivals ample scope for dominating America in specific areas, and perhaps across the board.

A close examination of contenders reveals that the reconfiguration of global wealth and power looming on the horizon does not necessitate Armageddon and is compatible with a continual improvement in global living standards. There is little immediate prospect of nuclear war among great powers (the United States, the European Union, Russia, China, and India), and technological diffusion should continue to increase planetary GDP. This good news, however, is tempered by several profound negatives. First, China and other rising stars remain wedded to authoritarian values, so that divine intervention aside, the post-U.S. global order will depart even further from the true democratic ideal than it does now. Second, China and many others likely to improve their seeding in the global competition are inclined toward protectionism and the use of power to profit at the expense of others, instead of abiding by the rule of law. Third, this propensity raises the specter of deglobalization and intensified world macroeconomic turmoil, compounding crises generated in the West. Fourth, the planetary race to control natural resources, including the arctic, will intensify.[7] Fifth, some upstarts are likely to be militarily belligerent in their neighborhoods, especially China.[8] Sixth, less developed nations will increasingly fall under non-Western spheres of influence because of democracy's tarnished guiding light.

The situation is complex. Leadership of the post-U.S. global order is apt to be bifurcated on economic and geopolitical grounds. On the economic

---

Intervening in these circumstances we become adherents not of liberty but of force and are made to seem fools for our naiveté.

[7] Stephen Blank, "The Chinese and Asian Impact on Russian Nuclear Policy," *Defense and Security Analysis* Vol. 28, No. 1, March 2012, pp. 36–54.

[8] Junko Ogura and Jethro Mullen, "Fallout widens from island dispute between China, Japan," CNN, September 17, 2012.

front, advanced nations with relatively honest and competitive elected governments should outstrip the United States' living standard. They will become the benchmark for second-best economic excellence.[9] A few advanced small powers like Taiwan and Singapore are poised to rapidly catch up with and overtake U.S. living standards based solely on their economic prowess, and some Western social democracies like Denmark are likely to surpass their transatlantic neighbor at a slower pace. [10]

In the international political arena, large developing nations such as China, India, and Brazil could become greater powers than the United States regionally and perhaps beyond, despite their systemic flaws. Russia's relative strength also could marginally improve.[11] There is no emerging hegemon, however, capable of becoming both an economic and geopolitical superpower in the foreseeable future as the United States was a quarter century ago. The West's economic paralysis and diminished military and political influence will have to be gauged by different national benchmarks.

ECONOMY

Picking tomorrow's economic frontrunners is never easy because performance is not governed solely by the economic and political systems of the different countries. Often, it is strongly affected by regional trends and global

---

[9] Less developed nations have catch-up possibilities that enable them to temporarily enjoy superior growth, but as the Japanese example demonstrates, these advantages of backwardness are ephemeral. The intrinsic merit of economic systems, adjusted for special factors, needs to be assessed with a better metric. There are many candidates. We employ per-capita income, as a proxy for living standard, even though it is merely a rule of thumb because the concept is easily understood and measured.

[10] Denmark's per-capita GDP exceeds Taiwan's slightly and is lower than Singapore's. The CIA is enthusiastic about Danish economic success:

This thoroughly modern market economy features a high-tech agricultural sector, state-of-the-art industry with world-leading firms in pharmaceuticals, maritime shipping and renewable energy, and a high dependence on foreign trade. Denmark is a member of the European Union (EU); Danish legislation and regulations conform to EU standards on almost all issues. Danes enjoy among the highest standards of living in the world and the Danish economy is characterized by extensive government welfare measures and an equitable distribution of income. (*CIA Factbook: Denmark*, December 2011).

[11] Russia's governance system and economy are worse than those of the United States. However, the nation's extreme economic backwardness provides room for modest catch-up. See Steven Rosefielde, "Economics of the Military-Industrial Complex," in Michael Alexeev and Shlomo Weber, *The Oxford Handbook of Russian Economy*, Oxford: Oxford University Press, 2013; Rosefielde, "Postcrisis Russia: Counting on Miracles in Uncertain Times," in Carolina Vendil Pallin and Bertil Nygren, eds., *Russian Defense Prospects*, New York: Macmillan, 2011; and Rosefielde, "The Impossibility of Russian Economic Reform: Waiting for Godot," US Army War College, Carlisle Barracks, 2012.

interdependencies. Nonetheless, Singapore and Taiwan provide suggestive examples illustrative of how Asia's Sino-subregion could become the globe's economic paragon. Living standards there already exceed the EU mean, and they are rapidly closing the gap with those of the United States.[12] The conventional expectation is for Sino-subregional per-capita income to converge toward, but not surpass the United States' because theorists assume that the United States is still an archetypal true democratic free-enterprise system, and Singapore and Taiwan are not. They are right about the Sino-subregion, but wrong about the United States, raising the possibility that after catching up, Singapore and Taiwan may set the new global standard despite conspicuous shortcomings. [13]

Taiwan's elected government is just beginning to find its footing, and Singapore is widely regarded as an authoritarian city-state (alpha city).[14] Civil liberties in the Sino-subregion are deficient. Also, Taiwan still retains elements of state ownership, together with insider-biased government economic management that impairs economic efficiency. Nonetheless, Taiwan and Singapore both possess compensating virtues that could leave U.S. politarchic living standards in the dust.

They prioritize self-reliance, entrepreneurship, and competitive individual wealth-seeking, especially in the export sector. They are competitively pro-productive, pro-business, pro-innovation, and technologically proficient, shunning policies and programs that impede private economic initiative and effort. Singapore's government may be the most market-friendly in the world and has a reputation for honesty.[15] Moreover, Singapore's and Taiwan's

---

[12] Estimated 2010 per-capita GDPs in the United States, Singapore, Taiwan, and the EU computed according to the purchasing power parity (PPP) methodology were respectively: 47.2, 62.1, 35.7 and 32.7 billion U.S. dollars (CIA *Factbooks* for the United States, Singapore, Taiwan, and the European Union. Singapore leads the pack, but not on an indigenous basis (roughly 54 percent of national income). When incomes accruing to foreign nationals are excluded, its living standard is on a par with Taiwan's, or roughly 75 percent of the U.S. benchmark. The outflows as in Singapore are to resident foreigners and resident foreign companies. They are included in GDP. See 2009, *Gross Domestic Product, Census and Statistics*, Department Hong Kong Special Administrative Region, February 2010, table A, p.153.

[13] Steven Rosefielde, *Asian Economic Systems*, Singapore: World Scientific Publishers, 2013.

[14] An alpha city is an important node in the global economic system. See Saskia Sassen, *The Global City: New York, London, Tokyo*, Princeton, NJ: Princeton University Press, 1991.

[15] "Singapore has a highly developed and successful free-market economy. It enjoys a remarkably open and corruption-free environment, stable prices, and a per capita GDP higher than that of most developed countries" (*CIA Factbook*, December 2011). Cf. http://www.transparency.org/policy_research/surveys_indices/cpi/2010/results "Corruption Perceptions Index 2010 Results," Transparency International, the Global Coalition against Corruption.

common-law judicial systems shelter businessmen from what otherwise would be a toxic rule of men, enabling them to partly offset efficiency losses from restricted civic freedom.

The net benefit of their governance strategy should fall far short of the true democratic ideal because the latter jointly optimizes civic and private rights. Nonetheless, the empowerment of free enterprise (subject to the social contract) at the expense of social justice should produce higher levels of per-capita income than the politarchic alternative, which stifles productivity, spawns crises, and feigns concern for national welfare. This is why the Sino-subregional strategy is apt to succeed in comparative terms, even though it falls far short of Western norms of social justice and democracy.[16]

HEGEMONY

These prospective accomplishments, however, cannot serve as a platform for international political and military superpower because Singapore and Taiwan are too small. Aspirants by default must come from the ranks of large nations that currently possess inferior economic systems. The primary candidates are the so-called BRIC group (Brazil, Russia, India, and China) of seemingly rapidly modernizing great regional powers, but all suffer serious handicaps. Their governments heavily manage their economies for insider gain, and their social stability is problematic. All have very low per-capita incomes, and the staying power of their growth is doubtful. Although Brazil's, India's, and China's recent economic performance have been impressive (albeit flagging),[17] even after correction for statistical irregularities, the benefits of relative economic backwardness are depleting, and their advances following Japanese precedent should eventually slow to a crawl. Russia's economic prospects are particularly dim. Contrary to media hype, there are no BRIC miracle economies, and there won't be even if they form an economic and political community with a BRIC bank as has been recently proposed.[18]

This does not mean that these countries are not regional powerhouses, only that they face an uphill battle displacing the United States and the European

---

[16] Singapore and Taiwan spend far less on social welfare as a share of their GDP than do the United States and the European Union. Confucian family and community obligations, however, pick up some of the slack.

[17] Samantha Azzarello and Blu Putnam, "BRIC Country Update: Slowing Growth in the Face of Internal and External Challenges," *CME, Market Insights*, July 29, 2012.

[18] C. Raja Mohan, "BRICS for a New Global Order" RSIS Commentaries, March 26, 2012.

Union as the globe's dominant economic and political forces. Brazil is the least likely to become a planetary hegemon because it is preoccupied with regional leadership, and Latin America is peripheral in the global scheme of things. Russia is a much better candidate because it possesses bountiful natural resources, is a nuclear superpower with strong conventional war-fighting capabilities, borders the European Union (Finland), Central Asia, China, and the arctic with easy access to other powerful states via the Baltic, Black and Caspian Seas, and the Pacific Ocean. The Kremlin additionally has spheres of influence throughout the former Soviet Republics, the former Comecon states, and parts of the Third World. Nonetheless, its commercial technologies are backward,[19] and its manufacturing capacities have not been integrated into the global network. Most important of all, Russia's economic system is dysfunctional, resistant to substantive reform, and cannot keep pace with its peers and the faltering West.[20] Russia's GDP and living standards are virtually the same today as they were in 1989 when Mikhail Gorbachev launched his destructive *perekhod* (market transition) campaign.[21] Under these circumstances, the Kremlin can bully weak states in its own neighborhood but cannot assume the mantle of world leader. It has become a weak sister in China's shadow.

This leaves India and China. Both have approximately a billion more people than the United States, including hundreds of millions of highly educated citizens.[22] They have vast territories with abundant resources

[19] Steven Rosefielde and Stefan Hedlund, *Russia since 1980: Wrestling with Westernization*, Cambridge: Cambridge University Press, 2008.

[20] Steven Rosefielde, "The Impossibility of Russian Economic Reform: Waiting for Godot," US Army War College, Carlisle Barracks, 2012. Rosefielde, "Russian Economic Reform 2012: "Déjà vu All Over Again," US Army War College, Carlisle Barracks, 2012.

[21] Steven Rosefielde, "After Soviet Communism: Authoritarian Economic Evolution in Russia and China," in Iikka Korhonen and Laura Solando, eds., *From Soviet Plans to Russian Reality*, WSOUpro, Helsinki, 2011, pp. 81–92.

[22] Sonia Luthra, "India's Economic Outlook: Implications and Trends: Interview with Nicholas Eberstadt," *National Bureau of Asian Research*, December 29, 2011: With about 1.2 billion people, India is the world's second most populous country and its largest democracy. Despite two decades of exceptionally rapid economic growth, material poverty is still widespread in India – the World Bank estimates that well over 50 percent of the country still lives on less than $2 a day. The U.S. Census Bureau and the UN Population Division (UNPD) offer broadly consistent pictures of India's population profile for the year 2030. Both the Census Bureau and the UNPD's medium variant projections envision India 2030 as a country with roughly 1.5 billion people. India will be about 40 percent urban, up from an estimated 30 percent today. China's current population is more than 1.3 billion, but India is on track to become the world's most populous country by 2025. Current projections envision that China will have entered into a long-term depopulation. China's working-age population is on track to peak around 2015 and will have been shrinking for a decade-and-a-half by 2030. By contrast, India's steadily growing working-age population

and excellent commercial access to the world economy. Both are rapidly mastering a wide range of technologies and benefit substantially from direct foreign investment and outsourcing. Their economies are state-managed, but markets nonetheless abound and are liberalizing.[23]

The sky then should be the limit, except insofar as they can expect to be hobbled by the same sorts of problems besetting the United States: economic privilege granting and seeking, paralytic regulation, monopoly power, institutionalized high unemployment, overtaxation and misallocated transfers, state-mandated forced substitution, adulterated public services including health, education, and the environment, social turmoil, financial speculation, excess money creation, excess debt (including China),[24] inferior domestic commercial technological innovation, foreign financial dependency, and government gridlock.

Recent Western experience shows that these sometimes elusive factors are palpable and should not be disregarded by assuming that governments will do the right thing. India and China are both notoriously corrupt, with Delhi leaning toward rudimentary politocracy, and Beijing toward monolithic Communist Party privilege granting and privilege seeking. In India elected officials and their private partners regulate, mandate, speculate, contract, transfer, and have amassed an enormous public debt at the expense of competitive efficiency, whereas in China these same games are played mostly among the unelected members of the Communist Party.

Both consequently are experiencing widening income and wealth inequality, stark regional disparities, and social strife that will intensify as the advantages of economic backwardness deplete. Catch-up growth

---

will be the world's largest well before 2030. Nonetheless, China will retain a number of demographic advantages bearing directly on economic potential. Today, China is substantially more urbanized than India. The UNPD estimates 48 percent of the country is urban today, as against 30 percent for India, and it projects that this gap will actually widen over the next two decades. For another, China's overall public-health conditions are substantially better. Life expectancy in China is about eight years longer than it is in India and is projected to remain significantly higher through 2030. Perhaps most importantly, China has a dramatic edge over India on mass educational attainment. As of today, almost everyone in China's working-age population is at least literate. By contrast, roughly a third of India's working-age population has never been to school. India is about half a century behind China in eliminating illiteracy. Even posting steady educational progress, India will still lag far behind China in attainment levels twenty years from now.

[23] World Bank, *China 2030: Building a Modern, Harmonious, and Creative High-Income Society*, 2012. "Indian Economic Reforms: A Welcome Boldness," *Economist*, September 14, 2012. Rosefielde, *Asian Economic Systems*, Singapore: World Scientific Publishers, 2013.

[24] Minxin Pei, "China's Ticking Debt Bomb," *The Diplomat Blogs*, July 5, 2011.

has brought a respite, but social polarization is apt to continue generating strong headwinds.[25]

Another way of looking at the matter that pierces the facade of those who rely on the trend always being their friend is to recall that theory strongly suggests that true democratic free enterprise is likely to be the best economic system, and that India and China are light-years from this standard. Progress here for India is apt to be excruciatingly slow given the twin demons of material and communal dissention and may never come to fruition in China. There is no need here to speculate about whether Indian politocracy or Chinese communist authoritarianism will eventually prove to be the superior engine of material advance.[26] The only issue on the table is whether one or both systems will prove its/their (their mettle) against the politarchic United States, and on this point the answer is moot, depending more on the United States than anything else. India and China have yet to demonstrate that their economic institutions can propel them forward after the easy gains of modernization have been exhausted.

China may not be destined to outshine India economically as some seem to believe, but it has three significant advantages when it comes to projecting global power: huge foreign reserves, communist authoritarianism, and location. First, the centralization of political authority gives Beijing the ability to monopolize more than $3 trillion of foreign reserves, enabling it to amass natural-resource and strategic industrial assets across the globe,[27] purchase and steal advanced civilian and military technologies, and wield enormous clout in international financial markets. India's foreign reserves by contrast are modest, although private individuals are estimated to hold more than a trillion dollars illegally abroad. Second, authoritarian nations frequently are able to devote more resources to defense than popularly elected governments. Third, China has a better strategic location for browbeating regional rivals. Japan and South Korea are dependent on Beijing's strategic metals. They rely heavily on the mainland as an export market and as a source of low-cost intermediate inputs for their manufactures. A similar story holds for Southeast Asia, buttressed by manifest Chinese nuclear arms superiority, and Beijing currently has the upper hand on Russia and North Korea.

---

[25] "The Wheels Are Coming Off China's Economy: Gordon Chang," Yahoo! News, December 20, 2011.

[26] Yi-chong Xu, ed., *The Political Economy of State-owned Enterprises in China and India*, London: Palgrave Macmillan, 2012.

[27] David Zweig and Bi Jianhai, "China's Global Hunt for Resources," *Foreign Affairs*, September/October, Vol. 85, No.5, 2005, pp. 25–38.

India's geostrategic position is more constrained. It cannot intimidate China. Pakistan is an unstable nuclear rival, and Iran is not much better, making it harder for Delhi to geopolitically lever its growing economic power. India already is a great regional power and will grow stronger, but Beijing's global hegemonic prospects are brighter, with adverse implications for the United States that echo the Great Depression and political turmoil of the interwar period.

The principal danger on the economic front stems from China's reflexive protectionism that allows it to overimport and underexport, causing high involuntary unemployment in the West,[28] reflected in Beijing's approximately \$3.4 trillion reserve accumulated since joining the WTO in 2001. Its policy is the modern-day equivalent of Washington's Hawley-Smoot tariff imposed in 1930,[29] which raised U.S. tariffs for more than 20,000 imports to record levels, seeking to preserve jobs at home by discouraging imports, and creating new employment by subsidizing exports, both at the expense of foreign workers. The gambit backfired because the world swiftly responded tit for tat to America's beggar-thy-neighbor policy, imposing countertariffs and subsidies that triggered a sharp contraction in international trade and intensified the Great Depression.

Western retaliation for contemporary Chinese beggar-thy-neighbor trade practices has been slow because Beijing has steadfastly denied wrongdoing, but retaliatory sentiment is rising.[30] China could relent, but it is reasonable

---

[28] Steven Rosefielde, "China's Perplexing Foreign Trade Policy: Causes, Consequences and a Tit for Tat Solution," *American Foreign Policy Interests*, Vol. 33, No. 1, January–February 2011, pp. 10–16. Rosefielde, "Export-led Development and Dollar Reserve Hoarding," in Rosefielde, Kuboniwa, and Mizobata, eds., *Two Asias: The Emerging Postcrisis Divide*, Singapore: World Scientific, 2011.

[29] The Tariff Act of 1930, better known as the Smoot–Hawley Tariff (P.L. 71–361) was signed into law on June 17, 1930. The overall level tariffs under the Tariff were the second-highest in U.S. history, exceeded by a small margin only by the Tariff of 1828 and the ensuing retaliatory tariffs by U.S. trading partners reduced U.S. exports and imports by more than half.

[30] Joe McDonald, "American Firms Say Chinese Protectionism Rising," Associated Press, April 20, 2011. Shanshan Zhu, "China Lambasts US Senate Currency Bill," *Global Times*, October, 13, 2011: "In defiance of China's repeated warnings, the Democrat-led Senate passed the Currency Exchange Rate Oversight Reform Act with a 63–35 majority Tuesday." The CEO of Dow, now the largest chemical firm in the world, who is Australian by nationality and in the United States on a green card, and is a major leader of U.S. business, described the evolution of the Chinese-U.S. business relationship as follows: First the Chinese were suppliers to Western firms; now they are customers (or "partners"); they are becoming competitors (especially the large state-owned enterprises) in the global marketplace. Chinese competitors lack transparency; their cost of capital is uncertain; they benefit from substantial raw-material subsidies. These are greater problems for U.S. competitors than the much-publicized low-wage costs of the Chinese firms. This latest stage, in

to worry that as its great power waxes, it will become more intransigent, plunging the global economy into a black pit that the U.S. Congress in 1930 failed to avoid.

China's protectionist impulse also provides a clue to how it is apt to operate as the new global political hegemon should it achieve this status. Beijing will try to create spheres of influence (coprosperity zones), not unlike Japan did in the 1930s, more fashionably describing them as economic communities and unions (like ASEAN).[31] It will try to overwhelm and annex Taiwan through persuasion, guile, or force as it did Tibet; enforce its claims on sea-based natural resources throughout the entire region and beyond, including the arctic, and it will try to dominate East Asian sea lanes.

As during the 1930s, there will be many who argue that these outcomes are agreeable. There will be peace and prosperity in our time, and a quarter of a loaf is better than none. China today, like Nazi Germany, Imperial Japan, and the Soviet Union yesterday, is growing faster than the United States, providing trickle-down benefits that partly compensate for the negatives.[32] On paper, the 1930s were not really so bad. Yes, there was a lost decade, but after 1933, all the world's major economies steadily recovered until the outbreak of World War II.[33] If Hitler and Hirohito hadn't opted for conquest, their regimes although oppressive, eventually might have mellowed after exterminating tens of millions of racial "undesirables."[34]

The same comforting thoughts apply today, and of course it can be plausibly argued that in the postcolonial era, China's hegemony will be

---

which Chinese firms compete with U.S. firms, may cause U.S. firms to more strongly back retaliatory U.S. government actions against Chinese trade practices. Quinn Mills, conference report, fall 2011.

[31] Yun Chen and Ken Morita, "Toward an East Asian Economic Community," in Steven Rosefielde, Masaaki Kuboniwa, and Satoshi Mizobata, eds., *Prevention and Crisis Management: Lessons for Asia from the 2008 Crisis*, Singapore: World Scientific Publishers, 2012. Fu-kuo Liu, "Beijing's Regional Strategy and China – ASEAN Economic Integration," *China Brief*, Vol. 8, Issue 10, May 13, 2008. Full text of Chinese Premier Wen's statement at the 14th China-ASEAN Summit, November 18, 2011. http://news.xinhuanet.com/english2010/china/2011–11/18/c_131255936.htm

[32] The GDP compound annual growth rates 1933–1940 computed in 1990 U.S. dollars respectively were: German 7.0 percent, Japan 5.7 percent, and the Soviet Union 6.8 percent. See Angus Maddison, *The World Economy: Historical Statistics*, OECD, Paris, 2006, pp. 428, 476, and 550. Official statistics computed in their own currencies were higher.

[33] Russia's post-Soviet experience is often given a positive gloss by mischaracterizing its recovery 1989–2008 after hitting rock bottom at almost 50 percent of its 1989 GGP as rapid growth.

[34] Steven Rosefielde, *Red Holocaust*, New York: Routledge, 2010.

less damaging than Japan's three quarters of a century ago.[35] However, in drawing up one's own balance sheet of the unintended international consequences of U.S. politocracy, it should be recognized that the deterioration in economic conditions in the ensuring decades may be much severer than in the 1930. The United States and Europe haven't even begun to seriously grapple with their national debt crises, and if they do not, it will turn out that the West is only in the first phase of a mega crisis, which when compounded by protectionist-driven de-globalization will make the economic aspect of the 1930s look like halcyon days.

GLOBAL DEMOCRATIC SETBACK

Prospects for global true democracy are similarly dispiriting. There is not a single champion of true democracy in Asia or among BRIC that can carry what once was the United States' torch. The leading nations of Europe succumbed to social democracy half a century ago, and most other governments around the globe are content to adorn their regimes with balloting in lieu of popular sovereignty vouchsafed by constitutional property and civil rights minority guarantees. If reason prevailed, the future should be truly democratic, but the trend is moving state governance in the wrong direction.[36]

---

[35] Mark McDonald, "Communist Bling: It's All the Rage in China," *International Herald Tribune Rendezvous*, March 11, 2012.

[36] Cf. Larry Diamond, "The Democratic Rollback," *Foreign Affairs*, March/April, 2008. http://www.foreignaffairs.org/20080301faessay87204/larry-diamond/the-democratic-rollback.html; Yun-Han Chu, Larry Diamond, Andrew Nathan and Doh Chull Shin, *How East Asians View Democracy*, New York: Columbia University Press, 2008. Sumit Ganguly, Larry Diamond, and Marc Plattner, *The State of India's Democracy*, Baltimore: Johns Hopkins University Press, 2007.

TWELVE

Recovering Lost Ground

True democracy is not a lost cause, and the United States can become a political, economic and international paragon again by vanquishing politocracy.

The nation does not have to accept politarchic rule with all its harmful consequences.[1] The true democratic global movement can be reempowered, world economic competitiveness bolstered, planetary social justice improved, the United States' microeconomic sclerosis reversed, and its macro-economy stabilized.[2] True democratic governments can spend

---

[1] Contemporary politarchs today act as if they are subconsciously driven by a death wish. The concept of death drive (*Todestrieb*), or innate human death wish was originally proposed by Sigmund Freud in his 1920 classic work, *Beyond the Pleasure Principle*, where he wrote of the "opposition between the ego or death instincts and the sexual or life instincts." It is frequently called *Thanatos* in post-Freudian thought, and viewed as the obverse of the drive to life. Freud applied his new theoretical construct in *Civilization and Its Discontents* (1930) to the difficulties inherent in Western civilization, postulating the need for a cultural superego to control human aggression, or again by extension, the politarchic death drive.

[2] The day of reckoning may soon be at hand. The United States is mimicking Greece, and the panic could begin well before the national debt hits 160 percent of GDP. See Andrew Taylor, "Obama Budget: New Spending with Recycled Tax Ideas," Yahoo! Finance, January 12, 2012:

The White House is focusing on re-election themes such as jobs and public works projects in President Barack Obama's new budget blueprint while relying on tax increases on the wealthy and corporations to reduce future deficits after four years of trillion dollar-plus shortfalls. Obama's 2013 budget, set for release Monday, is the official start to an election-year budget battle with Republicans. It did not result in a genuine effort to address the $15 trillion national debt or the entrenched deficits that keep piling on to it. The president's plan was laden with stimulus-style initiatives: sharp increases for highway construction and school modernization, and a new tax credit for businesses that add jobs. But it avoided sacrifice without any curbs on the unsustainable growth of Medicare, the government health-care program for the elderly, even as it proposed a 10-year, $61 billion "financial crisis responsibility fee" on big banks to recoup the 2008 Wall Street bailout. The president's budget plan predicted a deficit of $1.3 trillion for 2012 and a $901 billion deficit in the 2013 budget year, which starts Oct. 1. It claimed deficit savings of more than $4 trillion

prudently, regulate efficiently, eradicate financial speculation, restore sound money, limit indebtedness, prevent future economic crises, avoid foreign imbroglios, and vouchsafe national security.

Contemporary economic optimization theory points the way.[3] It proves that true democracies that limit the state's economic role to those activities where it has a comparative advantage are best, given competitive free enterprise. The ideal ratio of state to private production depends on the *demos*'s shifting preferences and its assessment of elected agents' integrity and competence. Elected officials of any stripe should never be permitted to undertake tasks unless it can be rigorously demonstrated that they can do them as well or better than the people. The burden of proof should always fall on elected agents, not their sovereign (the *demos*). "The people" here means the majority of the electorate subject to fundamental property and civil-rights guarantees, not minority segments of the electorate like big business and big social advocacy acting on their own behalves in conjunction with politarchs claiming to be the conscience of society.[4] "The people"

---

over a decade, mixing $1 trillion already banked through last summer's clampdown on agency operating budgets with $1.5 trillion in higher tax revenues reaped from an overhaul of the tax code that has yet to be implemented. An additional $1 trillion, more or less, is supposed to come from war savings, a move that budget watchdogs call an accounting gimmick, especially because the administration also wants to devote some of those savings to pay for $476 billion in road and bridge projects over the coming six years. Obama's 2014 budget proposal is more smoke and mirrors. See Thomas Eddlem, "Obama's 2014 Budget Proposal: Tax, Spend, elect – and Borrow," *New American*, April 12, 2013.

[3] For a thorough technical demonstration of this claim, see Steven Rosefielde, *Asian Economic Systems*, Singapore: World Scientific Publishers, 2013, chapter 1.

[4] True democracy won't remedy all that ails humankind. Freud and a host of scientists and philosophers have shown from multiple perspectives that the principles of Enlightenment democracy are not sufficient to obviate human discontent and discord. Freud, for example, contends that while civilization is intended to protect men against nature and "adjust their mutual relations," it restricts the possibilities of individual satisfaction without fulfilling its promise to adequately compensate the collective. This causes an intractable conflict between the forces of the libido and the superego, which Freud suggests will be won by aggression (politocracy?). Even if one of the main purposes of civilization is to bind each man's libidinal impulses to those of others, he contends that love and civilization eventually come into conflict with one another because family units tend to isolate themselves and prevent individuals from detaching and maturing on their own. Civilization also saps sexual energy by diverting it into cultural endeavors. It restricts love object choices and mutilates our erotic lives. Enlightenment democracy accordingly cannot eradicate all humanity's discontents. See James Strachey, ed., *The Standard Edition of the Complete Psychological Works of Sigmund Freud*, New York: Vintage, 1999; Sigmund Freud, *Introduction to Psychoanalysis*, New York: Boni and Liveright, ,917; Freud, *Beyond the Pleasure Principle*, London: International Psycho-Analytical, 1920; Freud, *The Ego and the Id*, New York: W.W. Norton1923; Freud, *Civilization and its Discontents*, New York: W.W. Norton, 1930. Enlightenment democracy, thus, is a pragmatic solution, not a panacea.

explicitly excludes foreigners claiming "stakeholder" sovereignty rights and entitlements.

Optimization theory further requires that agents fully inform themselves about the people's preferences even when circumstances occasionally compel them to employ their best judgment.[5] A true democratic best is an integrated optimum where individuals privately maximize their utility, and government efficiently fills in the gaps to further improve the people's well-being. These principles apply in the United States and universally across the globe both domestically and in foreign affairs.

Politarchs claim that they are trying to do this with government programs, taxes, subsidies, "tax expenditures," mandates, regulations, multinational, and transnational initiatives, but they are mendacious. As explained in Chapter 7, it is impossible to attain optimal results with their anticompetitive, command planning, directive and incentive methods, and outcomes invariably will be worse when elected officials are politocratically self-serving. Remember the Soviet Union.

The United States can attain true democratic economic outcomes today in accordance with the Constitution and Bill of Rights by reducing politocratic big government to the ideal democratic size,[6] and then raising the electorate's consciousness so voters appreciate the necessity of electing officials willing to serve the people,[7] instead of colluding with big business and

---

[5] The federal government may sometimes be able to constructively arbitrate disputes about the size and substance of public services within constitutionally set parameters, but it is not the people's conscience, and should not impose its will on the *demos*. From a Freudian perspective, politocrats usurp the role of the *demos*'s superego and divert libidinal energies to their own purposes, while reducing egos to a minor role. The "pleasure principle" and the "death drive" are both co-opted to serve politarch masters, and the people are their unwitting drudges. The same sort of tale can be spun substituting Benthamite utility seeking for the pleasure principle. Neurosis and psychosis are additional factors responsible for aberrant and deviant behavior, judged from the standard of the ideal human psychosexual pattern. Still, these problems probably can be mitigated by individuals adopting pain-avoidance strategies that create personal and/or transcendental values that make them virtuous enough to honor the people's ultimate sovereignty. Freud's narrow view of secular reality, which ignores existential paradox, inclined him toward pessimism.

[6] Steven Rosefielde, *Asian Economic Systems*, Singapore: World Scientific, 2013, chapter 1; Steven Rosefielde and R. W. Pfouts, *Inclusive Economic Theory*, draft 2013.

[7] Raising the electorate's consciousness is nontrivial, but some advance should be achievable. Cf. Erich Fromm, D. T. Suzuki, and Richard DeMartino, *Zen Buddhism and Psychoanalysis*, Harper and Row: New York, 1960, p. 108. Also see Sigmund Freud, *Civilization and its Discontents*, New York: W.W. Norton, 1930:

We may begin by saying that the average person, while he thinks he is awake, actually is half asleep.... The average person's consciousness is mainly "false consciousness," consisting of fictions and illusion, while precisely what he is not aware of is reality. We can thus differentiate between what a person is conscious of, and what he becomes conscious of. He

big social advocacy at home and abroad. This has the further advantage of empowering civil society, individual liberty, social justice, and national security.

The world can achieve similar outcomes by adopting true democratic principles. There is nothing heterodox in this prescription. Politarchs themselves offer the same advice, only their actions belie their words.

The goal necessitates paring bigness not for its own sake, but because politocracy causes microeconomic inefficiency and macroeconomic destabilization and makes nations vulnerable to foreign machinations. The objective is entirely pragmatic. The strategy is not failsafe, but it does provide good prospects for success.

SHRINKING GOVERNMENT AND DEFANGING POLITOCRACY

Advancing the cause of true democracy in the United States merely requires reducing big government, establishing laws that criminalize trafficking in state services, and vigorously enforcing them. For the rest of the world, it necessitates replacing other forms of government, both elected and authoritarian, with true democracy. The concept is simple, but the devil is in the details.

MACROECONOMIC POLICY, EXPENDITURES, AND PROGRAMS

First and foremost, Washington should get out of the macroeconomic leveraging business. This is a simple matter of policy that only requires limiting deficit spending to countercyclical stabilization, shunning inflationary increases of money and credit, and avoiding excessive national indebtedness. These goals can be facilitated by capping federal borrowing, limiting it to a fixed share of GDP, and by outlawing quantitative easing (printing and debasing money).[8] A debt to GDP cap in the vicinity of 25 percent could be manageable and is more flexible than banning public deficits outright as the Tea Party proposes.[9] It provides macroeconomic policymakers

is conscious, mostly, of fictions; he can become conscious of the realities which lie under these fictions.

From Freud's perspective, individual libidos cannot be beneficially controlled by collective superegos. This task is best left to "practical" individual egos responsible for balancing the libido and the superego.

[8]   The dollar has been debased to 3 percent of its 1914 level when the Federal Reserve system was inaugurated.

[9]   A U.S. populist movement championing tax reductions, small government, reduced national debt and deficits spending, and strict construction of the U.S. Constitution. Many

with considerable leeway while preventing sovereign debt obligations from soaring through the stratosphere.[10]

Quantitative easing (QE-infinity) unconscionably swells the coffers of politarchs and their Wall Street partners without stimulating employment as promised.[11] The Federal Reserve should be prohibited from deliberately fostering inflation to lighten the government's debt[12] and from indulging Wall Street financial speculators. [13]

of the policy recommendations advocated in this volume are compatible with the Tea Party movement's program, but for a different set of reasons. The Tea Party is inspired by libertarianism and conservatism. Our analysis is driven by Peircian scientific pragmatism. See Steven Rosefielde and Ralph W. Pfouts, *Inclusive Economics*, London: Oxford University Press, 2014 forthcoming.

[10] The IMF uses sovereign debt to GDP ratios as a condition for lending to less developed countries like Serbia, but the concept has not been extended to the United States or the European Union. See Gordana Filipovic, "Serbian Fiscal Council Says Wider Deficit 'Justified and Timely," *Bloomberg Businessweek*, October 2, 2011.

[11] John Carne, "Three Things Fed Did Today It's Never Done Before," Yahoo! Finance, September 13, 2012: "The Federal Reserve took a really aggressive stance Thursday when it announced its new round of quantitative easing. There are no definite size or time limits on QE3–prompting some to call it QE-Infinity."

[12] Jeff Cox, "Fed Wants Inflation Now, Will Clean Up 'Mess' Later: El-Erian," Yahoo! Finance, September 21, 2012. "The Federal Reserve and Chairman Ben Bernanke not only are willing to tolerate inflation but actually are trying to create it, with a 'mess' left behind for their successors to clean up, Pimco's Mohamed El-Erian told CNBC."

[13] Gretchen Morgenson, "Secrets of the Bailout, Now Told," *New York Times*, December 5, 2011:

Among all the rescue programs set up by the Fed, $7.77 trillion in commitments were outstanding as of March 2009, Bloomberg said. The nation's six largest banks – JPMorgan Chase, Bank of America, Citigroup, Wells Fargo, Goldman Sachs and Morgan Stanley – borrowed almost half a trillion dollars from the Fed at peak periods, Bloomberg calculated, using the central bank's data. Those six institutions accounted for 63 percent of the average daily borrowings from the Fed by all publicly traded United States banks, money management and investment firms, Bloomberg said. Numbers for individual companies were equally astonishing. For example, the Fed provided Bear Stearns with $30 billion to see it through its 2008 shotgun marriage with JPMorgan. This was in addition to the $29.5 billion in assets purchased by the Fed from Bear to assist in the buyout by JPMorgan. Citigroup, meanwhile, tapped the Fed for almost $100 billion in January 2009 – its peak during the crisis – and Morgan Stanley received $107 billion in Fed loans in September 2008. The fact is, investors didn't know how dire the situation was at these institutions. At the same time that these banks were privately thronging the teller windows at the Fed, some of their executives were publicly espousing their firms' financial solidity. During the first three months of 2009, for example, when Citigroup's Fed borrowing apparently peaked, Vikram Pandit, its chief executive, hailed the company's performance. Calling that first quarter the best overall since 2007, Mr. Pandit said the results showed "the strength of Citi's franchise." These disclosure lapses are disturbing to Lynn E. Turner, a former chief accountant at the S.E.C. Since 1989, he said, commission rules have required public companies to disclose details about material federal assistance they receive. The rules grew out of the savings and loan crisis, during which hundreds of banks failed and others received

Whether the required restraint is achieved by abolishing the Federal Reserve System in favor of a National Bank and placing legal restraints on deficit spending and Wall Street bailouts or by various alternative devices is unimportant; what matters is reining in big governmental deficit spending and monetary leveraging ("prosperity management").

$2 TRILLION OF FAT

These restrictions constitute a good start, but they are no substitute for drastically slashing public programs, grants-in-aid, mandates, pernicious regulations, and other forms of politocratic plunder. The easy profits afforded by the public-service business bear primary blame for the United States' economic woes because they provide politicians with an irresistible temptation to serve themselves rather than the *demos*. Absent this corruption, the federal government would be smaller, with most public services provided by states and municipalities. Small government may be blemished too, but reduced scale should drastically diminish waste, fraud, abuse, red tape, the tax burden on workers and the middle class, mandates, transfers to the rich, and macroeconomic destabilization. Small is beautiful on these grounds, even if true democracy continues to be tarnished by politarchic mischief.

Politarchs have torpedoed all attempts to prudently hold the line on public services by counterclaiming that there is no significant fat to trim in the

government help. The rules are found in a section of the S.E.C.'s Codification of Financial Reporting Policies titled "Effects of Federal Financial Assistance Upon Operations." They state that if any types of federal financial assistance have "materially affected or are reasonably likely to have a future material effect upon financial condition or results of operations, the management discussion and analysis should provide disclosure of the nature, amounts and effects of such assistance.

Given these rules, Mr. Turner said: "I would have expected some discussion in the management discussion and analysis of how this has had a positive impact on these banks' operating results. The borrowings had to have an impact on their liquidity and earnings, but I don't ever recall anybody saying 'we borrowed a bunch of money from the Fed at zero percent interest.'" It will be interesting to see whether the S.E.C. does anything to enforce its rules that companies disclose federal assistance in financial filings, either in the recent past or in the future. You could certainly argue that requiring such disclosures is even more important nowadays, given that so many banks are considered too big to fail and that the taxpayer will undoubtedly be asked once again to rescue them from their mistakes. "These banks and the Fed have never believed in transparency," Mr. Turner said. "I actually think their thought process is sorely flawed. If the banks knew this stuff was going to be made public they'd behave differently. Instead of runs on the bank you'd have bankers doing things intelligently to avoid getting into trouble."

federal budget[14] or from off-budget spending, insisting that any reduction in deficit spending will impose unacceptable hardships, even though many of these same politicians occasionally indulge in singing the praises of small government.[15] Congress currently classifies 55 percent of all federal spending as mandatory (nonnegotiable entitlements) and therefore exempt from spending reductions. Much higher figures for entitlements are often claimed as well. These are legalistic ploys to keep the subject of tax cutting and social security/Medicare privatization permanently off the table. The notion that federal government cannot be drastically shrunk in terms of both its regulatory reach and its expenditures is ludicrous,[16] entitlements notwithstanding.

As explained in Chapter 6 there is roughly $2 trillion of fat in the United States' $5.3 trillion federal budget, excluding social security and Medicare. This assessment was recently underscored by a report issued by the Institute of Medicine, an arm of the National Academy of Sciences, which found that the U.S. health-care system squanders $750 billion a year – roughly 30 cents of every medical dollar, much of which is paid for by Medicare and Medicaid as a form of disguised transfer to health-care businesses and political allies.[17] An epidemic of fraudulent lifetime disability claims by American males further underscores the corruption.[18]

[14] The failure of the Joint Select Committee on Deficit Reduction ("super-committee") to reach a budget-deficit-reduction agreement as required by the Budget Control Act of 2011 illustrates how stealthy politarchic trans-partisanship trumps "systems risk." The bill was supposed to cut $917 billion over ten years, and the super-committee was supposed to cut at least another $1.5 trillion over the next decade. See Kate Bolduan and Deirdre Walsh, "'Super Committee' Fails to Reach Agreement," CNN, November 21, 2011.

[15] "The era of big government is over." Bill Clinton, State of the Union Address, 1996. www.clinton4.nara.gov/WH/New/other/sotu.html

[16] Jonathan Karl, Richard Coolidge, and Sherisse Pham, "Murtha Airport, Brought to You by American Taxpayers," Yahoo! Finance, April 3, 2012: "The Murtha Airport in Johnstown, Pa., is a prime example of taxpayer spending that refuses to die. Representative John Murtha steered some 150 million of taxpayer dollars to this eponymous airport over the last decade and despite the fact he died more than a year ago, the money keeps on coming."

[17] Ricardo Alonso-Zaldivar, "Report: US Health Care System Wastes $750B a Year," Yahoo! Finance, September 6, 2012. Cf. Barry Meier and Katie Thomas, "Insurers Pay Big Markups as Doctors Dispense Drugs," *New York Times*, July 11, 2012: "When a pharmacy sells the heartburn drug Zantac, each pill costs about 35 cents. But doctors dispensing it to patients in their offices have charged nearly 10 times that price, or $3.25 a pill."

[18] Michael Barone, "American Men Find Careers in Collecting Disability," *The Washington Examiner*, December 1, 2012:

In 1960, some 455,000 workers were receiving disability payments. In 2011, the number was 8,600,000. In 1960, the percentage of the economically active 18-to-64-year-old population receiving disability benefits was 0.65 percent. In 2010, it was 5.6 percent.... Between 1996 and 2011, the private sector generated 8.8 million new jobs and 4.1 million people entered the disability rolls. The ratio of disability cases to new jobs has been even

Obviously, the problem is not that there is no fat to trim; there simply is no will to trim it.[19]

There are many superfluous programs that can be slashed or eradicated. The federal government currently pays $20 billion annually in direct "farm income stabilization" subsidies to farmers without regard to their income (mostly agribusiness). These programs which date back to the 1922 Grain Futures Act, the 1929 Agricultural Marketing Act, and the 1933 Agricultural Adjustment Act, have become detached from their original purpose and now just squander money. The United States has spent $704 billion on Iraq and Afghan national building operations since 2003, despite the fact that the Iraq War itself was won in a week.[20] An additional $159 billion was scheduled to be spent in 2011. Similar sums may soon be squandered in Syria primarily for the benefit of well-connected contractors, camouflaged by high-toned declarations of democratic humanitarianism. Terminating the hemorrhaging is just a matter of pulling the plug. These expenditures supplement the defense department's operating budget, which contains large volumes of nondefense categories like environmental defense, homeland defense, and sundry disguised social-welfare programs. It also includes monies for national ballistic missile defense, a capability that political leaders are unwilling to effectively deploy. Insofar as the government has lost its will to defend, hundreds of billions of dollars should be slashed from the defense budget, including withdrawal from NATO, which has morphed into a social club rather than a serious military organization, when it is not otherwise engaged in promoting politarchic defense contracting. It is too expensive to go on pretending.

worse during the sluggish recovery from the 2007–2009 recession. Between January 2010 and December 2011, there were 1,730,000 new jobs and 790,000 new people collecting disability.

See Nicholas Eberstadt, *A Nation of Takers: America's Entitlement Epidemic*, New York: Templeton Press, 2012.

[19] A Congressional oversight committee recently discovered that New York has overcharged Washington $15 billion dollars for mental health care since 1990. Jacob Gershman, "State Accused of $15 Billion Fraud Scheme," *Wall Street Journal*, September 21, 2012:

A congressional oversight committee on Thursday accused New York of overbilling Medicaid by billions of dollars by inflating reimbursement payments to its state-run institutions for the mentally disabled. In a scathing report, the Republican-led House Oversight and Government of New York charged a per-diem rate of $5,118 for residents of the institutions, a network of 11 centers that now house about 1,300 people with severe developmental disabilities. Over the course of a year, Medicaid spends $1.9 million for every resident or $2.5 billion in total – with half coming from the federal government. But the cost of running the institutions is only a quarter of that amount. "This is intentional fraud," said Arizona Rep. Paul Gosar, a Republican committee member.

[20] http://en.wikipedia.org/wiki/Financial_cost_of_the_Iraq_War

The list of cuts is easily expanded through every government agency,[21] including the State Department, which squanders fortunes on officer and staff perks. The essential point here is not to make a case for particular cuts, but to establish how easy it is for the federal government to live within its means while paying down the national debt, without imposing additional taxes.

Big government also can be shrunk by localizing. The federal government today needlessly operates as a middleman for state government collecting taxes that could be raised locally, transferring them as grants-in-aid to lower governmental entities.[22] It spent $653 billion this way in 2010.[23] These expenditures were quadruply prodigal. First, they entail duplicative administration. The state and local governments that actually devise and supervise programs do not need federal bureaucrats operating at arm's length with slender competency meddling from afar.[24] Duplicative activities that add substantial costs, including unnecessary red tape imposed on state and local administrators by their federal masters, can be eliminated by having states and localities tax, fund, and execute programs themselves.[25] Just as in the corporate world, delayering is a primary source of cost savings. Second, delayering automatically eliminates the politarchic component of the

---

[21] Alan Blinder and Mark Zandi, "How the Great Depression Was Brought to an End," July 27, 2010. http://www.economy.com/mark-zandi/document/End_of_Great_Recession. pdf. Congress continues to extend unemployment benefits well beyond the statutory limit, in what is becoming a permanent welfare payment.

[22] Grants-in-aid are part of a larger policy called "devolutionary federalism," or "new federalism." The concept was first applied in 1970 in the form of revenue sharing. Block grants for a wide range of activities from education to health care, transportation, housing, and counterterrorism were substituted in 1988. Grant-in-aid programs include entitlement programs that flow directly to state and local agencies. Block grants are discretionary or project grants for a wide range of federal programs from preventing juvenile delinquency to improving infant health outcomes. Contracts are issued for specified services. Demonstration grants are awarded for experimental programs. Direct payment are given to individuals who satisfy federal eligibility requirements, loan, or loan-guarantee programs enabling community-based organizations, public and private entities, and some private businesses to borrow funds, sometimes at below-market rates, from public or private lenders for specific purposes.

[23] U.S. Office of Management and Budget, *Budget of the United States Government, Historical Tables*, annual. See also http://www.whitehouse.gov/omb/budget

[24] States and localities may succumb to politocratic temptation, but being closer to the people, are more easily disciplined. If citizens fail in some states, adverse effects are still likely to be less than they are today in Washington.

[25] The counterargument is that states would choose different programs and be less attentive to civil-rights issues. These claims tacitly assume that the federal government is doing

federal public-service business, including mandates.[26] Concealed transfers to obligated associates vanish. Third, it bypasses mountains of superfluous rules and regulations affecting final recipients, and fourth, it assures that states and localities tax, fund, and undertake only projects the people actually desire. Paul Light estimates that the federal government could save $1 trillion over ten years by reducing management levels from eighteen to no more than six levels.[27]

OFF-BUDGET REDUCTIONS

Eliminating superfluous on-budget programs, waste, fraud, and abuse is essential, but it is only the tip of the iceberg. National welfare can be enhanced further to the tune of trillions of dollars by reining in off-budget "tax expenditures," subsidies, and diverse insurance schemes.

Consider the facts. The federal government as of 2008 sponsored more than $12 trillion of financial business activity through government-sponsored enterprises (GSE), nearly equal to the entire gross national product. Congress created the first GSE, Farm Credit System, in 1916, followed in 1932 by Federal Home Loan Banks, Sallie Mae (educational loans) in 1972, Fannie Mae (1938–2008), and Freddie Mac (1970–2008). Fannie Mae and Freddie Mac were publicly chartered but privately owned until 2008, when they were forced into conservatorship. The rationale for these operations is that GSEs save billions annually in interest costs for homeowners because of the risk discount provided by the federal government's implicit credit guarantee. Politicians gain merely by implicitly pledging to serve as creditor of last recourse, showering voters with allegedly cost-free benefits (alchemy).

---

things right, which it is not, and that civil rights cannot be properly defended at the state level. The first supposition is false, the second debatable.

[26] Most mandates are legislated. But there is also a vast underworld of hidden mandates where private organizations including charities are informally pressured and indirectly compensated for funding projects that politocrats favor. For a recent example of this arcane kickback system, see David Crary, "Charity Confronts Backlash over Grant Cuts," Associated Press, February 2, 2012. The Susan Komen foundation, a private charity, was pilloried for cutting its grants to Planned Parenthood by twenty-six senators, who apparently thought that they had the right to dictate the spending of private institutions to the groups they designated.

[27] Paul Light, "Opinion," *Wall Street Journal*, July 7, 2011. Specially, he recommends freezing all hiring at the senior and middle levels of government (possible savings: $250 billion); eliminating $300 billion delinquent federal income taxes owed by federal and congressional employees, contractors, and stimulus recipients, streamline, focus on productivity, eliminate automatic time-on-the-job pay increases, cut the number of contract employees by 500,0000.

However they were not content to limit assistance to implicit credit guarantees for the benefit of private owners of Fannie Mae and Freddie Mac and homeowners. Politicians pressed Fannie Mae into the subprime loans business (see Chapter 8) and Freddie Mac into the secondary-mortgage market (including derivative mortgage-backed securities), ultimately precipitating a housing bubble that culminated in the bankruptcies of Bear Stearns, Lehman Brothers, Morgan Stanley, Goldman Sachs, and AIG and the global financial crisis of 2008.[28] "Cost-free" benefits proved to be a taxpayer nightmare.[29]

From the public's perspective the cost of the bailout and the earlier Savings and Loan scandal lopsidedly outweigh any gains GSEs can possibly generate for the foreseeable future. Trillions of dollars of future catastrophic losses can be forestalled merely by having the federal government exit this politarchic business.[30] Of course, it can be counterargued that Congress will learn its lesson and discipline itself from abusing the GSE public-service business, but the evidence belies the hope.[31] Incredibly, the Obama administration,

---

[28] The bubble was predicted by Robert Shiller in 2000. See Shiller, *Irrational Exuberance*, Princeton, NJ: Princeton University Press, 2000; Shiller, *The Subprime Solution: How Today's Global Financial Crisis Happened, and What to Do About It*, Princeton, NJ: Princeton University Press, 2008.

[29] On December 24, 2009 the Treasury Department pledged unlimited support for the next three years to Fannie Mae and Freddie Mac, despite $400 billion in losses.

[30] "The Perfect Bailout: Fannie and Freddie Now Directly to Wall Street," Yahoo! Finance, February 2, 2011:

Treasury Secretary Tim Geithner is providing Fannie Mae and Freddie Mac with as much credit as they need to purchase toxic mortgages held by banks at prices that won't produce book losses. This amounts to a stealthy taxpayer funded bailout, giving a green light to all parties to repeat the reckless lending that caused the 2008 financial crisis confident that they will reap the gains, and taxpayers will eat the losses. The US government for the first time in its history is poised to become the largest source of outstanding loans for home mortgage and consumer credit, eclipsing the private sector. Government-financed borrowing for these purposes ran at $6.3 trillion (up from $4.4 trillion in 2006) in the first quarter of 2011. Private credit provision ran $6.6 trillion, down from $8.5 trillion in 2006. The trend suggests that government provided capital in the second quarter of 2011 already exceeds that from the private sector. See also Gillian Tett, "The State is Now the Dominant Force in US Capital Markets," *Financial Times*, July 1, 2011.

[31] Peter Wallison and Edward Pinto, "Bet the House: Why the FHA Is Going (for) Broke," *American Enterprise Institute*, January 19, 2012:

No serious observer of the Federal Housing Administration (FHA) believes its financial future is bright. But few recognize just how troubled this government agency really is. That is because it uses lax accounting standards that obscure real and present danger to its own bottom line and the American taxpayer. In fact, when measured against the accounting system used by private mortgage insurers, the FHA is deeply insolvent, with a capital shortfall of tens of billions of dollars. If it were a private firm, state regulators would

under the cover of the Frank-Dodd Act, already has begun mandating a massive expansion of the very same subprime loans largely responsible for the 2006 housing crisis and the financial meltdown that swiftly ensued.[32]

There is a simple solution for part of Congress's off-budget misbehavior. Abolish GSEs, and prohibit other institutions like the FHA from guaranteeing unfunded liabilities. If democratic federal representatives in their collective wisdom determine that homeowners deserve to be subsidized at the expense of renters they can supplement the mortgage interest deduction on IRS 1040 Schedule B with a partial tax credit. No new bureaucracy is needed. Just add a single entry to the tax form. The same approach can be applied to unnecessary federal outsourcing. The government pays AON immense fees to monitor cafeteria-plan tax incentives that could be just as easily achieved by increasing the IRS 1040 Schedule B cap on medical expenses.[33]

---

immediately shut it down. Even using its own rosy numbers puts the FHA's leverage at 840 to 1, a far more scandalous ratio than even Fannie Mae and Freddie Mac. As shown by Fannie and Freddie as recently as 2008 and the slow-motion collapse of the savings and loans (S&Ls) in the 1980s, if government-backed entities are allowed to continue operating when they are insolvent, their losses will only compound. Indeed, the FHA has almost tripled its insurance in force in only three years, in part to cover its losses. And Congress made matters worse last fall when it raised the FHA's conforming loan limit to $729,750. That pleased the powerful National Association of Realtors, but it simply poured fuel on the fire. Before the agency's losses skyrocket, triggering a massive taxpayer bailout that deepens our nation's debt, Congress should reverse that mistake and enact reforms to pull the FHA back from the brink."

[32] PeterWallison and Edward Pinto "How the Government Is Creating Another Bubble," AEI Articles and Commentary, December 27, 2010: Wallison and Pinto contend that the Dodd-Frank Wall Street Reform and Consumer Protection Act (July 2010) allow the administration to substitute the Federal Housing Administration (FHA founded as part of the National Housing Act of 1934) for Fannie Mae and Freddie Mac as the principal and essentially unlimited provider of subprime mortgages at taxpayers' expense. Since the 2008 government takeover of Fannie Mae and Freddie Mac, the government-sponsored enterprises' regulator has restricted them to purchasing high-quality mortgages, with affordable housing requirements mandated in 1992 relaxed. This reduces the future risk, but the good is entirely negated by shunting the old destructive practices to the FHA on the pretext of supporting the soundness of the entire mortgage industry. The gambit, in the usual way, allows the administration to present a prudent face with regard to Fannie Mae and Freddie Mac while recklessly reprising the Housing and Urban Development Administration's (HUD) prior destructive policies. Wallison, Pollock, and Pinto, "Taking the Government Out of Housing Finance: Principles for Reforming the Housing Finance Market," AEI Online, March 24, 2011. Peter Wallison, Alex Pollock, and Edward Pinto report that the U.S. government-sponsored 27 million subprime and alt-policies. To correct the situation they recommend that the government get out of the housing-finance business. Government regulation should be restricted to ensuring mortgage credit quality. Assistance to low-income families should be on-budget. Fannie Mae and Freddie Mac should be privatized.

[33] A cafeteria plan is an employee-benefit plan offered by the United States pursuant to Section 125 of the Internal Revenue Code.

Social Security and Medicare can be radically downscaled too by applying the same principles. Both can be gradually privatized by permitting workers the option of contributing FICA taxes to dedicated Roth IRAs (eliminating double taxation) for future retirement and medical services, or to other existing federal programs.[34] The people also can be permitted to withdraw some or all of their past contributions, with corresponding reductions in benefits.[35] If everyone opted to exit, federal expenditures would fall $700 billion, using current annual payouts as a benchmark, and administrative costs, including federal-employee wages, would be cut proportionally. Mixed privatization schemes would yield lesser savings. Whatever the exact figure might be, it would be appropriate for the government to transfer some part of the residual Old Age, Survivors and Disability Insurance Act (OASDI) outlays together with the taxes required for funding these programs to other portions of the budget as explicit welfare-tax transfers, and insurance-premium payments. Moral hazard and market risk are omnipresent, and it is possible that some private mutual funds might go bankrupt, leaving retirees indigent. The government can hedge this contingency by either establishing a catastrophic insurance fund, or leaving the task to the private insurance sector.[36] The same principle holds for Medicare ($250 billion).

---

[34] FICA and SECA taxes are levied on gross employee payroll and self-employed income before tax. When the monies are returned in the form of retirement benefits, up to 85 percent becomes taxable again for recipients filing joint returns with adjusted gross income in excess of $44,000. Cf. Max Skidmore, "The History and Politics of Health Care in America: From the Progressive Era to the Patient Protection and Affordable Care Act," *Poverty & Public Policy*, Vol. 3, No.1, pp.1–9. 2011.

[35] The term "Social Security" refers to the Old Age, Survivors and Disability Act (OASDI) of 1935 and subsequent amendments. The act now encompasses OASDI, unemployment benefits, Temporary Assistance to Needy Families (TANF), Medicare, Medicaid, State Children's Health Insurance Program (SCHIP), and Supplemental Security Income (SSI). SCHIP, TANF, Medicare, and SSI are welfare programs not limited to workers. Opponents of social-security privatization claim that the system is an "insurance," not a retirement program, but this is a dodge because the two elements can be easily separated, with the insurance component retained at a miniscule portion of the current expense. George W. Bush laid out a proposal for partial privatization in his 2005 State of the Union Address. Martin Feldstein and Jeffrey Liebman, eds., *The Distributional Aspect of Social Security Reform*, Chicago: University of Chicago Press, 2002; Andrew Achenbaum, *Social Security Visions and Revision*, A Twentieth Century Fund Study, New York: Cambridge University Press, 1986; Jeffrey Brown, Jeffrey Liebman, and David Wise, *Social Security Policy in a Changing Environment*, Chicago: University of Chicago Press, 2009.

[36] Various claims have been made about social security. Milton Friedman contended that it is unfair to the poor because the contribution of the rich is capped. Paul Samuelson drew attention to the fact that OASDI's funding structure resembles a Ponzi scheme, but others counterargue that the system is transparent. Cf. Nancy Altman, "The Current Battle in the Long Running War Over Social Security," *Poverty & Public Policy*, Vol. 3, No.1, Article 4, pp.1–4.2011.

Politarchs, claiming to have the people's welfare at heart, vehemently oppose privatization because unbundling OASDI exposes the complex transfers and parochial character of the program. OASDI has been a cash cow since 1983, taking in more money than it pays out. The residual is used derivatively to fund other programs (disguised income tax). But the string is being played out: OASDI alone is expected to show cumulative deficits in the trillions of dollars from 2016–2040.[37] The disability program also will start spilling red ink in 2016.[38] Both problems can be significantly ameliorated through privatization and enhanced transparency, allowing people to make rational choices instead of having superfluous debts piled on the nation's shoulders. The essential point is that OASDI, for those who choose to stay with the FICA system, should be transformed into a self-financing federal pension annuity fund, with all the social-welfare frills transferred from the trust fund to the federal budget, without mortgaging the future. There may be a case for establishing a minimum national income, but it should be made transparently, without contaminating the social-security system.[39]

Big government also must shun subsidizing the U.S. Postal Service's ever-mounting losses, running $11 billion in 2011, and slated to rapidly

---

[37] Status of Social Security and Medicare Programs, Summary of the 2010 Annual Reports, www.socialsecurity.gov Cf. Veronique de Rugy, "Social Security in Cash Flow Deficit," Mercatur Center, George Mason University, April 12, 2010.

[38] Henry Blodget, "GE Paid Less Tax Than You Last Year, Says the New York Times," Yahoo! Finance, March 29, 2011: "Our byzantine tax laws allow multinational companies not to pay U.S. taxes on overseas profits, carry forward losses." GE had $5.1 billion of domestic profit and still paid no tax. Readers should note that there is an alternative minimum tax on personal income tax that prevents GE type outcomes, but apparently not on corporate taxes. "Biggest Public Firms Paid Little U.S. Tax, Study Says," *New York* Times, November 3, 2011:

Warren E. Buffett, take note. It is not just a few wealthy individuals paying unusually low taxes to the federal government. Corporate America is not far behind. A comprehensive study (Citizens for Tax Justice) released on Thursday found that 280 of the biggest publicly traded American companies faced federal income tax bills equal to 18.5 percent of their profits during the last three years – little more than half the official corporate rate of 35 percent and lower than their competitors in many industrialized countries.... Wells Fargo Bank, which is a large holding of Mr. Buffett's company, Berkshire Hathaway reported a total of $49 billion in profits in 2008 through 2010, yet received a tax benefit of $651 million.

[39] See "Over 350 Experts Call for Entitlement Reform Now," letter to John Boehner (Speaker of the House), Harry Reid (Senate Majority Leader), Nancy Pelosi (House Minority Leader), and Mitch McConnell (Senate Minority Leader), April 4, 2011: "The President's National Commission on Fiscal Responsibility and Reform concluded that we are at a national 'moment of truth,' saying 'We cannot play games or put off hard choices any longer. Without regard to party, we have a patriotic duty to keep the promise of America to give our children and grandchildren a better life.'" http://americanactionforum.org/issues/over-350-experts-call-entitlement-reform-now

increase as demand for physical postal delivery drops as a consequence of internet competition.[40]

REGULATION

Regulatory simplification is another area for rolling back big government and can be combined with tighter supervision in critical sectors like banking and finance. This is a case where less often is more, and fine turning is imperative. The federal government routinely issues a torrent of rules and regulations, camouflaged as simplification. This proliferation stems from legislatures' and regulators' irrepressible urge to paper-microregulate everything no matter how peripheral the benefit or how great the cost. The exercise creates featherbedded federal jobs, imposes colossal reporting obligations, and wastes time, when the same revenue and control goals could be achieved by targeting a few strategic parameters. Politarchs have had no difficulty exempting 47 percent of income earners from federal-income taxation, and the same concept should be applied to regulation broadly. Authentic tax simplification would close the kinds of loopholes that allowed General Electric to pay no corporate tax in 2009, despite reporting $12 billion in profit,[41] and AARP to enjoy nonprofit status while earning more than a billion dollars in for-profit business income.[42] Duplicative regulation, moreover, can be eliminated by assigning primary responsibility to states and localities. Tighter banking and financial regulation only involves better supervision and prohibiting excess balance-sheet leveraging.

---

[40] Henry Blodget, "And Now the U.S. Postal Service is About to Go Belly up..." Yahoo! Finance, September 6, 2011. Cries for subsidies are certain to mount because the U.S. Postal Service employs 653,000 people with generous benefits and pensions. Labor costs are 80 percent of the Postal Service's expenses, compared with 35 and 40 percent for UPS and FedEx respectively. Jennifer Liberto, "Why Congress Can't Save the Postal Service Right Now," CNNMoney, November 29, 2011.

[41] Richard Burkhauser and Mary Daly, *Declining Work and Welfare of People with Disabilities: What Went Wrong and a Strategy for Change*, American Enterprise Press, 2011.

[42] Ricardo Alonso-Zaldivar and Stephen Ohlemacher, "House Republicans Seek IRS Probe of AARP," Yahoo! Finance, March 30, 2011: "Three veteran GOP representatives released a report that estimates AARP could make an additional $1 billion over 10 years on health insurance plans." The AARP is a key lobbyist for Obama care. "Royalties from licensing the use of AARP's name earned $657 million for the organization in 2009." AARP Services is a wholly taxable subsidiary of the AARP and sells insurance products. It is partnered with UnitedHealth Group and Aetna.

REMEDYING HARD TIMES

Recapitulating the key recommendations, the restoration of true democratic U.S. economic governance should proceed as follows:

First, a mandatory ceiling should be imposed on the national debt, and policymakers required to smooth normal business-cycle fluctuations within this constraint. The mandatory debt-GDP ratio should be set at 25 percent (roughly a quarter of the current figure).

Second, federal government spending (excluding social security and Medicare) should be cut by 50 percent to eliminate the current fiscal deficit.

Third, all spending by the State Department and Defense Department supporting multinational, transnational, and world government transfers of U.S. sovereignty to other individuals and bodies should be eliminated, together with all other foreign activities primarily promoting politarchic public-service trafficking abroad. These cuts are included in the 50-percent reduction suggested in point 2.

Fourth, federal grants-in-aid should be abolished, with responsibility for funding some or all of these programs assumed by the states. This will make state legislatures fully accountable for the cost of their activities, without what appears to them to be Washington's free money. The federal government can continue to provide emergency assistance to states to alleviate catastrophes. If state legislatures and local authorities deem it appropriate, some of these monies can be allocated to cooperative activities favored by advocates of participatory democracy.[43]

Fifth, a moratorium should be declared on federal mandates, followed by the establishment of a commission to eliminate all existing mandates except those needed to fill gaps in the people's ability to maximize their private utility. This rule is dictated by the integrated public-private economic optimization concept laid out at the beginning of the chapter. It means that all mandates enriching big business and big social advocacy must be abolished. Only mandates essential for efficiently carrying out routine administrative activities in accordance with the people's wishes should be retained.

---

[43] Some democratic theorists contend that government should be run directly by the people, understood as individuals and communities. The concept is participatory democracy. We appreciate the principle, and believe that the ideal is compatible with true democracy, but it should also be noted that participatory democracy in and of itself cannot solve the federal politocracy problem that is the central concern of this treatise unless politarchs are defanged. Participatory democratic theory is closely associated with Fabian socialism. See George Douglas Howard Cole, *Self-Government in Industry*, London: Bell, 1917.

Sixth, the federal government should drastically pare down and/or cease providing subsidies to business (including exports, technological innovation, and environmental protection).[44] The people's revenues should not be transferred to big business, big social advocacy, or anyone else on the pretext of optimally microregulating economic activity, whenever state agents are clearly incompetent to provide the benefits claimed. Bureaucrats rarely choose winners.

Seventh, judicial activism serving the same improper ends should be outlawed.

Eighth, federal monetary and financial regulation should be targeted primarily on preserving price and wage stability instead of providing windfall profits to Wall Street and other speculators under the guise of promoting full employment. This precludes QE-infinity.

Points 1, 5, 6, and 7 also are applicable to state governments and should be pursued there to achieve a complete true democratic solution.

None of these eight actions pose any serious technical hurdles. They are all matters of political will. Some may seem out of reach, but this is only because Americans have been indoctrinated to believe that government services provide the people with full value. Once the emperor's new clothes are rightly perceived as figments of popular imagination,[45] citizens can organize to shrink big government and defang politocracy.

ROLLING BACK, DOWNSIZING, DELAYERING, AND PRUNING

The eight steps elaborated in the true democratic framework above can be condensed into a simple four-pronged action plan: rolling back, downsizing, delayering, and pruning. First, contemporary federal spending should be rolled back to the pre-financial crisis, 2007 level. Second, individual programs should be downsized in accordance with true democratic demand. Third, the cost of these programs should be reduced by delayering

---

[44] Although the United States has been a top innovator for decades, one recent study estimates that its rate of progress in becoming a new, knowledge-based innovation economy is slower than that of all the other thirty-nine countries/regions that were evaluated. A troubling sign is that patents issued to American applicants have dropped recently while those issued to foreign applicants continue to increase. In contrast, Israel has been accelerating its progress as an innovation-based economy over the last fifteen years. Israel has attracted more than twice as much venture capital investment per person than the United States and thirty times more than Europe. Hudson Institute, Conference on Economic Lessons from Israel: Jumpstarting Trade and Investment, March 19, 2012.

[45] Hans Christian Andersen, *The Annotated Hans Christian Andersen*, New York: W. W. Norton & Company, 2008.

(eliminating duplication),[46] and finally, the assortment of public services within each budgetary category should be optimized by pruning programs,[47] mandates,[48] and \$1 trillion of tax expenditures (tax breaks),[49] that is, by cutting superfluous activities and retaining essentials.

The hemorrhaging cannot be completely staunched because politicians know how to wage trench warfare in the battle to preserve programs, noncompetitive purchases, tax expenditures, and mandates. Nonetheless, much

[46] Ben Feller, "Obama Seeks Power to Merge Agencies," Yahoo Finance!, January 13, 2012. The president has other parsimonious options: "President Barack Obama on Friday took aim at his government's own messy bureaucracy, prodding Congress to give him greater power to merge agencies and promising he would start by collapsing six major economic departments into one. Pressing Republicans on one of their own political issues, Obama said it was time for an 'effective, lean government.'"

[47] Christina Sommers, "How the CDC is Overstating Sexual Violence in the US," *Washington Post*, January 30, 2012: "The CDC's National Intimate Partner and Sexual Violence Survey found that, in the United States in 2010, approximately 1.3 million women were raped and an additional 12.6 million women and men were victims of sexual violence." It reported, "More than 1 in 3 women and 1 in 4 men have experienced rape, physical violence and/ or stalking by an intimate partner in their lifetime." Health and Human Services Secretary Kathleen Sebelius hailed the report for giving "a clear picture of the devastating impact these violent acts have on the lives of millions of Americans." "In fact, what the study reveals is the devastating impact that careless advocacy research can have on truth. The agency's figures are wildly at odds with official crime statistics. The FBI found that 84,767 rapes were reported to law-enforcement authorities in 2010. The Bureau of Justice Statistics' *National Crime Victimization Survey*, the gold standard in crime research, reports 188,380 rapes and sexual assaults on females and males in 2010."

[48] Kimberly Hefling, "College Presidents Wary of Obama Cost-control Plan, Yahoo! News, January 29, 2012:

"Fuzzy math," Illinois State University's president called it. "Political theater of the worst sort," said the University of Washington's head. President Barack Obama's new plan to force colleges and universities to contain tuition or face losing federal dollars is raising alarm among education leaders who worry about the threat of government overreach. Particularly sharp words came from the presidents of public universities; they're already frustrated by increasing state budget cuts. The reality, said Illinois State's Al Bowman, is that simple changes cannot easily overcome deficits at many public schools. He said he was happy to hear Obama, in a speech Friday at the University of Michigan, urge state-level support of public universities. But, Bowman said, given the decreases in state aid, tying federal support to tuition prices is a product of fuzzy math.

[49] The Congressional Joint Committee on Taxation estimates tax expenditures annually for more than 180 special programs listed in the U.S. tax code. The figure for 2009 was \$1 trillion. The major recipient was wealthy homeowners. The majority of tax expenditures are targeted at individual social benefits and services. See Christopher Faricy, "The Politics of Social Policy in America: Indirect Versus Direct Social Spending," *The Journal of Publics*, Vol. 73, No. 1, January 2011, pp. 74–83; Kim Dixon, "Analysis: Tax Breaks on Autopilot with Little Debate," Yahoo! News, January 16, 2012: "Recipients of more than \$30 billion of tax breaks hope to catch a ride on the payroll tax legislation expiring next month, with special interests – from Diageo to Nascar racetrack owners to major U.S. banks – lobbying to win renewals of their preferences in the sprawling U.S. tax code." It is impossible to make head or tail of social benefits on an item-by-item basis.

can be accomplished with caps, cuts, and sequestration. The public can demand that tax expenditures be reduced gradually, or in one fell swoop, leaving the fine print to the legislators. Additionally, the president can refuse to spend monies that Congress appropriates if they are unwarranted and can instruct his administrators to refrain from enforcing onerous mandates. Both the Congress and the president are to blame from mandate abuse.

The repeated claim that Congress and the president cannot responsibly extricate the United States from its economic plight therefore is false. Rolling back, downsizing, delayering, pruning, eradicating politocratic subsidies to big business and big politocracy are feasible and beneficial. They haven't been accomplished because politarchs are unwilling to put the people's welfare ahead of their own well-being.[50] They must be pressured with organized civic campaigns.

Rolling back, downsizing, delayering, and pruning will undo America's microeconomic paralysis. However, they alone won't prevent high unemployment, inflation, trade imbalances, and financial crises because federal officials can still overborrow, print money, and manipulate the Fed funds rate. Washington is capable of running budgetary deficits at half the current level of spending. Moreover, nothing prevents the Federal Reserve chairman from providing cheap credit and subsidies to insiders[51] or monetizing the debt (QE-infinity). Nor is there anything that deters federal

---

[50] Media treatment of the "fiscal cliff" illustrates the point. Democrats and Republicans are using apocalyptic rhetoric to persuade the public that they are making Herculean efforts to cut the 2013 federal budget deficit which will probably run $1.3 trillion. But the "fiscal cliff" and cutting they describe on close reading is chicken feed. See Damian Paletta, "White House Say Government May Help Firms Buffer Cost of Sequester," *Wall Street Journal*, September 29, 2012: "Democrats and Republicans are expected to work between the Nov. 6 election and the end of the year on an effort to avoid the cuts, but so far lawmakers remain far apart. The cuts, referred to in Washington as the 'sequester,' were put in place last year as part of a deal to raise the debt ceiling. The cuts would total $109 billion in annual spending reductions over nine years." Cf. Andrew Taylor, "CBO: Debt Crisis Looms Absent Major Policy Changes," Yahoo! Finance, June 22, 2011: "CBO, the nonpartisan agency that calculates the cost and economic impact of legislation and government policy, says that the nation's rapidly growing debt burden increases the probability of a fiscal crisis in which investors lose faith in U.S. bonds and force policymakers to make drastic spending cuts or tax increase." This is characterized as a European-style debt crisis. John Huntsman, former Governor of Utah, and a Republican presidential candidate recently vetted a plan to cut obstructive government regulation, kill Obama's health-care program and simplify taxation, but failed to address the need to go beyond repackaging to wholesale downsizing. See "Huntsman's Good Economic Plan," *Wall Street Journal*, September 2, 2011.

[51] "Bernanke Doubling Down on Housing Bet Asks Government to Help: Mortgages," Yahoo! Finance, January 11, 2012:

authorities from laxly regulating the speculative activities of banks and financial institutions (shadow banks), or Congress from granting various tax incentives and subsidies to the real-estate, natural-resources, and other hard-asset industries. These and other abuses need to be remedied with stern restrictions on deficit spending, money emission, credit creation, insurance guarantees,[52] speculative financial practices,[53] leveraging,[54] and private speculation.[55]

Macroeconomic stability today is sacrificed by paying lip service to the imperative of full employment. No cost, it is claimed, is too heavy to bear if everyone has a job, even though deficit spending and low interest rates have not cured the problem since 2008 and didn't make a significant dent during the 1930s. Making a fetish of full employment is nonsense. The right goal is to maximize national well-being, not to ruin the country providing entitlements. The right policy is to prohibit Congress from deficit spending and accumulating national debt beyond prudent ceilings and to compel the

Since the Fed started buying $1.25 trillion of mortgage bonds in January 2009, the value of U.S. housing has fallen 4.1 percent, and is down 32 percent from its 2006 peak, according to an S&P/Case-Shiller index. The central bank is poised to buy about $200 billion this year, or more than 20 percent of new loans, as it reinvests debt that's being paid off. Some Fed officials have said they may support additional purchases that Barclays Capital estimates could total as much as $750 billion.... The central bank's purchases of mortgage bonds with yields at record lows is increasing the risk of eventual losses for the Fed, said Anthony B. Sanders, a professor of real-estate finance at George Mason University in Fairfax, Virginia.... Though the bigger ideas in Bernanke's report may sound good, "'repercussions" would include further entangling banks and the government in housing, said Jim Vogel, a debt analyst at FTN Financial in Memphis, Tennessee. That could limit financial companies' access to capital and make it impossible for the U.S. to unwind its involvement in mortgages for decades, he said. The study said it avoided discussions of "longer-term restructuring of the housing-finance market.

[52] The U.S. government for the first time is poised to become the largest source of outstanding loans for home mortgage and consumer credit loans, eclipsing the private sector. Government-financed borrowing for these purposes now runs at $6.3 trillion per year (up from $4.4 trillion in 2006) in the first quarter of 2011. Private mortgage and consumer credit by contrast was $6.6 trillion, down from $8.5 trillion in 2006. Gillian Tett, "The State is Now the Dominant Force in US Capital Markets," *Financial Times*, July 1, 2011.

[53] The EU may be on the cusp of doing this. See Huw Jones, "EU Lawmakers Back Curbs on High Frequency Share Trade," *Chicago Tribune*, September 26, 2012.

[54] Steven Rosefielde, Masaaki Kuboniwa, and Satoshi Mizobata, (eds.), *Prevention and Crisis Management: Lessons for Asia from the 2008 Crisis*, Singapore: World Scientific Publishers, 2012.

[55] William Cohan, "How Wall Street Turned a Crisis Into a Cartel," Yahoo! Finance, January 10, 2012. "Today, there are far fewer than 17 firms in control of the investment-banking business and rules the IPO market. The renewed power of the Wall Street cartel may be the worst consequence of the 2008 decision to rescue Wall Street rather than let it collapse under the weight of its broken business model."

Federal Reserve to restore sound money.[56] Under these new rules, Congress will retain limited power to counter-cyclically deficit spend, and the Federal Reserve will still have some monetary discretion, but both will be enjoined to stabilize the economic system first and alleviate employment within that constraint.

Competitive economic theory teaches that true democracy, free from politocratic distortion and avoidable destabilization, will inter-temporally maximize individual and public utility, taking full advantage of the opportunities afforded by science and technological progress. Second-best versions of the same theory that acknowledge the unlikelihood of perfectly competitive outcomes, similarly imply that true U.S. democracy will provide superior outcomes, and lead the United States to dramatically outperform China's, India's, Brazil's, Russia's, and Japan's economies as they are currently configured.

America's economic paralysis, crisis, and decline from this perspective are not inevitable. Nor are they attributable to the founding fathers' flawed paradigm. The fault rests entirely at the doorstep of true democracy's elected enemies who have beguiled voters into believing that they can have whatever they wish if they trust their politicians and wink at their transgressions.

REASON AND RAINBOWS

It can be counterargued that the real world is too complicated to be adequately appraised with true democratic theory, either in a perfectly or workably competitive framework;[57] that important variables have been omitted in reducing the United States' economic and foreign policy woes to a single cause. This certainly was Keynes's claim, and is Paul Krugman's view today.[58] However, they and innumerable others, including Karl Marx, Vladimir Lenin, Joseph

---

[56] "Fed's Latest Easing Could Cost $1 Trillion: Economists," Yahoo! Finance, January 19, 2012. The Federal Reserve is expected to purchase $1 trillion of mortgage-backed securities (MBS) to further reduce interest rates in an effort to shore up the real-estate market. This will drastically impair the balance sheet of the Federal Reserves and threatens a bout of rampant inflation but also will provide income to the banking sector. As usual, politarchs are willing to impose immense economic risks on the public for narrow insider benefit.

[57] The term "workably competitive" means that economic activity is marred to some extent by anticompetitive private and public forces, including media manipulation.

[58] Paul Krugman, "Nobody Understands Debt," Op Ed, *New York Times*, January 1, 2012: "So yes, debt matters. But right now, other things matter more. We need more, not less, government spending to get us out of our unemployment trap. And the wrongheaded, ill-informed obsession with debt is standing in the way."

Stalin, Jean Monnet, and Robert Schuman, have had their day in court,[59] with little positive to show for it. Indeed, it is our contention that the obdurate belief that big elected government is intrinsically better than true democracy lies at the root of the United States' economic tribulations, and even if we are mistaken, opponents must acknowledge that neither grand counter-theories nor muddling have yet saved the day.

It will cost little to test our hypothesis. A program based on these principles could hardly make matters worse, and any adverse social consequence can be lessened by tweaking taxes,[60] fine-tuning state and local programs, and appealing to private charity. There is a true national democratic option. All Americans need do is embrace practical reason and drive the politocrats from the temple.[61]

---

[59] Jakub Grygiel, "One Market, One Currency, One People: The Faulty Logic of Europe," Foreign Policy Research Institute, Endnotes, January 10, 2012:

Were the EU a term paper, a lenient professor would likely give it a D+... The project of a united Europe is based on the belief that economic unity (itself poorly defined) will lead to political unity. Such a line of causation demanded a technocratic approach. Missing the underlying national unity, the establishment of a common market and a common currency had to be pursued by a supranational elite with a very tenuous electoral accountability. Absent a *demos*, the technocrats had to take over the decision-making process. The hope, based on the assumption that a common economy creates a unified people, was that at a certain point a European demos would arise allowing the functioning of a European democracy. But until then, technocracy would have to suffice, and indeed, it was the only way to manage European affairs. The "democratic deficit" of EU institutions is, therefore, a direct outcome of the faith in the transformative powers of economic structures.

[60] Once politarchic tax and subsidies are purged from the system, there can be a reasoned debate on the level and incidence of taxes and transfers.

[61] Henry Blodget, "Yes, it is a New Year – And the United States is Still Broke," *The Daily Ticker*, January 3, 2012: "The U.S. government General Account Office end fiscal year 2011 annual report concludes that the country is also clearly on an unsustainable course. Here are the highlights: The U.S. ran a $1.3 trillion budget deficit in 2011, flat with 2010 and the third year in a row of deficits over $1.3 trillion. The U.S. federal debt load continues to climb as a percentage of GDP and is expected to explode over the next few decades. The big problem in our current and future finances is NOT spending on defense, education, the environment, and the other government programs that Democrats and Republicans love to fight about. The big problem in our budget is a combination of taxes that are currently off their peak as a percentage of GDP and future unfunded commitments to Medicare and Social Security. The amount of the "unfunded liability" for our social-insurance programs (Medicare and Social Security) is now $34 trillion. This is an increase of $3 trillion from last year. This number has increased at about $1.7 trillion per year for the past ten years. If not for some absurd assumptions about how Congress is going to eventually chop the cost of Medicare (the so-called "doc-fix" that pays doctors more for Medicare procedures than Congress passes every year), the liability would be $46 trillion. So, what's the implication and solution? Over the long haul, the intelligent solution is a combination of modestly higher taxes and reductions in Medicare and social-security benefits. The other option is bankruptcy."

GOOD FOR THE GANDER

The revitalization of a true democratic United States on balance should be good news for the rest of the world. Revived U.S. prosperity will spur domestic innovation, increase international trade and investment, and stimulate economic activity abroad. Living standards everywhere should broadly rise, although some whose wealth and power were linked with U.S. politocracy will be deprived of their privileges. On the political front, faith in the tarnished democratic paradigm will be restored, accelerating nation-based democratic globalization. This development will be welcome by all who prefer true democracy to alternative forms of governance. What is good for the goose in this regard should be good for the gander. Paraphrasing Mikhail Gorbachev, true democracy should be beneficial "for our country and the world,"[62] even though it is not a panacea.

CLARION CALL

Many Americans believe that history is purposive, driven by reason, and therefore will culminate in true democracy. Their faith has multiple secular roots that can be traced diversely to Gottfried Leibniz, Emmanuel Kant, Georg Wilhelm Friedrich Hegel, Karl Marx, and Francis Fukuyama. The conviction cannot be disproven despite Voltaire's scathing eighteenth-century satire because the end of days is unspecified.[63] Every failure is construed as a bump in the road,[64] and every reform is a reset opportunity for believers.[65] This doublethink makes it difficult for Americans to grasp that their democracy has been usurped and to contemplate how the problem can be redressed.

Hope has its charm but is also a refuge for politicians because it encourages the public to believe that balloting comes to the same thing as sovereign popular rule, and that whatever is wrong, the United States' electoral system will remedy itself soon. Providence, however, is not enough. Politicians will continue blowing smoke in people's eyes until they are driven out of electoral government or cut down to size.

---

[62] Mikhail Gorbachev, *Perestroika: New Thinking for Our Country and the World*, New York: Harper & Row, 1988.

[63] Voltaire, *Candide, or the Optimist*, London: Penguin, 1759.

[64] Westerners are susceptible to other types of wishful thinking like getting something for nothing, free lunches, the money tree, and manna from heaven.

[65] Brigitte Geissel and Kenneth Newton, eds., *Evaluating Democratic Innovations: Curing the Democratic Malaise?* London: Routledge, 2012.

Americans can't have it all – politocracy, true democracy, and the best of everything providence provides. If the nation really desires prosperity, stability, social justice, well-being and national security for our country and the world, the American people must choose true democracy, eschewing sociocracy and rolling back the politarchic tide. [66]

---

[66] All of these disorders were grasped in their essentials by Enlightenment democrats like John Locke and the United States' founding fathers and the safeguards they recommended remain valid. Solutions for the West and the rest therefore can be readily found by returning to basics (including an appreciation of minority-property rights), and purging what purports to be superior modern democracy of its antidemocratic accretions.

Conclusion

America's hard times and fading international stature are due to the usurpation of its elected political system by politicians in collusion with big business and big social-welfare-state advocates promoting excess big government to feather their own nests. Their machinations have not only diminished living standards, inured high unemployment, and widened inequalities, but they also threaten to trigger a financial mega crisis driven by excessive national debt and imperil U.S. national security.[1]

Usurpation has been a "noiseless revolution" because, among other reasons, Americans have become accustomed to speaking as if any elected government is a democracy. This has prevented most observers from appreciating that elected governments that do as they please without adhering to

---

[1] There has been a lively debate about whether debt to GDP ratios in excess of 90 percent retard long-term growth. The controversy is primarily about statistics rather than causality, and doesn't directly address the likelihood that stratospheric American debt GDP ratios will trigger a global megacrisis. Cf. Carmen Reinhart and Kenneth Rogoff, "Growth in a Time of Debt," NBER Working Paper No. 15639, January 2010, http://www.nber. org/papers/w15639, and Thomas Herndon, Michael Ash, and Robert Pollin, "Does High Public Debt Consistently Stifle Economic Growth? A Critique of Reinhart and Rogoff," University of Massachusetts Working Paper, No.322, April 2013, http://www.peri.umass. edu/fileadmin/pdf/working_papers/working_papers_301–350/WP322.pdf

Stephen Ziliak and Diedre McCloskey, "We Agree that Statistical Significance Proves Essentially Nothing: A Rejoinder to Thomas Mayer," *Economic Journal Watch*, Vol.10, No.1, January 2013, pp. 1–11.

As stated in the preface we have shown that: (1) the U.S. economy is micro-inefficient and macro-destabilized by bad state governance; (2) bad governance is caused by insider self-seeking; (3) excessive bigness is an aspect of insider self-seeking; (4) insider goals (codetermined by politicians, big business and big social advocacy) conflict with the people's will; (5) the people's will as reflected in the Constitution requires drastic governmental downsizing; and (6) if the rollback is accomplished the principal sources of the U.S. micro- and microeconomic disorders will be significantly ameliorated. Each of these propositions was rigorously formulated, analyzed, and objectively tested in the preceding chapters.

the detailed wishes of the majority, subject to constitutional property and civil-rights protections, are antidemocratic.

Economic theory clearly teaches that the more elected officials and their bureaucracies and collaborators use the people's resources to enrich themselves, the more damage they do to the nation's economy, welfare, social justice, and security. The evidence compiled in this volume confirms the hypothesis. U.S. politocracy has straitjacketed competition, misallocated resources, overtaxed the middle class, inured high unemployment, reduced real wages, spawned income inequality and social injustice, depressed initiative and innovation, fueled financial speculation, set the stage for a mega debt crisis, embroiled the nation in foreign imbroglios, degraded national security, and shed an immense amount of needless blood.[2]

America's leaders concede nothing about the damage they have done and continue to do. They claim credit for anything that plausibly can be considered an achievement, blame everybody else for failures, and press inexorably for more resources to cure problems they themselves have created. Denial has served them well.

Things are going badly for the nation, and could turn calamitous unless the United States and Europe shed their denial and face up to looming financial mega crises driven by national debt and the growing risks of great power conflict. It is not too late.[3]

Americans can still stand up for their Constitutional rights. Transpartisan politarchy can be eradicated by slashing big government and rationalizing domestic and foreign policy strictly in accordance with Enlightenment democratic principles. If properly executed, a few simple adjustments will install true democracy, insure national prosperity, promote national security, advance the cause of global security, enhance the United States' global standing, and restore democracy's tarnished beacon. The fate of universal true democracy may well hang in the balance. These virtuous outcomes won't come to pass without a new Kuhnian political paradigm shift that replaces partisan wrangling over government spoils

---

[2] Larry Kudlow, "Global Recession? Warning Signs Everywhere," Yahoo! Finance, June 14, 2012.

[3] Alkman Granitsas and Marcus Walker, "Greece's Fringe Parties Surge Amid Bailout Ire," *The Wall Street Journal*, March 28, 2012. "The election, not yet scheduled but expected in April or May, is shaping up as a public revolt against Greece's political establishment, which has backed the austerity policies that are the price of financial life support from Europe and the International Monetary Fund. Mainstream politicians are increasingly painted as leading Greece into a debt trap, then impoverishing it in trying to escape." With regard to defense, the United States has surrendered it strategic independence and is rapidly compromising its nuclear deterrent. See Chapter 9.

with a popular struggle to roll back trans-partisan politocracy. Partisan competition between the Democratic and Republican parties cannot do the job, and the invisible hand does not offer a viable alternative. The American people must purge the nation of its elected enemies themselves through direct political action.[4]

---

4 "If we can but prevent the government from wasting the labors of the people, under the pretense of taking care of them, they must become happy" (Thomas Jefferson to Thomas Cooper, November 29, 1802).

Bibliography

Achenbaum, Andrew. *Social Security Visions and Revision*, New York: Twentieth Century Fund, 1986.

Adams, John. "The Foundation of Government," 1776.

Altman, Nancy. "The Current Battle in the Long Running War Over Social Security," *Poverty & Public Policy*, Vol. 3, No.1, Article 4, 2011, pp. 1–4.

Altman, Roger. "The Great Crash, 2008," *Foreign Affairs*, January/February 2009.

Andersen, Hans Christian. *The Annotated Hans Christian Andersen*, New York: W. W. Norton & Company, 2008.

Anderson, Perry. *Lineages of the Absolutist State*, London: Verso, 1974.

Arrow, Kenneth. *Social Choice and Individual Values*, New York: Wiley, 1951.

Barro, Robert. "The Ricardian Approach to Budget Deficits," *The Journal of Economic Perspectives* Vol. 3, No. 2, 1989, pp. 37–54.

Barth, James R., Li, Tong, Phumiwasana, Triphon, and Yago, Glenn. *A Short History of the Subprime Mortgage Market Meldown*, Santa Monica, CA: Milken Institute, 2008.

Benabou, Roland, and Jean Tirole. "Individual and Corporate Social Responsibility," *Economica*, 2010, Vol. 77, pp. 1–19.

Bergson, Abram. "A Reformulation of Certain Aspects of Welfare Economics," *Quarterly Journal of Economics*, Vol. 52, No. 1, February 1938, pp. 310–34.

"Social Choice and Welfare Economics under Representative Government," *Journal of Public Economics*, Vol. 6, No. 3, October 1976, pp. 171–90.

Berle, Adolf and Means, Gardner. *The Modern Corporation and Private Property*, New York: Macmillan, 1932.

Berliner, Joseph. *Innovation in Soviet Industry*, Cambridge, MA: MIT Press, 1975.

Blank, Steven, ed. *Russian Nuclear Weapons: Past, Present and Future*, Carlisle Barracks, PA: Strategic Studies Institute, U.S. Army War College, 2012.

Blank, Stephen. "The Chinese and Asian Impact of Russian Nuclear Policy," *Defense & Security Analysis* XXVIII, No. 1, 2012, pp. 36–54

Blinder, Alan and Zandi, Mark. "How the Great Depression Was Brought to an End," July 27, 2010. http://www.economy.com/mark-zandi/documents/end-of-great-recession.pdf

Blumenthal, Daniel. "How Many Nuclear-Armed Countries Does Obama Want in Asia?" *Foreign Policy*, Nov 29, 2011. http://www.defensestudies.org/cds/2011/11/

Bolton, John. "The Innocents Abroad," *National Review*, Sept 6, 2011.

Borchert, Jens and Zeiss, Jurgen, eds. *The Political Class in Advanced Democracies*, New York: Oxford University Press, 2003.

Brody, Dan. *The Haliburton Agenda: The Politics of Oil and Money*, New York: John Wiley and Sons, 2004.

Brogan, Hugh. *Alexis De Tocqueville: A Life*, New Haven: Yale University Press, 2008.

Brown, Nathan J., ed. *The Dynamics of Democratization: Dictatorship, Development and Diffusion*, Baltimore: Johns Hopkins Press, 2011.

Brown, Jeffrey, Liebman, Jeffrey and Wise, David. *Social Security Policy in a Changing Environment*, Chicago: University of Chicago Press, 2009.

Buchanan, James. *Democracy in Deficit: The Political Legacy of Lord Keynes*, Indianapolis, IN: Liberty Fund, 1999.

Buchanan, James and Tollison, Robert. *The Limits of Liberty Between Anarchy and Leviathan*, Chicago: University of Chicago Press, 1975.

Budget of the United States Government: Browse Fiscal Year 2011, Historical Tables, Section 3, Federal Outlays by Function, Table 11.2, p. 222.

Burkhauser, Richard and Daly, Mary. *Declining Work and Welfare of People with Disabilities: What Went Wrong and a Strategy for Change*, Washington, DC: American Enterprise Press, 2011.

Chomsisengphet, Souphala and Pennington-Cross, Anthony. "The Evolution of the Subprime Mortgage Market," *Federal Reserve Bank of St.Louis Review*, Vol. 88, No.1, January/February 2006, pp. 31–56.

"A Look at Subprime Mortgage Originations: 2000–2007." http://www.ftc.gov/be/workshops/mortgage/presentations/Cross_Chomsisengphet_Subprime_2008.pdf

Chu, Yun-Han, Diamond, Larry, Nathan, Andrew and Shin, Doh Chull. *How East Asians View Democracy*, New York: Columbia University Press, 2008.

Clinton, Bill. "The era of big government … over." *State of the Union Address*, 1996.

Coase, Ronald. "The New Institutional Economics," *American Economic Review*, Vol. 88, No. 2, May 1998, pp. 72–74.

Condorcet, *Life of Voltaire, in Works*, Vol. IV, Paris: Gale ECCO, 2010, pp. 176–77.

Congelton, R., Hillman, A. and Konrad, K. *Forty Years of Rent Seeking*, Berlin: Springer Verlag, 2008.

Cooper, Robert. *The Breaking of Nations: Order and Chaos in the Twenty-First Century*, New York: Atlantic Monthly Press, 2003.

Copland, James. *Trial Lawyers Inc.: Attorneys General – A Report on the Alliance between State AGs and the Plaintiffs' Bar 2011*, Manhattan Institute's Center for Legal Policy, 2011.

Dadush, Uri. "Global Rebalancing: The Dangerous Obsession," Carnegie Endowment for International Peace, Policy Brief 90, February 2011.

Dallago, Bruno and Guglielmetti, Chiara. "Eurozone and Global Imbalances: Two Europes?" in Rosefielde, Steven, Kuboniwa, Masaaki and Mizobata, Satoshi., eds., *Two Asias: The Emerging Postcrisis Divide*, Singapore: World Scientific, 2011.

Delong, J. Bradford and Magin, Konstati. "A Short Note on the Size of the Dot-Com Bubble," National Bureau of Economic Research Working Paper 12011, January 2006.

Descartes, Rene. *Meditationes de Prima Philosophia*, 1641.

Diamond, Larry. "The Democratic Rollback," *Foreign Affairs*, March/April 2008, pp. 36–48. http://www.foreignaffairs.org/20080301faessay87204/larry-diamond/the-democratic-rollback.html

Eaton, Jonathan and Fernandez, Raquel. "Sovereign Debt," in Grossman, Gene and Rogoff, Kenneth, eds., *Handbook of International Economics*, Vol. 3, Amsterdam: Elsevier Science B.V., 1995, chapter 39.

Faricy, Christopher. "The Politics of Social Policy in America: Indirect Versus Direct Social Spending," *The Journal of Publics*, Vol. 73, No. 1, January 2011, pp. 74–83.

Financial Audit, Resolution Trust Corporation's 1995 and 1994 Financial Statements, *U.S. General Accounting Office*, July 1996, pp. 8, 13.

Feldstein, Martin and Liebman, Jeffrey, eds., *The Distributional Aspect of Social Security Reform*, Chicago: University of Chicago Press, 2002.

Fleming, Thomas. *The New Dealers' War*, New York: Basic Books, 2001.

Fonte, John. *Sovereignty or Submission: Will Americans Rule Themselves or Be Ruled by Others?*, New York: Encounter Books, 2011.

Freud, Sigmund. *Introduction to Psychoanalysis*, 1917.
Beyond the Pleasure Principle, 1920.
The Ego and the Id, 1923.
Civilization and Its Discontents, 1930.

Fromkin, David. "Entangling Alliances," *Foreign Affairs*, Vol. 48, Issue 4, July 1970, p. 688.

Fromm, Erich, Suzuki, D. T. and DeMartino, Richard. *Zen Buddhism and Psychoanalysis*, New York: Harper and Row, 1960.

Frum, David. *How We Got Here: The '70s*, New York: Basic Books, 2000.

Fukuyama, Francis. *The End of History and the Last Man*, New York: Free Press, 1992.

Galbraith, John Kenneth. *The New Industrial State*, New York: Houghton-Mifflin, 1967.
Economics and the Public Purpose, New York: Houghton-Mifflin, 1973.
The Good Society, New York: Mariner Books, 1997.

Ganguly, Sumit, Diamond, Larry and Plattner, Marc. *The State of India's Democracy*, Baltimore: Johns Hopkins University Press, 2007.

Geissel, Brigitte and Newton, Kenneth., eds., *Evaluating Democratic Innovations: Curing the Democratic Malaise?*, London: Routledge, 2012.

Gerth, Hans, and Mills, C. Wright. *From Weber, Max*. London: Routledge and Kegan Paul, 1970.

Gorbachev, Mikhail. *Perestroika: New Thinking for Our Country and the World*, New York: Harper & Row, 1988.

Grauwe, Paul De. *Economics of Monetary Union*, New York: Oxford University Press, 2000.

Gregory, Paul. "Was Stalin Really Necessary?" The International Conference on Stalinism, Moscow, Dec 5, 2008.

Grotius, Hugo. *De jure belli ac pacis (On the Law of War and Peace)*, 1625.

Grygiel, Jakub. "One Market, One Currency, One People: The Faulty Logic of Europe," Foreign Policy Research Institute, Endnotes, January 10, 2012.

Halbwachs, Maurice. Rousseau:*The Social Contract, Book III*, Chapter XV, Paris: Aubier, 1943, pp. 339–40.

Hecht, Marie B. *John Quincy Adams*, New York: American Political Biography Press, 1972, pp. 330–31.

Hedlund, Stefan. *Invisible Hands, Russian Experience, and Social Science: Approaches to Understanding Systemic Failure*, Cambridge: Cambridge University Press, 2011.

Hegel, Georg Wilhelm Friedrich. *Lectures on the Philosophy of World History: Introduction, Reason in History*, New York: Cambridge University Press, 1975.

Herman, Arthur. *Commentary*, Vol. **132**, No. 5, Dec 2, 2011, p. 19.

Herman, Edward and Chomsky, Noam. *Manufacturing Consent: The Political Economy of the Mass Media*, Boston: Pantheon, 1988.

Herndon, Thomas, Michael Ash, and Robert Pollin. "Does High Public Debt Consistently Stifle Economic Growth? A Critique of Reinhart and Rogoff," University of Massachusetts Working Paper, No.322, April 2013, http://www.peri.umass.edu/fileadmin/pdf/working_papers/working_papers_301–350/WP322.pdf

Heston, Alan and Kuman, Vijay. "Institutional Flaws and Corruption Incentives in India," *Journal of Development Studies*, Vol. 44, No. 9, 2008, pp. 1243–61.

Hoffer, Erick. *The True Believer: Thoughts on the Nature of Mass Movements*, New York: Harper and Row, 1951.

Horowitz, David. *America's Political Class Under Fire: The Twentieth Centuries Great Culture Wars*, New York: Routledge, 2003.

Huntington, Samuel. "The West: Unique, Not Universal," *Foreign Affairs*, Vol. 75, No. 6 (Nov/Dec 1996), pp. 28–46.

Ikenberry, G. John. *Liberal Leviathan: The Origins, Crisis, and Transformation of the American System*, Princeton, NJ: Princeton University Press, 2011.

"The Rise of China and the Future of the West," *Foreign Affairs* January–February 2008, Vol. 87, No. 1, pp. 23–37.

Jung, Karl. *The Structure of Pysche, Collected Works*, Vol. 8, Princeton: Princeton University Press, 1927.

Kant, Immanuel. *Kritik der reinen Vernunft (Critique of Pure Reason)*, 1781.

Kant, Emmanuel. *Answering the Question: What is Enlightenment?*, 1784.

Kenen, Peter B. "Toward a Supranational Monetary System," in G. Pontecorvo, R.P. Shay, and A.G. Hart, eds., *Issues in Banking and Monetary Analysis*, New York: Holt, Reinhart, and Winston, 1967.

Kenneth, Arrow. *Social Choice and Individual Values*, Wiley: New York, 2nd ed., 1963.

Kerber, Linda K. "The Meanings of Citizenship," *Journal of American History* Vol. 84, No. 3, Dec 1997, pp. 833–54.

Keynes, John Maynard. *The Economic Consequences of the Peace*, New York: Harcourt, Brace and Howe, 1920.

The General Theory of Employment, Interest and Money, London: Macmillan Cambridge University Press, for Royal Economic Society, 1936.

Kimmenl, Michael. *Absolutism and Its Discontents: State and Society in Seventeenth-Century France and England*, New Brunswick, NJ: Transaction Books, 1988.

Knight, Frank. *The Ethics of Competition and Other Essays*, New York: Harpers and Brothers, 1935.

Koh, T. Harold. "Why Transnational Law Matters," *Penn State International Law Review* 24, 2006.

Krause, Karl. *The Archetype of Humanity*, 1811.

Krugman, Paul. *The Return of Depression Economics and the Crisis of 2008*, New York: W. W. Norton Company, 2009.

Kuhn, Thomas. *The Structure of Scientific Revolutions*, Chicago: Univ. of Chicago Press, 1962.

Kupchan, Charles. "NATO's Final Frontier: Why Russia Should Join the Atlantic Alliance," *Foreign Affairs*, May 2010, Vol. 89, No. 3, pp. 100–112.

Laffont, Jean-Jacques and Tirole, Jean. *A Theory of Incentives in Procurement and Regulation*, Cambridge: MIT Press, 1993.

László, Csaba. *Innovation, Imitation and Adaptation: The Experience of Fifteen Years of Upscaling Hungarian Economic Higher Education*, Budapest: Akademiai Kiado, 2005.

Lehne, Stefan. "How to Strengthen the European External Action Service," Camegie Foundation, Dec 16, 2011.

Lewis, Tracy and Sappington, David. "Ignorance in Agency Problems," *Journal of Economic Theory*, Vol. 61, 1993, pp. 169–83.

Lewis, Michael. *Boomerang: Travels in the New Third World*, New York, W.W. Norton Company, 2011.

Locke, John. *Two Treatises on Government*, London: Bettesworth, 1728.

Lowell, James Russell. *Democracy*, New York: Riverside Press, 1902.

Lucas, Robert. "Macroeconomic Priorities," *American Economic Review*, Vol. 93, No. 1, 2003, pp. 1–14.

Luthra, Sonia. "India's Economic Outlook: Implications and Trends: Interview with Nicholas Eberstadt," National Bureau of Asian Research, Dec 29, 2011.

Macaulay, Thomas Babington. "History," *Edinburgh Review*, May 1828.

Maddison, Angus. *The World Economy: Historical Statistics*, OECD, Paris, 2006, pp. 428, 476, and 550.

Madison, James . *Federalist Paper No. 10, 1787*.

Mahbubani, Kishore. "The Case Against the West," *Foreign Affairs*, Vol. 87, No. 3 May/June 2008, pp. 111–24.

Marx, Karl. *The Communist Manifesto*, New York: Penguin, 1998 (1848).

Das Kapital, Verlag von Otto Meisner, 1867.

Maskin, Eric and Tirole, Jean. "The Principal-Agent Relationship with an Informed Principal, I: Private Values," *Econometrica*, Vol. 58, 1990, pp. 379–410.

"The Principal-Agent Relationship with an Informed Principal, II: Common Values," *Econometrica*, Vol. 60, 1992, pp. 1–42.

McCloskey, Donald. *The Bourgeois Era*, Chicago IL: University of Chicago Press, 2010.

McKinnon, Ronald I. "Optimum Currency Areas," *The American Economic Review*, Vol. 53, No. 4, Sept 1963, pp. 717–25.

McNally, Robert and Levi, Michael. "A Crude Predicament," *Foreign Affairs*, Vol. 90, No. 4, 2011, pp. 100–11.

McVay Athanasius D. and Luciuk, Lubomyr Y., eds., *The Holy See and the Holodomor*, Toronto: Kastan Press, 2011.

Meade, James. *Principles of Political Economy: The Just Society*, Chicago: Aldine Press, 1965.

Liberty, Equality and Efficiency, New York: New York University Press, 1993.

Mill, John Stuart. *On Liberty*, 1859.

Miller, Ken. "Coping with China's Financial Power: Beijing's Financial Foreign Policy," *Foreign Affairs*, Vol. 89, No. 4, July 2010, pp. 96–109.

Mills, C. Wright. *The Power Elite and the State: How Policy is Made in America*, New York: Oxford University Press, 1956.

Mills, Quinn. *World Financial Crisis 2008-2010: What Happened, Who Is to Blame, and How to Protect Your Money*, CreateSpace, 2009.

Morita, Ken and Chen, Yun. "Toward an East Asian Economic Community," in Rosefielde, Steven, Kuboniwa, Masaaki, and Mizobata, Satoshi., eds., *Prevention and Crisis Management: Lessons for Asia from the 2008 Crisis*, Singapore: World Scientific Publishers, 2012.

Mosca, Gaetano. *The Ruling Class*, 1896.

Mouffe, Chantal. *The Democratic Paradox*, New York: Verso, 2000.

Mundell, Robert. "A Theory of Optimum Currency Areas," *American Economic Review*, Vol.51, Sept 1961, pp. 657–64.

Niall, Ferguson. *The Ascent of Money: A Financial History of the World*, New York: Penguin, 2008.

"Complexity and Collapse," *Foreign Affairs*, March/April 2010, Vol. 89, No. 2, pp.18–32.

North, Douglass. *Understanding the Process of Economic Change*, Princeton: Princeton University Press, 2005.

Nove, Alec. *Was Stalin Really Necessary?*, Routledge: London, 1964.

The Economics of Feasible Socialism, London: Routledge, 1983.

Nye, Joseph. *Soft Power: The Means to Success in World Politics*, Public Affairs, 2004.

"The Decline of America's Soft Power," *Foreign Affairs*, May/June, 2004.

Okara, Andrei. *Sovereign Democracy: A New Russian Idea or PR Project, Russia in Global Affairs*, Vol. 5, No. 3, July–Sept 2007, pp. 8–20.

O'Neill, Eugene. *Long Day's Journey into Night*, New Haven: Yale University Press, 2002.

Osborne, Peter. *The Triumph of the Political Class*, New York: Simon and Schuster, 2007.

Ostrom, Elizabeth. *Understanding Institutional Diversity*, Princeton, NJ: Princeton University Press, 2005.

Owah, Emmanuel Oneyemaghani. "Government of the Crooks, by the Crooks, for the Crooks," *Kleptocracy Nigeria Expose*, Xlibris, 2011.

Packer, George. "The Broken Contract," *Foreign Affairs*, Vol. 90, No. 6. Nov-Dec. 2011, pp. 20–31.

Parent, Joseph M. and MacDonald, Paul K. "The Wisdom of Retrenchment," *Foreign Affairs*, Vol. 90, No. 6, Nov–Dec 2011, pp. 32–47.

Pareto, Vilfredo. *Cours d'économie politique professé a l'université de Lausanne*. Vol. I, 1896; Vol. II, 1897.

Phillips, William. "The Relationship Between Unemployment and the Rate of Change of Money Wages in the United Kingdom 1861–1957," *Economica*, Vol. 25, No. 100, 1958, pp. 283–99.

Pennington-Cross, Anthony. "Credit History and the Performance of Prime and Nonprime Mortgages," *Journal of Real Estate Finance and Economics*, Vol. 27, No. 3, Nov 2003, pp. 270–301.

Putnam, Robert. *The Comparative Study of Political Elites*, New York: Prentice Hall, 1976.

Rahman, K. Sabeel. "Democracy and Productivity: The Glass-Steagall and the Shifting Discourse of Financial Regulation," *Journal of Policy History*, Vol. 24, No. 4, Oct 2012.

Rajan, Raghuram. "The True Lessons of the Recession," *Foreign Affairs*, Vol. 91, No. 3, May/June 2012, pp. 69–79

Rawls, John. *A Theory of Justice*, Cambridge, MA: Belknap Press of Harvard University Press, 1971.

Lectures on the History of Moral Philosophy, Cambridge, MA: Belknap Press of Harvard University Press, 1971.

Razin, Assaf and Rosefielde, Steven. "Currency and Financial Crises of the 1990s and 2000s," *CESifo Economic Studies, CESifo Economic Studies*, Vol. 57, Issue 3, 2011, pp. 499–530. doi:10.1093/cesifo/ifr016.

"A Tale of a Politically-Failing Single-Currency Area," *Israel Economic Review*, Vol. 10, No. 1, 2012, pp. 125–38.

"PIIGS," in Steven Rosefielde, Masaaki Kuboniwa and Satoshi Mizobata, eds., *Prevention and Crisis Management: Lessons for Asia from the 2008 Crisis*, Singapore: World Scientific, 2012.

"What Really Ails the Eurozone?: Faulty Supranational Architecture," *Contemporary Economics*, Vol. 6, Issue 4, Dec 2012, pp. 10–18.

Realty Trac Staff, "More than 1.2 Million Foreclosure Filings Report in 2006," February 8, 2007.

"U.S. Foreclosure Activity increase 75 Percent in 2007," January 29, 2008.

Reinhard, Carmen and Kenneth Rogoff. *This Time is Different: Eight Centuries of Financial Folly*, Princeton: Princeton University Press, 2009.

"Growth in a Time of Debt," NBER Working Paper No. 15639, January 2010, http://www.nber.org/papers/w15639,

Reves, Emery. *The Anatomy of Peace*, Smith: Peter Publisher, 1945.

Rives, J. B. *Tacitus: Germania*, Oxford: Oxford University Press, 1999.

Roche, David and McKee, Bob. *Democrisis*, London: Lulu, 2012.

Rodrik, Dani. *The Globalization Paradox: Democracy and the Future of the World Economy*, New York and London: W.W. Norton, 2011.

Rogoff, Kenneth, *The Second Great Contraction*, Project Syndicate, http://www.project-syndicate.org/commentary/rogoff83/English, 2011.

Rosecrance, Richard. "Bigger is Better: the Case for a Transatlantic Economic Union," *Foreign Affairs*, Vol. 89, No. 3, May 2010, pp. 42–50.

Rosefielde, Steven. *Soviet International Trade in Heckscher-Ohlin Perspective*, Lexington, MA: Heath-Lexington, August, 1973.

Russia in the 21st Century: The Prodigal Superpower, New York: Cambridge University Press, 2005.

Russian Economy from Lenin to Putin, New York: Wiley, 2007.

Red Holocaust, New York: Routledge, 2010.

"China's Perplexing Foreign Trade Policy: Cause, Consequences, and a Tit for Tat Solution," *American Foreign Policy Interests*, Winter 2011, pp. 10–16.

"Postcrisis Russia: Counting on Miracles in Uncertain Times," in Pallin, Carolina Vendil and Nygren, Bertil, eds., *Russian Defense Prospects*, New York: Macmillan, 2011.

"After Soviet Communism: Authoritarian Economic Evolution in Russia and China," in Korhonen, Iikka and Solando, Laura, eds., *From Soviet Plans to Russian Reality*, Helsinki: WSOUpro, 2011, pp. 81–92.

"Export-led Development and Dollar Reserve Hoarding," in Rosefielde, Steven, Kuboniwa, Masaaki, and Mizobata, Satoshi, eds., *Two Asias: The Emerging Postcrisis Divide*, Singapore: World Scientific, 2011.

"The 'Impossibility' of Russian Economic Reform: Waiting for Godot," in Blank, Stephen., ed., *Russian Reform*, Carlisle Barracks: US Army War College, 2012, pp. 37–60.

"Economics of the Military-Industrial Complex," in Alexeev, Michael and Weber, Shlomo, eds., *The Oxford Handbook of Russian Economy*, Oxford: Oxford University Press, 2012.

"Russian Economic Reform 2012: "Déjà vu All Over Again," Carlisle Barracks: US Army War College, 2012.

Asian Economic Systems, Singapore: World Scientific Publishers, 2013.

Rosefielde, Steven and Hedlund, Stefan. *Russia Since 1980: Wrestling With Westernization*, Cambridge: Cambridge University Press, 2008.

Rosefielde, Steven, Kuboniwa, Masaaki, and Mizobata, Satoshi (eds.) *Two Asias: The Emerging Postcrisis Divide*, Singapore: World Scientific, 2012.

Rosefielde, Steven, Kuboniwa, Masaaki, and Mizobata, Satoshi (eds.), *Prevention and Crisis Management: Lessons for Asia from the 2008 Crisis*, Singapore: World Scientific Publishers, 2012.

Rosefielde, Steven and Pfouts, R.W. "Egalitarianism and Production Potential in Postcrisis Russia," in Rosefielde, Steven, ed., *Efficiency and the Economic Recovery Potential of Russia*, Aldershot: Ashgate, 1998.

Inclusive Economic Theory, Singapore: World Scientific, 2014.

Rosefielde, Steven and Mills, Quinn. *Masters of Illusion: American Leadership in a New Age*, Cambridge: Cambridge University Press, 2007.

Ross, Stephen. "The Economic Theory of Agency: The Principal's Problem," *American Economic Review*, Vol. 63, No. 2, 1973, pp. 134–39.

Sandel, Michael. *Justice: What is the Right Thing to Do?*, New York: Macmillan, 2010.

Sassen, Saskia. *The Global City: New York, London, Tokyo*, Princeton, NJ: Princeton University Press, 1991.

Schroeder, Gertrude. "The Soviet Economy on a Treadmill of Reforms," in *Soviet Economy in a Time of Change*, Washington, D.C.: Joint Economic Committee of Congress, 1979, pp. 312–66.

Scott, Bruce. *Capitalism: Its Origins and Evolution as a System of Governance*, Berlin: Springer, 2011.

Sen, Amartya. *The Idea of Justice*, Cambridge, MA: Harvard University Press, 2009.

Shevtsova, Lilia. "Russia's Choice: Change or Degradation?" in Stephen Blank, ed., *Can Russia Reform? Economic, Political and Military Perspectives*, Carlisle Barracks: U.S. Army War College, 2012, pp. 1–36.

Shiller, Robert. *Irrational Exuberance*, Princeton, NJ: Princeton University Press, 2000.

The Subprime Solution: How Today's Global Financial Crisis Happened, and What to Do about It. Princeton, NJ: Princeton University Press, 2009.

Shiller, Robert and Akerlof, George. *Animal Spirits: How Human Psychology Drives the Economy and Why It Matters for Global Capitalism*, Princeton, NJ: Princeton University Press, 2009.

Skidmore, Max. "The History and Politics of Health Care in America: From the Progressive Era to the Patient Protection and Affordable Care Act," *Poverty & Public Policy*, Vol. 3, No. 1, 2011, pp. 1–9.

Slaughter, Anne-Marie. "The Real New World Order," *Foreign Affairs*, Vol. 75, No. 5, Sept/Oct 1997, pp. 184–87.

Stone, Ralph., ed., *Wilson and the League of Nations: Why America's Rejection*, New York: Krieger Publishing Company, 1978.

Strachey, James., ed., *The Standard Edition of the Complete Psychological Works of Sigmund Freud*, New York: Vintage, 1999.

Stiglitz, Joseph. *Freefall: America, Free Markets, and the Sinking of the World Economy*, New York: W. W. Norton & Company, 2010.

Surrey, Stanley. *Pathways to Tax Reform: The Concept of Tax Expenditures*, Cambridge, MA: Harvard University Press, 1974.

Taleb, Nassim. *The Black Swan: The Impact of the Highly Improbable*, New York: Random House, 2007.

Taylor, John. "Divine Coincidence and the Fed's Dual Mandate," *Economist's View*, January 29, 2011.

Toward a Euro-*Atlantic Security Community*, Carnegie Endowment for International Peace, Euro-Atlantic Security, Euro-Atlantic Security Initiative EASI Final Report, February 2012.

Tselichtchev, Ivan. *China versus the West: The Global Power Shift of the 21st Century*, Singapore: John Wiley & Sons, 2012.

United States Department of State FY2010 Agency Financial Report.

U.S. Bureau of Labor Statistics, Employment and Wages Annual Averages, 2008, Bulletin 2718, January 2010, Table 645 (Employment and Wages: 2000 to 2008).

"US Government's 2010 Financial Report Shows Significant Financial Management and Fiscal Challenges," Government Accountability Office, January 2011.

Voltaire, *Candide, or the Optimist*, 1759.

Von Mises, Ludwig. "The Economic Calculation in the Socialist Commonwealth," in Von Hayek, Fredrich, ed., *Collectivist Economic Planning*, London: Routledge, 1935.

Socialism: An Economic and Sociological Analysis, London: J. Cape, 1936.

Omnipotent Government: The Rise of the Total State and Total War, New York: Libertarian Press, 1985.

Wagemann, Claudius. *Breakdown and Change of Private Interest Governments*, New York: Routledge, 2011.

Weber, Max. "Politics as a Vocation," in Gerth, H. and Mills, C. Wright, eds., *From Max Weber: Essays in Sociology*. London: Routledge and Kegan Paul, 1970.

Wedel, Janine. *Shadow Elite: How the World's New Power Brokers Undermine Democracy, Government and the Free Market*, New York: Basic Books, 2009.

Weidenbaum, Murray. "The Employment Act of 1946: A Half Century of Presidential Policymaking," *Presidential Studies Quarterly*, Vol. 26, Issue 3, Summer 1996, pp. 880–85.

Weitzman, Martin. "The New Soviet Incentive Model," *The Bell Journal of Economics*, Vol. 7, 1976, pp. 251–57.

Western, Jon and Goldstein, Joshua S. "Humanitarian Intervention Comes of Age," *Foreign Affairs*, Vol. 90, No. 6, Nov–Dec 2011, pp. 48–59.

Wilhelm Georg and Hegel, Friedrich. *Phenomenology of Spirit*, trans. A. V. Miller, 1977.

Wilkie, Wendell. *One World*, New York: Simon & Schuster, 1943.

Williamson, Oliver. *Markets and Hierarchies*, New York: The Free Press, 1975.

The Economic Institutions of Capitalism: Firms, Markets and Relational Contracting, New York: The Free Press, 1985.

Mechanisms of Governance, Oxford: Oxford University Press, 1996.

"The New Institutional Economics: Taking Stock, Looking Ahead," *Journal of Economic Literature*, Vol. 38, No. 3, Sept 2000, pp. 595–613.

World Bank, *China 2030: Building a Modern, Harmonious, and Creative High-Income Society*, 2012.

Xu, Yi-chong., ed., *The Political Economy of State-owned Enterprises in China and India*, London: Palgrave Macmillan, 2012.

Zafirovski, Milan. *The Enlightenment and its Effect on Modern Society*, New York: Springer, 2001.

Zakaria, Fareed. *The Future of Freedom: Illiberal Democracy at Home and Abroad*, New York: W. W. Norton, 2007.

"The Rise of Illiberal Democracy," *Foreign Affairs*, Vol. 76, Issue 6, Nov/Dec 1997, pp. 22–43.

Ziliak, Stephen and Diedre McCloskey. "We Agree that Statistical Significance Proves Essentially Nothing: A Rejoinder to Thomas Mayer," *Economic Journal Watch*, Vol.10, No.1, January 2013, pp.1–11.

Zmora, Hillary. *Monarchy, Aristocracy, and the State in Europe – 1300–1800*, New York: Routledge, 2001.

Zweig, David and Bi Jianhai, "China's Global Hunt for Resources," *Foreign Affairs*, Vol. 84, No. 5, Sept/Oct 2005, pp. 25–38.

Index